Printed for J. Hinxman

Return of judicial rents fixed by Sub-Commissioners and Civil Bill Courts

Notified to Irish Land Commission, March and April 1889

Printed for J. Hinxman

Return of judicial rents fixed by Sub-Commissioners and Civil Bill Courts
Notified to Irish Land Commission, March and April 1889

ISBN/EAN: 9783742805829

Manufactured in Europe, USA, Canada, Australia, Japa

Cover: Foto ©ninafisch / pixelio.de

Manufactured and distributed by brebook publishing software
(www.brebook.com)

Printed for J. Hinxman

Return of judicial rents fixed by Sub-Commissioners and Civil Bill Courts

Irish Land Commission.

The Land Law (Ireland) Act, 1881, 44 & 45 Victoria, ch. 49

The Land Law (Ireland) Act, 1887, 50 & 51 Victoria, ch. 33.

RETURN

ACCORDING TO PROVINCES AND COUNTIES

OF

JUDICIAL RENTS

FIXED BY

SUB-COMMISSIONS

AND

CIVIL BILL COURTS,

AS NOTIFIED TO THE IRISH LAND COMMISSION DURING THE MONTHS OF

MARCH AND APRIL, 1889,

SPECIFYING DATES AND AMOUNTS RESPECTIVELY OF THE LAST INCREASES OF RENT WHERE ASCERTAINED;

ALSO

RENTS FIXED UPON THE REPORTS OF VALUERS APPOINTED BY THE IRISH LAND COMMISSION ON THE JOINT APPLICATIONS OF LANDLORDS AND TENANTS.

Presented to both Houses of Parliament by Command of Her Majesty.

DUBLIN:

PRINTED FOR HER MAJESTY'S STATIONERY OFFICE,

BY

ALEXANDER THOM & CO. (LIMITED),

And to be purchased, either directly or through any Bookseller, from Eyre and Spottiswoode, East Harding-street, Fetter-lane, E.C., or 32, Abingdon-street, Westminster, S.W.; or Adam and Charles Black, 6, North Bridge, Edinburgh; or Hodges, Figgis, and Co., 104, Grafton-street, Dublin.

1889.

INDEX.

MARCH, 1889.

SUMMARIES FOR MARCH, 1889.

Summary showing, according to Provinces and Counties, the Number of Cases in which Judicial Rents have been Fixed by Sub-Commissions, under the Land Law (Ireland) Act, 1881, during the Month of March, 1889; and also the Acreages, Tenement Valuations, Former Rents, and Judicial Rents of the Holdings.

Province and County.	Number of Cases in which Judicial Rents have been fixed.	Acreage. (Statute Acres) A.	R.	P.	Tenement Valuation. £	s.	d.	Former Rent. £	s.	d.	Judicial Rent. £	s.	d.
ULSTER—													
Antrim, ...	9	158	1	11	150	6	0	161	13	5	151	11	1
Armagh, ...	78	1,191	1	38	1,059	0	0	1,096	1	8	887	11	8
Cavan, ...	60	918	0	4	639	1	0	666	11	9	488	18	0
Donegal, ...	17	815	1	6	164	17	0	166	14	9½	122	8	9
Down, ...	139	2,376	3	5	2,088	18	10	1,840	13	1	1,480	8	0
Monaghan, ...	163	3,137	0	25	1,761	1	0	1,836	6	8	1,378	9	0
Tyrone, ...	24	1,153	1	24	861	3	4	961	9	1	807	8	0
Totals, ...	455	8,456	0	33	8,114	6	1	6,006	13	3½	4,570	1	2
LEINSTER—													
Carlow, ...	63	1,070	0	36	830	7	0	683	16	11	499	16	8
Kilkenny, ...	33	1,197	1	36	685	10	0	793	19	9	599	17	10
Longford, ...	68	2,364	2	25	1,401	6	0	1,536	6	5	1,313	19	10
Meath, ...	14	443	2	26	317	5	0	362	3	5	479	9	3
Westmeath, ...	31	537	3	38	608	10	0	478	7	4	371	11	8
Wexford, ...	31	486	1	4	322	18	0	418	0	0½	310	1	4
Wicklow, ...	6	803	3	23	163	0	0	185	4	4	188	18	0
Totals, ...	216	6,704	3	37	3,938	11	0	4,661	18	5½	3,593	4	7
CONNAUGHT—													
Galway, ...	62	1,731	2	9½	780	8	0	511	13	4	479	5	10
Mayo, ...	116	2,363	0	25	553	4	0	816	4	10	491	2	10
Roscommon, ...	44	760	2	38	607	6	0	441	16	5	383	13	7
Sligo, ...	52	1,186	0	31½	374	2	0	360	5	3	280	13	8
Totals, ...	264	5,531	2	14	1,825	0	0	1,995	19	10	1,564	15	9
MUNSTER—													
Clare, ...	65	3,612	2	38	976	0	0	1,399	10	4	956	16	0
Cork, ...	45	3,623	2	7½	857	11	0	1,363	8	3	1,110	13	9
Kerry, ...	5	119	0	4	41	3	0	68	0	0	68	5	0
Limerick, ...	58	659	3	18	358	5	1	511	9	3	401	19	0
Tipperary, ...	11	811	3	37	374	18	0	376	5	1	300	3	4
Waterford, ...	21	1,161	0	15	738	17	9	833	6	4	498	8	0
Totals, ...	215	7,507	0	39½	3,197	14	8	4,605	13	6	3,516	14	6

IRELAND.

		A.	R.	P.	£	s.	d.	£	s.	d.	£	s.	d.
ULSTER, ...	455	8,456	0	33	8,114	5	4	6,006	13	9½	4,570	1	2
LEINSTER, ...	216	6,704	3	37	3,939	11	0	4,664	19	5½	3,593	4	7
CONNAUGHT, ...	264	5,531	2	14	1,825	0	0	1,999	19	10	1,564	15	9
MUNSTER, ...	215	7,507	0	39½	3,497	14	6	4,605	13	6	3,516	14	6
TOTALS, ...	1,150	26,200	0	8½	18,365	10	7	17,276	5	1	16,220	16	2

NOTE.—For Rents Fixed upon Reports of Valuers see pages [illegible].
[illegible]

LEASEHOLDERS.

SUMMARY FOR MARCH, 1889.

Summary showing, according to Provinces and Counties, the number of Cases in which Judicial Rents have been fixed by Sub-Commissions, under the Land Law (Ireland) Act, 1887, during the Month of March, 1889, and also the Acreages, Tenement Valuations, Former Rents, and Judicial Rents of the Holdings.

Province and County.	Number of Cases in which Judicial Rents have been fixed.	Acreage. Statute Acres. A. R. P.	Tenement Valuation. £ s. d.	Former Rent. £ s. d.	Judicial Rent. £ s. d.
ULSTER—					
Antrim, ...	60	1,633 2 20	575 5 0	1,038 17 8½	769 10 0
Armagh, ...	31	564 0 35	584 10 0	749 13 1	541 3 6
Cavan, ...	6	245 3 4	188 10 0	198 16 8	148 5 0
Donegal, ...	5	180 3 1	109 10 0	115 8 0	83 8 8
Down, ...	63	458 2 19	481 6 0	550 0 10	400 17 0
Londonderry, ...	5	71 2 36	86 5 0	63 14 10	55 7 4
Monaghan, ...	1	31 3 30	26 0 0	30 13 0	19 0 0
Tyrone, ...	15	590 0 31	275 18 0	364 1 6	230 9 6
Totals, ...	115	3,234 1 36	2,579 5 0	3,083 9 0½	2,310 16 9
LEINSTER—					
Carlow, ...	61	1,611 3 39	739 10 0	1,306 5 0	960 15 4
Dublin, ...	8	343 3 29	388 10 0	434 3 6	303 0 9
Kildare, ...	3	173 3 13	149 10 0	218 0 0	140 13 0
Kilkenny, ...	34	3,190 3 1	1,225 0 0	3,703 6 6	1,890 13 11
Longford, ...	9	333 3 26	457 5 0	405 0 5	463 19 0
Louth, ...	1	25 3 37	30 5 0	16 16 9	15 0 0
Meath, ...	19	1,613 1 5	1,044 10 0	2,020 13 5	1,530 0 1
Westmeath, ...	39	5,377 0 30	3,814 7 0	4,846 11 8	4,371 4 11
Wexford, ...	11	823 0 35	427 15 0	836 10 7	539 11 8
Wicklow, ...	2	387 3 18	581 15 0	643 17 0	618 0 0
Totals, ...	167	13,416 3 30	8,769 7 0	13,150 5 4	9,091 18 10
CONNAUGHT—					
Galway, ...	6	733 3 34	394 18 0	511 1 6	304 0 0
Mayo, ...	2	43 1 16	53 0 0	33 0 0	23 0 0
Roscommon, ...	20	506 1 6	236 7 0	380 15 4½	239 15 6
Sligo, ...	1	113 2 18	64 10 0	51 0 0	59 13 6
Totals, ...	29	1,396 3 25	643 12 0	975 16 10½	585 8 0
MUNSTER—					
Clare, ...	73	3,360 1 38	1,916 17 0	2,453 15 0	1,705 14 0
Cork, ...	61	4,195 3 24	2,125 14 10	3,107 7 6	2,343 8 8
Kerry, ...	35	1,585 1 14	844 5 0	1,333 5 4	931 6 0
Limerick, ...	30	2,405 3 13	1,425 10 0	2,097 11 3	1,646 16 3
Tipperary, ...	11	1,044 2 35	427 9 0	776 18 11	504 4 2
Waterford, ...	34	3,741 1 10	1,450 17 0	2,233 18 11½	1,759 2 0
Totals, ...	253	16,187 2 15	8,380 6 10	12,602 18 11½	9,190 6 7

IRELAND.

ULSTER, ...	115	3,234 2 38	2,579 3 0	3,083 3 0½	2,310 15 9
LEINSTER, ...	167	13,416 3 30	8,769 7 0	13,150 5 4	9,091 18 10
CONNAUGHT, ...	29	1,396 3 25	643 12 0	975 15 10½	585 8 0
MUNSTER, ...	253	16,187 2 15	8,380 6 10	12,602 18 11½	9,190 6 7
Totals, ...	564	32,218 0 38	20,371 10 10	29,781 18 2½	21,078 8 2

PROVINCE OF

COUNTY OF

Names of Assistant Commissioners by whom Cases were decided.	No.	Name of Tenant.	Name of Landlord.	Townland.
Assistant Commissioners—				
R. Gibbs (Legal). R. Spencer. J. M. Weir.	3672	John McCormick, ...	Jane Shannon and others, by Samuel Farquhar their Guardian, Reps. of Mrs Jane Means, deceased.	Carnmoney, ...
	3673	John Jamison, ...	do.	do. ...
	3674	Hugh Smyth, ...	Sir Richard Wallace, Bart.,	1 P. Kilcorig, ...
	3675	Thomas McGarrell, ...	do.	Fanmore, ...
	3676	Robert McKnight, ...	do.	Drumshill, ...
	3677	Philip Magee, ...	do.	Ballymacward, Lower,
	3678	Joshua Henley, ...	Marquis of Hertford, ...	Larganore, ...
	3679	John Tate, ...	do.	Broughmore, ...
	3680	Richard Thompson, ...	do.	do. ...

ULSTER.

ANTRIM.

Extent of Holding, Statute.	Poor Law Valuation.	Former Rent.	Judicial Rent.	Observations.	Value of Tenancy.
A. R. P.	£ s. d.	£ s. d.	£ s. d.		£ s. d.
4 1 15	--	10 0 0	10 0 0		
6 0 4	—	11 17 0	11 17 0		
5 0 1	6 5 0	4 18 0	4 11 0		
16 3 23	unascertained,	16 7 8	11 10 0		
7 2 0	11 15 0	8 12 8	6 0 0		
13 1 30	20 0 0	15 3 1	13 2 1		
37 2 25	40 0 0	40 1 6	30 0 0	£ s. d.	
38 3 35	41 0 0	30 15 0	21 0 0	Rent changed in 1860 from . . 14 8 1	
24 1 38	33 5 0	26 7 4	20 10 0	1882 26 7 4	
158 1 11	150 5 0	161 10 8	131 11 1		

ARMAGH.

2 2 0	3 15 0	3 14 8	2 0 0	By consent.	
21 1 35	24 0 0	23 6 8	16 13 0		
10 3 15	15 0 0	11 11 8	8 0 0		
11 3 8	16 0 0	10 17 5	9 0 0		
27 0 25	28 10 0	27 13 4	24 0 0		
12 1 20	14 15 0	15 9 4	10 15 0		
23 3 20	28 0 0	26 5 5	21 10 0		
18 2 0	27 0 0	26 8 7	20 0 0		
13 3 0	20 10 0	15 14 8	13 10 0		
7 1 15	11 10 0	7 9 4	7 9 4		
10 1 6	10 0 0	4 6 8	7 10 0		
11 3 20	unascertained,	8 6 10	7 5 0		

D. Tuohy (Legal).
H. Jameson.
H. E. Stewart.

5681	George H. S. Dun
5682	Sarah Gibson,
5583	James Corrigan,
5684	Do., ...
5685	Henry Gaughter,
5686	Do., ...
5687	James P. Barrett,
5688	Do., ...
5689	Do., ...
5690	John West,
5691	Do., ...
5692	Robert Willis,
5693	John Allen, ...
5694	John Cromwell,
5695	Samuel Farley,
5696	David McMullen,
5697	Mary Porter, Admix. of John
5698	Jackson Pillow,
5699	Thomas McClellan
5700	Jackson Pillow,
5701	Do., ...
5702	John Black, ...
5703	Hugh Cleland,
5704	Mary Hughes,
5705	John Muckle,
5706	Do., ...
5707	Robert Willis,

ARMAGH—*continued.*

Extent of Holding. (Statute.)	Poor Law Valuation.	Former Rent.	Published Rent.	Observations.	Value of Tenancy.
A. R. P.	£ s. d.	£ s. d.	£ s. d.		£ s. d.
27 3 28	25 0 0	20 5 8	21 0 0		
21 0 25	25 0 0	19 7 8	15 0 0		
12 3 34	9 0 0	5 8 0	7 0 0		
6 2 0	1 5 0	4 9 6	3 0 0		
15 1 2	19 0 0	27 5 0	14 0 0		
10 1 23	unascertained,	9 17 6	9 9 0		
28 3 31	do.	20 12 0	20 10 0		
9 1 19	do.	8 0 1	7 0 0		
7 3 0	do.	8 0 0	5 0 0		
7 2 15	11 10 0	6 7 0	7 0 0		
3 1 14	6 15 0	8 5 9	8 0 0		
5 3 20	unascertained,	6 0 0	6 5 0		
63 0 16	51 10 0	55 15 0	60 0 0		
18 2 0	19 5 0	15 3 4	11 10 0		
24 1 20	27 10 0	18 0 0	18 0 0		
19 1 35	19 5 0	14 9 0	19 15 0		
15 0 [illegible]	15 10 0	15 0 0	10 0 0		
18 3 12	20 10 0	18 11 0	15 0 0		
8 3 11	4 0 0	3 0 6	5 5 0		
12 3 3	unascertained,	18 12 10	9 0 0		
7 3 24	do.	7 10 0	8 0 0		
7 0 0	9 10 0	7 7 0	5 10 0		
60 1 20	unascertained,	45 0 4	31 0 0		
30 3 20	36 5 0	38 15 3	25 0 0		
14 1 8	unascertained,	18 1 0	9 5 0		
15 2 19	16 5 0	14 16 0	11 15 0		
11 1 37	11 5 0	11 0 0	5 5 0		
4 0 10	unascertained,	4 17 6	4 4 0		
3 2 33	do.	4 0 0	3 5 0		
4 0 13	do.	5 3 3	4 10 0		
3 0 38	3 0 0	3 6 5	3 10 0		
14 1 31	15 10 0	13 17 0	10 15 0		
12 1 0	13 15 0	16 17 8	10 10 0		
35 1 20	34 0 0	30 15 0	25 0 0		
8 3 20	18 0 0	10 18 5	7 10 0		

Names of Assistant Commissioners by whom Cases were decided.	No.	Name of Tenant.	Name of Landlord.
Assistant Commissioners—			
D. Tuohy (Legal). H. [illegible]. H. E. [illegible].	5716	John Lenby, ...	Rev. Richard Johnston
	5717	Patrick White, ...	Colonel G. M. Dobbin

ARMAGH—*continued.*

Extent of Holding. Statute.	Poor Law Valuation.	Former Rent.	Judicial Rent.	Observations.	Value of Tenancy.
A. R. P.	£ s. d.	£ s. d.	£ s. d.		£ s. d.
26 1 18	27 0 0	27 0 0	21 0 0		
31 1 0	unascertained,	23 9 10	20 10 0		
17 0 13	19 0 0	17 16 6	18 0 0		
7 1 18	unascertained,	5 15 0	5 5 0		
15 0 17	13 5 0	15 3 0	10 10 0		
10 1 6	11 5 0	8 16 7	7 10 0		
5 0 14	8 15 0	4 17 1	5 0 0		
10 0 13	4 10 0	6 3 6	6 0 0		
19 3 37	16 10 0	18 19 0	11 10 0		
16 0 7	unascertained,	16 3 6	19 0 0		
8 3 5	11 16 0	11 1 7	9 0 0		
4 0 24	4 3 0	4 6 7	3 15 0		
30 3 33	33 0 0	34 18 3	21 10 0		
17 3 36	18 10 0	14 17 10	18 0 0		
16 1 30	16 16 0	14 1 10	31 10 0		
38 3 14	40 0 0	41 6 0	36 0 0		
3 0 13	4 5 0	3 14 3	3 15 0		
20 0 3	26 0 0	23 14 8	16 10 0		
11 0 31	13 0 0	10 4 8	8 0 0		
8 0 36	8 0 0	9 0 3	7 0 0		
71 1 38	71 6 0	16 10 8	15 10 0		
16 3 18	20 10 0	19 15 9	15 0 0		
8 3 8	3 18 0	8 5 11	1 16 0		
17 3 30	18 0 0	18 5 10	13 15 0		
71 3 30	23 15 0	27 14 1	16 0 0		
20 0 0	20 5 0	17 0 0	13 10 0		
9 0 37	9 10 0	7 7 4	6 5 0		
21 0 30	19 10 0	18 8 8	15 10 0		
12 0 18	13 0 0	9 18 8	8 10 0		
1,172 1 33	1,030 0 0	1,035 4 5	837 11 4		

Names of Assistant Commissioners by whom Cases were decided.	No.	Name of Tenant.	Name of Landlord
Assistant Commissioners—			
W. E. Bailey (Legal). S. Byrne. J. Patterson	2864	Rose Kelly, Ltd. Admix. of Pat Kelly.	Josiah Adams, ...
	2865	Charles Lackey, ...	Thomas C. Burrowes,
	2866	William Spence, ...	do. ...
	2867	Patrick Boyle, ...	Captain O. D. Barnett
	2868	James Malone, ...	do. ...
	2869	Henry McCauley, ...	Maxwell J. Boyle,
	2870	Jane McKnight, Ltd. Admix. of John McKnight.	Theophilus Clements,
	2871	Benjamin Armstrong, ...	do. ...
	2872	Patrick Kelly, ...	do. ...
	2873	Honoria Keel, ...	do. ...
	2874	Bernard Coyle, ...	do. ...
	2875	Margaret McCann, ...	do. ...
	2876	Andrew Semple, ...	do. ...

CAVAN.

Extent of Holding. Statute.	Poor Law Valuation.	Former Rent.	Judicial Rent.	Observations.	Value of Tenancy.
A. R. P.	£ s. d.	£ s. d.	£ s. d.		£ s. d.
5 0 31	5 10 0	6 10 0	7 10 0		
11 3 34	5 10 0	8 5 0	6 15 0		
33 3 20	33 10 0	40 0 0	30 0 0		
7 3 18	6 18 0	5 15 6	6 15 0		
8 0 15	4 15 0	7 5 0	6 0 0		
21 0 36	15 0 0	17 2 0	14 0 0		
23 0 5	25 0 0	25 0 0	18 10 0		
15 1 8	9 5 0	9 0 0	7 10 0		
18 0 34	11 5 0	11 15 6	6 5 0		
14 0 10	9 15 0	10 0 0	5 5 0		
11 2 8	9 0 0	10 0 0	7 0 0		
18 3 34	10 15 0	12 0 0	[illegible] 0 0		
30 0 11	19 5 0	24 0 0	16 5 0		
5 2 19	5 0 0	5 0 0	3 5 0		
17 0 1	11 5 0	11 0 0	9 5 0		
33 3 13	26 10 0	18 0 0	13 10 0		
[illegible] 3 [illegible]	31 10 0	[illegible] 0 0	16 0 0		
9 3 1	7 5 0	7 10 0	5 15 0		
23 0 5	19 15 0	18 15 0	14 10 0		
29 0 1	20 15 0	22 0 0	17 5 0		
13 3 18	13 0 0	11 18 11	8 10 0		
15 0 3	18 0 0	12 0 0	6 10 0		
27 1 24	18 10 0	20 0 0	18 0 0		
11 2 21	8 10 0	10 0 0	8 10 0		
15 0 0	12 10 0	11 5 0	8 0 0		
14 0 30	11 10 0	11 10 0	6 0 0		
33 3 20	25 0 0	24 0 0	17 0 0		
9 0 30	5 0 0	7 10 0	5 10 0		
27 1 6	12 0 0	17 5 0	15 10 0		
18 0 11	8 10 0	8 8 8	6 0 0		
20 0 14	17 0 0	11 5 0	11 10 0		
24 0 0	16 17 0	16 16 7	13 0 0		

COUNTY OF

Names of Assistant Commissioners by whom Cases were decided.	No.	Name of Tenant.	Name of Landlord.	Townland.
Assistant Commissioners—				
W. F. Bailey (Legal). E. Bryan. J. Fitzgerald.	2899	Michael Carroll, ...	R. G. Shaw, ...	Ballagim, ...
	2900	Michael Duffy, ...	George McCabe and another,	Larraweelan, ...
	2901	Owen Lynch, ...	do.	do. ...
	2902	William Cronan, ...	do.	do. ...
	2903	Thomas Lynch, ...	do.	do. ...
	2904	Edward Kinsella, ...	do.	do. ...
	2905	James Fairbairn, ...	Mrs. Isabella Smith and anor., Trustees of late Edw. Smith,	Portlisky, ...
	2906	Patrick Kiernan, ...	do.	Drumman, ...
	2907	Thomas Leary, ...	do.	Bawnlk, ...
	2908	Michael McCabe, ...	do. ...	Killinkelly, ...
	2909	Alice McDonald, ...	do. ...	Shibllen, ...
	2910	Catherine Smith & anor.,	do.	Drumaneghill, ...
	2911	John McKeown & anor.,	do.	Derage, ...
	2912	John Brady, ...	do.	Ballymahala, ...
	2913	Thomas Leary, ...	do.	Shabbilen, ...
	2914	Owen Keown, ...	do.	Bawnlk, ...
	2915	John McCabe, ...	do.	Shibbilen, ...
	2916	Do., ...	do.	Bawnlk, ...
	2917	Philip Dinning, ...	do.	Drumvahill, ...
	2918	Michael Dillon, ...	do.	Muff, ...
	2919	Philip Smith, ...	do.	do. ...
	2920	Bridget Martin, ...	do.	Corlea, ...
	2921	Jane Brady, ...	do.	Drumaneghill, ...
	2922	John McCabe, ...	do.	Ballymahala, ...
	2923	Thomas Connolly, ...	do.	Drumrohill, ...
				Total, ...

COUNTY OF

Assistant Commissioners—	6383	Daniel Doherty & anor.,	Christopher Metcalf, ...	Kinnaggin and another,
D. Tierney (Legal). G. N. Gallagher. J. H. McCormick.	6384	Hannah Doherty, ...	Wm. Rankin, ...	Gortlarry, ...
	6385	Patk. Doherty, ...	do.	do. ...
	6386	Rep. Hugh Doherty, ...	do.	Carrick, ...

CAVAN—*continued.*

Extent of Holding.	Poor Law Valuation.	Present Rent.	Judicial Rent.	Observations.	Value of Tenancy.
A. R. P.	£ s. d.	£ s. d.	£ s. d.		£ s. d.
15 2 25	10 15 0	11 6 4	6 5 0		
11 8 39	6 5 0	8 5 0	5 10 0		
6 5 5	4 5 0	4 10 0	3 10 0		
10 0 15	5 5 0	6 11 0	4 10 0		
9 3 4	4 5 0	6 6 0	5 0 0		
13 1 0	8 5 0	8 18 0	6 10 0		
11 3 5	11 10 0	11 6 8	9 0 0		
1 5 5	9 8 0	4 10 0	2 5 0		
12 3 [illegible]	9 15 0	11 8 9	7 10 0		
13 [illegible] [illegible]	6 15 0	9 18 4	7 0 0		
24 [illegible] 12	15 5 0	19 5 0	13 10 0		
10 0 [illegible]	6 15 0	6 10 0	5 0 0		
7 3 24	unascertained.	7 1 0	5 10 0		
5 1 [illegible]	8 5 0	3 10 8	2 5 0		
5 0 0	3 0 0	3 18 0	8 0 0		
8 3 6	unascertained.	6 18 0	6 5 0		
5 2 17	6 5 0	4 7 8	3 5 0		
6 3 10	5 10 0	4 18 0	3 10 0		
16 1 37	10 5 0	11 8 8	8 10 0		
10 3 4	7 0 0	7 9 6	5 10 0		
15 1 18	9 5 0	10 4 6	8 5 0		
12 3 14	7 10 0	5 10 8	9 10 0		
12 0 8	6 15 0	10 6 6	7 10 0		
4 0 [illegible]	3 5 0	8 12 6	3 0 0		
8 3 14	3 10 0	5 0 0	3 5 0		
[illegible] 0 4	[illegible] 1 0	[illegible] 11 8	[illegible] 18 0		

DONEGAL.

COUNTY OF

Names of Assistant Commissioners by whom Cases were decided.	No.	Name of Tenant.	Name of Landlord.	Townland.
Assistant Commissioners—				
D. Tuckey (Legal). G. N. Caldwell. J. H. McConnell.	6387	Michael Gallaghan, ...	William Rankin, ...	Lisa, ...
	6388	Rose Lynch, ...	do.	Milltown, ...
	6389	James Toland, ...	Fanny Rankin, ...	do. ...
	6390	William Kearney, ...	Fanny Thompson and others,	Lisa, ...
	6391	William Murphy, ...	Norris Thompson and others,	Kinnygling, ...
	6392	Pat Mat. Leeney, ...	do.	Benbeg, ...
	6393	Henry Doherty, ...	do.	do. ...
	6394	Francis Bradley, ...	do.	Milltown, ...
	6395	Philip Doherty, ...	do.	Gortlury, ...
	6396	Rose McCaigue, ...	do.	do. ...
	6397	Michael McGonagle, ...	do.	Kinnygling, ...
	6398	Daniel Doherty, ...	do.	do. ...
D. Tuckey (Legal). F. O'Callaghan. S. Byrne.	6399	William Gregg, ...	Robert G. Montgomery, ...	Magheramphin.
				Total, ...

COUNTY OF

Head Commission.	4988	Agnes Aiken, ...	Viscount Bridport and anor., Trustees of Marquis of Downshire.	Drumlough, ...
	4989	Patrick Ritchie, ...	John B. Houston, ...	Ballyroney, ...
	4990	Patrick Lennon, Rep. of Bernard Lennon.	John Meade Amner, surviving Trustee of Hon. R. Meade.	Drumlough, ...
	4991	James Maginn, ...	do.	Cross, ...
	4992	Margaret Graham and another, Reps. of James Graham, deceased.	do.	Drumlough, ...
Assistant Commissioners— E. Greer (Legal). J. Cunningham. T. Smyth.	4993	William Nicholson, Rep. of Richard Nicholson.	Earl of Kilmorey, ...	Derryogue, ...
	4994	Edward Fearon, ...	do.	Ballinlare, ...
	4995	Patrick Hughes, ...	do.	do. ...
	4996	James Stewart, ...	do.	Moneydarragh, ...
	4997	John McIlgan, ...	do.	Drumsesk, ...
	4998	Patrick Hagan, ...	do.	Derryogue, ...

DONEGAL—*continued.*

Extent of Holding. Statute, &c.	Poor Law Valuation.	Former Rent.	Judicial Rent.	Observations.	Value of Tenancy.
a. r. p.	£ s. d.	£ s. d.	£ s. d.		£ s. d.
8 0 26	4 5 0	4 8 8	3 10 6	By consent.	
11 1 38	7 10 0	7 10 0	5 0 0	do.	
12 1 5	10 5 0	9 0 4	8 10 0	do.	
11 2 36	7 15 0	8 14 0	6 10 0	do.	
13 3 22	6 0 0	5 0 0	4 0 0	do.	
8 0 0	4 10 0	3 11 8	2 13 0	do.	
17 0 0	5 19 0	4 13 8	3 18 9	do.	
3 0 0	—	3 0 0	3 4 0	do.	
5 0 0	3 3 0	3 1 8½	1 10 0	do.	
10 0 0	4 10 0	4 5 10	3 5 0	do.	
22 1 8	10 0 0	3 18 1	4 16 0	do.	
18 3 10	16 5 0	13 8 1	10 0 0	do.	
131 1 10	74 0 0	69 14 7	59 0 0		
316 1 6	164 17 0	164 14 9½	122 3 9		

DOWN.

60 0 27	63 15 0	40 15 0	34 15 6	The rent in this case was fixed by consent of the parties at the sitting of the Court in Dublin.	
15 3 33	16 10 0	17 10 4	13 15 0	do.	
18 0 25	13 10 0	13 18 8	11 0 0	do.	
34 2 0	25 15 0	29 16 0	21 0 0	do.	
38 0 30	27 15 0	35 5 0	24 0 0	do.	
16 3 30	20 0 0	15 8 4	16 5 0		
10 3 29	13 10 0	8 18 4	7 5 6		
4 3 35	8 10 0	8 2 8	6 0 0		
10 3 34	14 0 0	8 1 10	6 5 0		
67 1 10	67 0 0	56 16 4	40 0 0		
3 0 30	5 0 0	2 8 8	2 0 0	By consent.	

COUNTY OF

Names of Assistant Commissioners by whom Cases were decided.	No.	Name of Tenant.	Name of Landlord.	Townland.
Assistant Commissioners—				
R. Greer (Legal) J. Christal T. Smith.	4999	Margaret Sloan, ...	Earl of Kilmorey, ...	Ballintra, ...
	5000	John Maginn, ...	do.	Clontdrummond,
	5001	Patrick Carr, Rep. of James Carr.	do.	Derrygegan, ...
	5002	Bernard Devlin, ...	Earl Annesley, ...	Moyadd, ...
	5003	Nicholas Hanna, ...	R. Kerr Boyd, ...	Dunavil, ...
	5004	Hugh Morgan, ...	do.	do. ...
	5005	William Spears, ...	Estate of John Moore and others, Owners, Mary Best, Petitioners.	Aughnaloopy, ...
	5006	James Fitzpatrick, ...	do.	do. ...
	5007	Mary Doran and another,	do.	do. ...
	5008	Patrick Rodgers, ...	Charles Orr, ...	do. ...
	5009	William White, ...	John McCartan, ...	Moygannon, ...
	5010	John Bradley, ...	do.	do. ...
	5011	Michael Grant, ...	do.	do. ...
	5012	John Maginn, ...	Earl of Kilmorey, ...	Ballynagaugh, ...
	5013	John Cummin, ...	do.	Maghery, ...
	5014	Henry Baird, ...	do.	Aughrim, ...
	5015	Patrick McKeys, ...	do.	Ballynahcarn, ...
	5016	Peter O'Hagan, ...	do.	do. ...
	5017	James McVeigh, ...	do.	do. ...
	5018	Hugh Morgan, ...	do.	do. ...
	5019	Rose Grant, ...	do.	Derrygegan, ...
	5020	Mary Colgan, ...	do.	Tullyframe. ...
	5021	Ellen and James Quinn,	do.	Ballynahatten, ...
	5022	Ellen Doran, ...	do.	Ballymageough,
	5023	Patrick Cunningham, ...	do.	Ardinall, ...
	5024	Sarah Foy, ...	do.	do. ...
	5025	Patrick Burke, ...	do.	Aughnaloughill, ...
	5026	John Fearon, ...	do	do. ...
	5027	James Traynor, ...	do.	Ballymageough.
	5028	Thomas Traynor, ...	do.	do. ...
	5029	Patrick Fitzpatrick, ...	do.	Ardinall, ...
	5030	Felix Monaghan, ...	do.	Aughrim, ...
	5031	Patrick Tinline, ...	do.	do. ...
	5032	Charles Woods, ...	do.	do. ...

DOWN—*continued.*

Extent of Holding. Statute.	Poor Law Valuation.	Former Rent.	Judicial Rent.	Observations.	Value of Tenancy.
A. R. P.	£ s. d.	£ s. d.	£ s. d.		£ s. d.
3 6 31	3 15 0	1 8 0	5 15 0	By consent.	
15 3 0	13 0 0	10 6 1	8 5 0	do.	
14 7 5	19 10 0	14 3 6	18 5 0	do.	
10 3 6	unascertained.	5 5 0	6 10 0		
8 1 7	4 15 0	3 16 0	3 0 0	Rent changed in 18[illegible] from . . . £ s. d. 4 8 10	
1 3 18	5 5 0	1 18 0	1 10 0	do. 8 0 0	
6 3 0	3 18 0	6 11 5	8 10 0		
8 5 3	1 3 0	1 15 0	1 5 0		
11 1 30	8 6 0	7 14 0	6 5 0		
9 0 10	5 12 0	7 15 8	6 0 0	1884 20 0 0	
8 0 15	2 6 0	7 10 0	6 10 0		
4 2 16	4 10 0	5 0 0	6 0 0		
9 2 35	9 5 0	6 0 0	7 0 0		
14 3 1	unascertained.	8 17 2	3 10 0	By consent.	
8 0 13	10 10 0	10 18 0	7 15 0	do.	
17 1 6	13 15 0	13 6 2	10 0 0	do.	
12 1 0	11 10 0	20 12 6	9 2 2	do.	
13 8 19	13 10 0	11 14 0	10 7 6	do.	
5 9 37	8 10 0	8 17 6	8 0 0	do.	
49 3 10	37 15 0	28 18 6	28 3 0	do.	
13 1 30	18 20 0	16 5 10	18 3 0	do.	
4 1 16	1 0 0	4 9 8	2 10 0	do.	
34 0 10	20 0 0	37 7 6	19 0 0	do.	
17 0 20	8 5 0	8 18 10	6 0 0	do.	
28 0 30	16 6 0	11 14 8	10 8 8	do.	
8 2 35	8 0 0	6 9 4	6 10 6	do.	
7 1 30	4 0 0	3 1 0	2 10 0	do.	
8 3 10	8 10 0	7 3 0	5 0 0	do.	
8 8 30	3 14 0	4 0 8	5 10 0	do.	
11 5 5	6 0 0	4 18 6	6 8 8	do.	
11 3 10	7 10 0	6 8 2	4 10 0		
8 1 20	3 10 0	2 0 8	2 10 0		
6 8 21	8 15 0	2 18 10	3 0 0		
3 5 8	5 10 0	5 18 2	2 10 0		

COUNTY OF

Names of Assistant Commissioners by whom Cases were decided.	No.	Name of Tenant.	Name of Landlord.	Townland.
Assistant Commissioners— E. Greer (Legal). J. Cunningham. T. Smith.	5033	Thomas Cunningham (Crown),	Earl of Kilmorey,	Anglerins,
	5034	Mathew Sloan,	do.	Drummenisnore,
	5035	Henry Magee,	do.	Largamore,
	5036	Richard Mackin,	do.	Ballynahatton,
	5037	John Coll,	do.	Ballymageogh,
	5038	Edward L. Moore,	do.	Derryoge,
	5039	Do.,	do.	do.
	5040	Catherine Martin,	do.	do.
	5041	Jane McLoughlin,	do.	do.
	5042	Richard Caulfield,	do.	Ballygowan,
Assistant Commissioners— E. Greer (Legal). R. Garland. S. Chambers.	5043	Agnes Bell,	Lord Trevor,	Carnagar,
	5044	John Patterson, junior,	John Mulholland, surviving Trustee of R. W. B. Ker,	Burren,
	5045	Hamilton Patterson,	do.	Creevytenant,
	5046	Johnston Hill,	do.	do.
	5047	James Irvine,	do.	do.
	5048	William Smyth,	do.	Magheraknock,
	5049	Do.,	do.	Glasdrummond,
	5050	William Davidson,	do.	do.
	5051	Samuel Armstrong,	do.	Ballyvarren,
	5052	William McMurray and another,	do.	Ballykine Lower,
	5053	John Hamilton,	do.	do.
	5054	John Blakely,	do.	do.
	5055	Robert Ireland,	do.	do.
	5056	John McIlveen,	do.	do.
	5057	James McIlveen,	do.	do.
	5058	Do.,	do.	Ballykine Upper,
	5059	Sampson Smythe,	do.	do.
	5060	Alexander Reid,	do.	do.
	5061	Do.,	do.	Ballymaglaive,
	5062	William Shanks,	do.	Clontaganland,
	5063	William Shelly,	Viscount Bridport and another, Trustees of Marquis of Downshire,	Drumadoney
	5064	David McAuley,	do.	do.
	5065	Samuel Kerr,	do.	do.
	5066	Robert McNeill,	do.	do.

DOWN—*continued.*

Extent of Holding. Statute.	Poor Law Valuation.	Former Rent.	Judicial Rent.	Observations.		Value of Tenancy.
a. r. p.	£ s. d.	£ s. d.	£ s. d.		£ s. d.	£ s. d.
9 1 8	8 10 0	8 11 0	6 15 0			
21 0 25	20 10 0	19 16 0	14 10 0			
12 0 8	16 15 0	16 6 9	14 0 0	Rent changed in 1854 from	6 9 5	
7 3 29	8 15 0	7 7 0	5 1 0			
10 0 4	10 10 0	8 13 4	7 10 0	1876	8 5 4	
67 2 15	71 0 0	61 9 0	58 0 0			
11 1 24	6 0 0	5 9 8	1 5 0			
7 0 23	9 0 0	10 0 10	6 6 0			
6 3 20	11 0 0	6 7 0	6 15 0			
1 2 39	4 15 0	5 1 0	4 0 0			
31 3 0	37 0 0	27 1 0	20 10 0			
28 3 15	16 0 0	11 16 0	10 0 0			
33 3 28	46 5 0	21 0 0	18 18 0			
30 1 25	24 16 0	20 0 0	18 14 0	1850	24 18 0	
34 0 20	28 10 0	31 0 0	25 0 0	do.	27 17 0	
12 0 0	7 16 0	6 11 0	6 0 0			
12 1 10	6 5 0	6 10 0	6 16 0			
6 1 0	4 0 0	3 18 0	3 0 0			
38 1 25	43 0 0	40 0 0	26 10 0			
12 0 23	8 0 0	8 0 0	8 0 0			
15 1 20	8 16 0	9 2 0	6 14 0			
6 3 20	6 12 0	5 9 0	4 12 0			
16 2 0	14 9 0	18 19 0	8 12 0			
9 0 15	9 0 0	6 2 0	6 12 0	1852	6 12 0	
8 2 10	5 0 0	4 10 0	3 15 0	1850	5 9 0	
6 2 5	6 0 0	5 16 0	4 15 0			
14 2 10	14 18 0	19 1 0	6 8 0			
5 0 0	6 5 0	4 10 0	4 10 0			
8 3 0	8 0 0	9 11 0	9 0 0			
14 2 25	12 10 0	10 11 0	6 18 0			
24 1 26	24 15 0	19 13 5	14 10 0			
22 3 21	29 10 0	28 13 0	19 10 0			
16 2 32	20 0 0	16 1 0	11 10 0			
15 1 32	14 10 0	18 1 0	11 0 0			

COUNTY OF

Names of Assistant Commissioners by whom Cases were decided.	No.	Name of Tenant.	Name of Landlord.	Townland.
Assistant Commissioners.—				
E. [illegible] (Legal).	5067	Robert Martin, ...	Viscount Bridport and anor., Trustees of Marquis of Downshire.	Drumadoney, ...
R. [illegible]	5068	James [illegible], ...	do.	Coravarny & anor.
S. [illegible]	5069	James Beatty, ...	do.	do. ...
	5070	James Beck, ...	do.	Moydalgan & anor.
	5071	James Bryson, ...	Omar C. Nelson and another, Trustees of H. Nelson, decd.	Lappagan, ...
	5072	John Rickie, ...	Robert J. Kennedy, ...	Ballydavey, ...
	5073	William Graham, ...	do.	do. ...
	5074	William J. Walker, ...	do.	Ballygrainey, ...
	5075	William M'Calla, ...	Visct. Bridport & anor., Trustees of Marquis of Downshire.	Moydalgan, ...
	5076	John Shelly, ...	do.	Dromara, ...
	5077	William J. Martin, ...	do.	Moydalgan, ...
	5078	Jonathan Turner, ...	do.	Ballykillcarataloney
	5079	Do., ...	do.	Coravarny, ...
	5080	James Nelson, ...	do.	Drumadoney, ...
	5081	Joseph Dawson, ...	do.	Backnamullagh,
	5082	William Gamble, ...	Omar C. Nelson and another, Trustees of H. Nelson, decd.	Lappagan, ...
	5083	Samuel Crown, ...	do.	do. ...
	5084	David Gibson and anor., Exors. of Thos. H. Shaw.	James Graham, ...	Drevy, ...
	5085	Do. ...	do.	do. ...
	5086	Daniel Rice, junior, and another, Exors. of James M'Loughlin.	John Mulholland, surviving Trustee of R. W. B. Ker.	Creevytenant, ...
	5087	David Reid ...	do.	Barvey, ...
	5088	Alexander Reid, ...	do.	Ballymacarn, ...
	5089	John Campbell, junior,	do.	Carrickmaddyroe?, ...
	5090	William M'Kelvey, ...	do.	Barvey, ...
	5091	John Patterson, ...	do.	do. ...
	5092	Marcia Cranberry, ...	do.	Magheraknock, ...
	5093	George Bell, ...	do.	do. ...
	5094	William Gibson & anor. ...	do.	Creevytenant, ...
	5095	David Simpson, ...	do.	do. ...
	5096	William S. Reid, Exor. of Elizabeth Lyons.	do.	Ballymacarn, ...
	5097	Hugh R. Douglas, ...	do.	Glendrumgand?,
	5098	Robert John Moore, ...	General H. G. Magennis, ...	Moybrick Upper,
	5099	Francis Sheppard, ...	James S. Price, ...	Glasdrummond,
				Total, ...

DOWN—*continued*.

Extent of Holding, Statute.	Poor Law Valuation.	Former Rent.	Judicial Rent.	Observations.		Value of Tenancy.
A. R. P.	£ s. d.	£ s. d.	£ s. d.		£ s. d.	£ s. d.
18 0 0	20 15 0	18 2 0	16 10 0			
173 3 10	133 15 0	116 3 0	90 0 0			
43 1 17	46 0 0	37 18 0	31 10 0			
7 3 34	9 15 0	5 6 0	5 5 0	Rent changed in 1880 to	6 2 0	
35 3 0	34 16 0	27 5 6	30 0 0			
30 3 3	22 0 0	23 1 8	16 12 0			
43 2 18	45 10 0	46 15 10	37 0 0			
65 3 0	65 5 0	66 15 4	58 0 0			
61 0 35	51 10 10	40 0 0	32 0 0			
53 3 24	50 0 0	53 0 0	41 0 0			
34 0 35	25 0 0	19 12 0	15 5 0			
18 3 21	—	15 16 0	18 10 0			
16 1 7	15 10 0	18 16 0	18 0 0			
19 0 32	23 0 0	15 8 0	12 10 0			
34 0 16	33 0 0	31 0 0	23 10 0			
7 0 14	7 0 0	5 10 6	4 10 0			
10 0 0	11 0 0	9 5 2	6 5 0	1855	6 5 0	
17 3 30	6 15 0	11 4 0	8 10 0			
15 0 10	8 10 0	7 11 0	8 0 0			
13 2 23	8 16 0	20 3 0	5 0 0			
70 3 20	36 10 0	25 7 9	31 0 0			
6 1 20	4 10 0	7 0 0	4 15 0			
13 3 5	8 0 0	8 14 0	5 10 0			
65 1 30	22 10 0	24 5 0	15 15 0			
24 1 5	18 0 0	18 0 0	10 10 0			
54 3 10	30 0 0	30 10 0	42 10 0			
30 0 5	19 0 0	17 1 0	13 10 0			
40 1 0	38 5 0	35 0 8	35 10 0			
10 0 0	7 5 0	7 3 0	5 10 0			
55 3 35	67 0 0	34 13 0	18 0 0			
60 1 15	50 10 0	27 5 0	23 10 0			
34 2 30	25 5 0	23 7 4	17 10 0			
19 1 10	13 0 0	11 4 8	5 10 0			

COUNTY OF

Names of Assistant Commissioners by whom Cases were decided.	No.	Name of Tenant.	Name of Landlord.	Townland.
Assistant Commissioners— W. F. Bailey (Legal). J. R. Hamilton. J. A. Kerr.	3778	Mary Mohan, ...	S. E. Shirley, ...	Lisnagunogue, ...
	3779	Laurence Murphy, ...	do.	do. ...
	3780	Henry McGuinness, ...	do.	Cabblen, West, ...
	3781	Mary McGeough, ...	do.	do. ...
	3782	Peter Murphy, ...	do.	Carramore and another.
	3783	Owen Mohan, ...	do.	Kilbarne, ...
	3784	Patrick Murphy, ...	do.	do. ...
	3785	John Murphy, ...	do.	Lossetts, ...
	3786	Edward McArdle, ...	do.	Lisanisk, ...
	3787	Bernard Mohan, ...	do.	Carramore and another.
	3788	Mathew McEnaney, Ld. Admr. of Cormack McEnaney.	do.	Mullanteleevan, ...
	3789	Hugh McEntee, ...	do.	do. ...
	3790	Michael Muldoon, ...	do.	Greaghlin, ...
	3791	Bernard McCabe, ...	do.	Rough, ...
	3792	John McCabe, ...	do.	Ballyvartan and another.
	3793	John Murray, ...	do.	Derrynaglogh, ...
	3794	James McCabe, ...	do.	Derrynascoble, ...
	3795	Thomas Mohan, ...	do.	Knockancran, West.
	3796	Bryan McMahon, ...	do.	Drumcarrigan-bog.
	3797	Laurence McDermott, ...	do.	Drumbracken and another.
	3798	Hugh McMahon, ...	do.	Drumbracken and others.
	3799	Ellen McMahon, Ld. Admix. of Oliver McMahon.	do.	Raferagh, ...
	3800	Thomas McEnaney, ...	do.	do. ...
	3801	Patrick Murtagh, ...	do.	do. ...
	3802	Owen McEnaney, ...	do.	do. ...
	3803	Patk. McMahon, Ld. Admr. of Cath. McMahon.	do.	Raferagh and another.
	3804	Edward McCluskey, ...	do.	do. ...
	3805	Pat McCluskey, ...	do.	do. ...
	3806	Hugh Morgan, ...	do.	do. ...
	3807	Michael McCluskey, ...	do.	Corgreagh, ...
	3808	Peter McEnaney, ...	do.	do. ...
	3809	Ross McCahey, ...	do.	do. ...
	3810	Patrick McEntee, ...	do.	do. ...
	3811	John McEntee, ...	do.	do. ...
	3812	Owen McCaul, Ld. Admr. of John McCaul.	do.	do. ...

MONAGHAN.

Extent of Holding. Statute.	Poor Law Valuation.	Former Rent.	Judicial Rent.	Observations.	Value of Tenancy.
A. R. P.	£ s. d.	£ s. d.	£ s. d.		£ s. d.
11 2 8	6 0 0	9 11 0	4 10 0		
17 3 0	11 10 0	12 10 0	8 17 6		
10 1 25	8 0 0	9 2 0	5 8 0		
6 0 5	4 0 0	3 12 0	3 15 0		
16 1 30	13 15 0	15 0 0	10 5 0		
10 1 20	7 5 0	9 9 0	6 5 0		
8 2 0	3 5 0	2 12 0	1 17 6		
6 0 0	5 10 0	5 15 0	5 0 0		
16 0 35	9 15 0	10 12 0	7 10 0		
7 2 10	5 10 0	5 16 0	4 5 0		
9 1 0	7 10 0	7 13 0	5 0 0		
4 1 5	3 15 0	4 18 0	2 10 0		
69 0 30	55 10 0	54 0 0	34 0 0		
18 2 5	15 15 0	14 0 0	9 10 0		
16 0 33	12 15 0	14 1 0	9 0 0		
16 2 24	15 5 0	16 4 0	11 15 0		
8 0 25	6 10 0	7 5 0	6 0 0		
11 0 2	9 10 0	10 15 0	8 10 0		
34 0 30	27 0 0	29 11 0	20 15 0		
71 5 16	58 10 0	62 2 0	44 0 0		
41 2 25	30 5 0	34 11 0	24 10 0		
14 2 20	9 10 0	7 18 0	8 0 0		
18 1 0	10 0 0	10 9 0	6 15 0		
8 2 20	6 18 0	6 9 0	3 17 6		
11 0 0	7 10 0	7 1 0	6 0 0		
15 3 10	14 5 0	10 6 0	6 0 0		
15 2 0	11 4 0	10 2 0	7 10 0		
27 1 25	18 0 0	18 15 0	12 10 0		
11 3 0	9 0 0	6 12 0	8 0 0		
34 2 15	25 0 0	27 11 0	18 5 0		
6 2 5	6 0 0	5 15 0	4 2 6		
23 1 24	25 0 0	25 0 0	15 0 0		
6 0 10	5 5 0	5 12 0	4 0 0		
31 1 8	21 0 0	22 14 0	16 10 0		
6 2 20	5 5 0	6 10 0	4 10 0		

Names of Assistant Commissioners by whom Cases were decided.	No.	Name of Tenant.	Name of Landlord.	Townland.
Assistant Commissioners— W. F. Bailey (Legal). J. R. Hearnden. J. A. Rice.	3813	James McCluskey,	S. E. Shirley,	Cargaboge,
	3814	James Gargan, Ld. Admor. of Patrick Gargan.	do.	Greaghlone,
	3815	Michael McGrane,	do.	Knocknamaroe,
	3816	James McMahon,	do.	Drumbracken & another.
	3817	Pat McCabe,	do.	Avery,
	3818	Michael McCluskey,	do.	Cargalougue,
	3819	Patrick McArdle,	do.	Carrickashedoge,
	3820	Patrick Murray,	do.	Corrinenty,
	3821	James McBride,	do.	Corraghy,
	3822	Bernard McBride, Ld. Admor. of Bridget McBride.	do.	do.
	3823	Mary McBride,	do.	Corraghy & anor.,
	3824	Do.,	do.	Corraghy,
	3825	Patrick McBride,	do.	Cargaghmore,
	3826	Francis McMillan,	do.	do.
	3827	Mary McCabe,	do.	Carrickashedoge,
	3828	Owen McCabe,	do.	do.
	3829	Pat McCabe,	do.	do.
	3830	Bernard McCluskey,	do.	do.
	3831	Catherine McGovern,	do.	Corrinenty,
	3832	Ellen McBride, Ld. Admx. of Michl. McBride.	do.	Lisirril,
	3833	Michael McCahery	do.	do.
	3834	Francis McCahery, Ld. Admor. of Cath. McCahery.	do.	do.
	3835	Michael McGovern,	do.	Corrinenty,
	3836	James McGovern,	do.	do.
	3837	Catherine McCabe,	do.	do.
	3838	Mathew McConnon,	do.	Faraghy,
	3839	Peter McCarby,	do.	do.
	3840	Francis McCabe,	do.	do.
	3841	Francis Murphy,	do.	do.
	3842	Philip McKenna,	do.	Corraghy,
	3843	Michael McKenna,	do.	do.
	3844	James McConnell,	do.	do.
	3845	Thomas Marron, Ld. Admor. of Cath. Marron.	do.	Umerafree
	3846	Bridget McEntee,	do.	Cargaghmore,
	3847	Thos. McEnaney (Fanny).	do.	Ardragh,

Extent of Holding, Statute.			Poor Law Valuation.			Former Rent.			Judicial Rent.			Observations.	Value of Tenancy.		
A.	R.	P.	£	s.	d.	£	s.	d.	£	s.	d.		£	s.	d.
36	2	20	38	0	0	34	14	0	31	10	0				
23	1	34	19	0	0	21	6	0	16	5	0				
10	2	0	8	6	0	6	14	0	6	0	0				
30	2	6	17	16	0	21	2	0	18	10	0				
8	3	30	6	0	0	8	8	0	7	18	0				
23	2	10	17	0	0	13	7	0	11	15	0				
13	3	15	8	5	0	7	18	0	5	5	0				
14	3	10	8	0	0	7	19	0	5	5	0				
15	2	20	12	2	0	10	0	0	7	5	0				
9	1	15	6	15	0	5	14	0	4	4	0				
17	1	0	10	14	0	11	0	0	8	10	0				
30	0	20	20	0	0	21	18	0	16	5	0				
12	3	10	5	0	0	4	11	0	3	10	0				
20	0	0	7	15	0	7	1	0	4	10	0				
4	0	10	3	10	0	3	4	0	2	2	0				
10	0	6	10	5	0	10	0	0	7	4	0				
8	0	20	6	18	0	6	8	0	2	17	6				
20	2	10	17	10	0	28	10	0	13	10	0				
13	2	30	9	10	0	8	14	0	5	5	0				
13	1	15	7	2	0	8	2	0	4	12	6				
20	2	0	14	15	0	15	1	0	8	15	0				
8	1	36	5	0	0	5	4	0	3	8	0				
8	1	24	4	5	0	4	3	0	3	6	0				
9	2	15	5	12	0	5	5	0	4	15	0				
13	1	30	9	0	0	10	1	0	7	5	0				
11	1	10	5	5	0	7	8	0	6	0	0				
5	3	30	4	15	0	4	9	0	3	0	0				
6	1	15	5	0	0	4	7	0	2	15	0				
6	1	36	4	15	0	4	2	0	3	0	0				
5	3	14	3	10	0	3	10	0	2	15	0				
3	1	0	2	10	0	2	0	0	1	10	0				
10	0	20	5	0	0	5	5	0	5	0	0				
9	3	30	5	5	0	5	15	0	4	10	0				
14	3	15	8	10	0	8	8	0	6	0	0				
11	1	10	8	15	0	6	1	0	6	2	6				

COUNTY OF

Names of Assistant Commissioners by whom Cases were decided.	No.	Name of Tenant.	Name of Landlord.	Townland.
Assistant Commissioners—				
W. F. Bailey (Legal). J. R. Heasmon. J. A. Kenny.	3848	Peter McEnarney, ...	S. E. Shirley, ...	Ardragh, ...
	3849	Bridget McGrive, ...	do.	Corrickinlonoy, ...
	3850	Mathew McCusam, ...	do.	Corrinkinale, ...
	3851	Francis McEnaney, ...	do.	Lurgey, ...
	3852	Sarah McCormack, ...	do.	Cavry, ...
	3853	Peter McCusam, ...	do.	do. ...
	3854	Elizabeth McCallen. ...	do.	do. ...
W. F. Bailey (Legal). J. D. Lynch. W. S. Rutgers.	3855	Luke McGovern, ...	Miss Henrietta Westenra, a lunatic, by H. O. Lewis, her Committee.	Dromturish, ...
	3856	Patrick Keenan, ...	Earl of Dartrey, ...	Oghavory, ...
	3857	Mary Kieran, ...	Lord Rossmore, ...	Crovanaige, ...
	3858	Thomas Kieran, ...	do.	Aughnagogh, ...
	3859	Joseph Tilby, ...	do.	Drumillany, ...
	3860	Patrick Glenn, ...	do.	Drumskerry and Stilbey,
	3861	Edward Murphy, ...	do.	Erinaghan, ...
	3862	Terence Connolly, ...	do.	Aughanagh, ...
	3863	James McMahon, ...	do.	Crovanaige, ...
	3864	Mary Kieran, ...	do.	do. ...
	3865	James Kieran, ...	do.	do. ...
	3866	Peter Cassidy, ...	do.	Annaleagh, ...
	3867	Robert Wilson, ...	do.	Aughnaskeary,
	3868	Bernard McPhillips, ...	do.	Annaghleigh, ...
	3869	Charles Connolly, ...	do.	Cruise, ...
	3870	Thomas McMurray, ...	do.	Drumgarranay and Cluan.
	3871	Pat Connolly, ...	do	Cruise, ...
	3872	Owen Connolly, ...	do.	Aughanagh, ...
	3873	Felix Sherry, ...	do.	do. ...
	3874	James Connolly, ...	do.	do. ...
	3875	John Connolly (Ross) ...	do.	Annaghleigh, ...
	3876	John Glenn, ...	do.	Colliagh, ...
	3877	Patrick McGuirk, Lcl. Admor. of Rose McGuirk.	do.	do. ...
	3878	Philip Bergin, ...	do.	do. ...
	3879	Anne McArdle, ...	do	Cornamaddy, ...

MONAGHAN—*continued.*

Extent of Holding. Statute.	Poor Law Valuation.	Former Rent.	Judicial Rent.	Observations.	Value of Tenancy.
A. R. P.	£ s. d.	£ s. d.	£ s. d.		£ s. d.
15 0 0	8 5 0	7 9 0	6 7 8		
10 3 0	8 0 0	5 18 0	4 5 0		
11 3 10	6 0 0	7 5 0	5 0 0		
18 1 28	10 15 0	11 15 0	8 0 0		
10 1 10	7 0 0	5 10 0	4 18 6		
11 2 8	7 5 0	6 3 0	4 0 0		
23 3 20	14 15 0	14 7 0	10 17 6		
55 0 8	53 10 0	65 9 4	50 0 0		
81 2 25	83 0 0	79 14 0	63 10 0		
12 3 15	5 15 0	9 10 0	7 0 0		
6 1 5	4 15 0	5 0 10	5 10 0		
15 3 18	11 0 0	15 7 11	8 0 0		
14 3 20	11 0 0	20 13 10	8 0 0		
21 1 25	15 5 0	18 5 0	11 0 0		
7 2 5	5 0 0	3 0 0	3 15 0		
15 0 25	9 0 0	9 14 0	6 10 0		
12 0 5	5 0 0	5 13 0	4 10 0		
15 0 15	10 10 0	10 17 6	7 10 0		
18 1 0	12 15 0	10 10 0	7 0 0		
55 3 20	30 0 0	33 5 0	25 0 0		
10 1 23	7 0 0	7 18 0	5 5 0		
12 1 5	6 15 0	9 18 6	8 0 0		
71 3 31	45 5 0	53 0 0	35 0 0		
5 0 0	5 10 0	6 13 10	3 10 0		
5 1 20	6 10 0	4 8 0	5 0 0		

COUNTY OF

Names of Assistant Commissioners by whom Cases were decided.	No.	Name of Tenant.	Name of Landlord.	Townland.
Assistant Commissioners— W. F. Bailey (Legal). J. D. Bell. W. S. Richardson.	3880	Bernard Duffy, ...	Lord Rossmore, ...	Shanrahan, ...
	3881	Ellen McGivin, ...	do.	do. ...
	3882	Margaret Coyle, ...	do.	Corrancarby and another.
	3883	Patrick McArdle, ...	do.	do. ...
	3884	Lawrence Duffy, ...	do.	Tandragee & another.
	3885	Henry Jackson, ...	do.	Tandragee, ...
	3886	Peter Crenlan, Ltd. Admr. of Thomas Crenlan,	do.	Ballymurgh, ...
	3887	Robert Jackson, ...	do.	do. ...
	3888	Alexander Hughes, ...	do.	Carrowm, ...
	3889	Patrick Connolly, ...	do.	do. ...
	3890	Anne Murphy, ...	do.	do. ...
	3891	Rachel Thompson, ...	do.	do. ...
	3892	John Murphy, ...	do.	do. ...
	3893	Catherine Boylan, ...	do.	Tullygillen, ...
	3894	John Boylan, ...	do.	do. ...
	3895	Susan Murphy, ...	do.	Rough Knock,
	3896	Mary Haughey, ...	do.	do. ...
	3897	James McKenna, ...	do.	Lisnarow & anor.
	3898	John O'Neill, ...	do.	do. ...
	3899	Michael Connolly, ...	do.	do. ...
	3900	Jane Henderson, ...	do.	Lough, ...
	3901	Hugh Henderson, ...	do.	do. ...
	3902	George Harkness, ...	do.	Tullyloan, ...
	3903	Francis Donaghy, ...	do.	Mullyknock and another.
	3904	Do.	do.	do. ...
	3905	Henry Jackson, ...	do.	do. ...
	3906	Thomas Brown, ...	do.	Lough, ...
	3907	James Connolly, ...	do.	Lisnaroe, ...
	3908	Francis Duffy, ...	Earl of Dartrey, ...	Conaboy, ...
	3909	Owen Johnston, ...	do.	do. ...
	3910	H. J. Allen, ...	Lord Rossmore, ...	Drumanevine, ...
	3911	Do.	do	Lisnalee, ...
	3912	George Thompson, ...	J. C. Wilson and others, ...	Aghadrumsee,
	3913	James Allen, ...	Lord Rossmore, ...	Lisnalee, ...
	3914	Owen Cogan, ...	John Hamilton, ...	Corraville, ...

MONAGHAN—*continued.*

Extent of Holding. Statute.	Poor Law Valuation.	Former Rent.	Judicial Rent.	Observations.	Value of Tenancy.
A. R. P.	£ s. d.	£ s. d.	£ s. d.		£ s. d.
10 3 20	7 0 0	8 1 6	5 10 0		
11 1 8	6 0 0	8 11 0	5 10 0		
13 0 20	9 15 0	10 13 1	6 0 0		
8 1 1	6 10 0	6 16 5	5 3 0		
19 0 10	18 0 0	11 5 0	9 15 0		
11 0 30	6 5 0	9 1 6	6 15 0		
16 1 0	10 15 0	11 3 8	8 0 0		
13 3 16	8 0 0	10 2 8	7 0 0		
20 2 30	20 5 0	13 17 6	13 0 0		
10 1 15	6 10 6	8 1 0	6 0 0		
9 1 33	6 10 8	6 9 2	4 15 0		
9 2 4	5 15 0	8 12 5	3 8 0		
16 1 0	10 0 0	9 8 0	7 10 0		
5 2 10	4 10 0	3 15 0	5 0 0		
8 2 5	6 15 0	6 0 7	5 0 0		
7 0 25	4 0 0	4 6 0	3 0 0		
20 0 25	17 15 0	18 0 0	14 0 0		
22 3 25	15 10 0	16 10 0	18 0 0		
8 1 35	5 5 0	5 0 2	4 5 0		
20 1 10	6 6 0	7 13 8	5 5 0		
26 0 10	22 15 0	21 17 0	15 10 0		
15 1 20	11 10 0	18 4 10	9 0 0		
67 0 31	23 15 0	67 1 6	18 0 0		
23 2 27	14 5 0	14 11 0	11 10 0		
3 0 20	2 0 0	1 17 5	1 6 0		
20 2 30	15 15 0	15 19 5	13 0 0		
22 3 10	20 2 0	21 18 4	16 0 0		
7 3 20	4 15 0	4 1 6	6 0 0		
8 0 0	5 0 0	6 18 0	3 15 0		
5 0 10	3 10 0	5 4 0	3 15 0		
5 0 16	5 5 0	6 3 4	3 10 0		
13 1 0	9 15 0	8 10 4	5 10 0		
19 2 20	16 10 0	16 10 0	13 0 0		
20 2 20	21 0 0	18 15 6	14 0 0		
7 6 13	8 10 0	5 14 0	8 10 0		

COUNTY OF

Names of Assistant Commissioners by whom Cases were decided.	No.	Name of Tenant.	Name of Landlord.	Townland.
Assistant Commissioners—				
W. F. Bailey (Legal). J. D. Bell. W. S. Richardson.	3915	Owen Johnston, ...	John Hamilton, ...	Carrsville, ...
	3916	John Tumelty, ...	do.	do. ...
	3917	Anne Sherry, ...	do.	do. ...
	3918	Owen Tumelty, ...	do.	do. ...
	3919	Arthur Johnston, ...	do.	do. ...
	3920	Mary Smith, ...	do.	do. ...
	3921	Felix O'Neill, ...	do.	do. ...
	3922	Felix Hughes, ...	do.	do. ...
	3923	Hugh O'Neill, ...	do.	do. ...
	3924	Daniel McNally, ...	do.	Brockwallace, ...
	3925	James Owens, ...	do.	do. ...
	3926	John McAdam, ...	do.	do. ...
	3927	Francis Mohan, ...	do.	do. ...
	3928	James Connolly, ...	do.	do. ...
	3929	Anne Devlin, ...	do.	do. ...
	3930	Francis McElearney, ...	do.	do. ...
	3931	Philip Ward, ...	do	do ...
	3932	Bridget Farrell, ...	do.	do. ...
				Total, ...

COUNTY OF

Assistant Commissioners—	7353	Sam Cunningham, ...	Major J. G. Smyly, ...	Ballylennon Scott,
D. Tierney (Legal). A. S. Drake. A. Doran.	7354	Caldwell Cunningham,	do.	do. ...
	7355	James Porter, ...	do.	Bridgetown, ...
	7356	Samuel Fox, ...	do.	do. ...
	7357	William Henderson, ...	do.	Ballylennon Scott,
	7358	Michael McLoughlin, ...	Robert F. Gordon and anor.,	Pluglish, ...
	7359	William McLoughlin, ...	do.	do. ...
	7360	James Sheridan, ...	do.	Drumnyvish, ...
	7361	Francis McCanny, Rep. of Thomas McCanny,	do.	Annaghlough, ...
	7362	Michael McCanny, Rep. of Thomas McCanny.	do.	do. ...

MONAGHAN—*continued.*

	Extent of Holding Statute.	Poor Law Valuation.	Former Rent.	Judicial Rent.	Observations.	Value of Tenancy.
	A. R. P.	£ s. d.	£ s. d.	£ s. d.		£ s. d.
	6 0 12	1 10 0	1 16 0	1 5 0		
	6 1 37	6 5 0	6 6 0	4 10 0		
	11 3 6	6 10 0	9 18 0	6 10 0		
	13 0 35	8 15 0	10 16 0	7 0 0		
	9 3 35	7 5 0	7 10 0	5 10 0		
	3 3 10	2 15 0	3 0 0	3 0 0		
	6 1 0	5 8 0	8 5 0	5 10 0		
	8 1 0	4 10 0	4 10 0	8 0 0		
	15 3 0	9 13 0	10 10 0	7 10 0		
	16 0 20	14 0 0	16 0 0	10 10 0		
	11 0 20	12 10 0	12 4 0	5 10 0		
	15 2 20	10 10 0	13 6 0	8 0 0		
	25 2 20	19 10 0	27 18 0	16 10 0		
	12 2 36	5 15 0	6 11 0	4 10 0		
	9 0 10	5 5 0	4 18 0	4 10 0		
	7 3 0	8 10 0	3 5 0	3 0 0		
	20 1 10	17 0 0	15 15 0	12 15 0		
	13 1 15	10 6 0	11 8 0	8 10 0		
	5,435 0 25	1,761 1 0	1,886 5 8	1,372 8 0		

TYRONE.

	33 3 30	19 10 0	20 0 0	16 0 0		
	22 3 13	15 10 0	14 1 10	11 0 0		
	36 1 20	20 0 0	27 19 0	22 0 0		
	16 1 10	11 0 0	10 17 0	5 0 0		
	15 2 25	10 10 0	9 4 0	7 0 0		
	47 3 30	10 5 0	8 14 0	6 10 0		
	57 2 20	6 10 0	6 5 0	5 5 0		
	4 2 30	2 10 0	2 0 0	1 12 0		
	12 0 25	4 5 0	3 1 0	3 0 0		
	13 2 0	7 5 0	6 18 0	6 5 0		

COUNTY OF

Names of Assistant Commissioners by whom these were decided.	No.	Name of Tenant.	Name of Landlord.	Townland.
Assistant Commissioners—				
D. Tuckey (Legal). A. E. Deane. A. Dickie.	7363	Charles McDermott, ...	Robert F. Gordon and another,	Annaghlough, ...
	7364	Edward Devany, continued in name of John Monaghan,	do.	Lisnagh, ...
	7365	Thomas E. Sparrick, ...	do.	Mossbeg, ...
	7366	Letty Kane, ...	do.	Praghlish, ...
	7367	John McCabe, ...	do.	do. ...
	7368	James McCanny, ...	do.	Annaghlough, ...
	7369	John Sproule, ...	James Orr, ...	Ardamoyra, Lower,
	7370	John Connolly, senior, ...	Earl of Caledon, ...	Shanagragan, ...
	7371	John Kelly, ...	do.	Claghernagh, ...
	7372	Ellen McNinch, ...	Robert S. Mansfield, ...	Williamount, ...
	7373	David Walker, ...	do.	Meaghan, ...
	7374	William McGlinchy, ...	Mathew Nelson, ...	Laughtmorris, ...
	7375	Francis McQuaid, ...	William Sproule, ...	Carrowshandrum,
	7376	Charles Sproule, ...	Robert A. Tennant and anor.,	Edenaragh, ...
				Total, .

PROVINCE OF

COUNTY OF

Assistant Commissioners—				
R. Bervin, Q.C. (Legal). S. Murphy. F. F. Jeffares.	765	Joseph Daly, Rep. of Honoria Daly,	Sir Thomas Butler, Bart., ...	Aughana, ...
	766	Patrick Murphy, ...	Right Hon. H. Bruen, ...	Ballyryan, ...
	767	Anne Nolan, Rep. of H. Nolan,	do.	Newtown, ...
	768	Patrick Curran, ...	Mrs. Sarah J. B. Cooper and another,	Tomard, Upper,
	769	John Sharpe, ...	Sir Robert Macy, Bart., ...	Carrymore, ...
	770	Richard Butler, ...	Colonel W. C. Conlin, ...	Ballyellen, ...
	771	Michael Byrne, ...	Rev. Dr. J. Whiting, ...	Rathglasscarra, ...
	772	Do., ...	do.	do. ...
	773	Thomas Neill, ...	John Kelson, ...	Mountneill, ...
	774	Patrick Dowling, ...	Mrs. A. B. de Montmorency,	Broughillstown,

TYRONE—*continued.*

Extent of Holding. Statute.			Poor Law Valuation.			Former Rent.			Judicial Rent.			Observations.
A.	R.	P.	£	s.	d.	£	s.	d.	£	s.	d.	
19	3	30	7	0	0	6	10	0	6	0	0	
6	1	13	9	10	0	3	4	0	1	14	0	
325	0	0	15	10	0	13	0	0	19	0	0	
11	3	36	4	0	0	9	0	0	3	6	0	
26	1	3	8	10	0	6	12	0	5	5	0	
34	0	9	6	0	0	6	17	0	5	12	0	
30	3	0	20	10	0	21	19	10	17	0	0	
15	3	25	6	10	0	5	13	4	4	0	0	
53	1	15	8	0	0	10	5	0	8	0	0	
31	3	0	17	10	0	13	0	0	13	0	0	
34	2	6	19	15	0	11	17	6	9	0	0	
12	0	0	5	0	0	8	0	0	5	0	0	
*—			30	7	6	34	0	0	25	0	0	*Undivided moiety of 150a. 1r.
78	3	36	10	15	0	14	5	7	10	10	0	
1,183	1	24	201	8	5	201	9	1	227	2	0	

LEINSTER.

CARLOW.

COUNTY OF

Names of Assistant Commissioners by whom Cases were decided.	No.	Name of Tenant.	Name of Landlord.	Townland.
Assistant Commissioners—				
R. Reeves, Q.C. (Legal). S. Mowbray. F. F. Jeffers.	775	John Donnelly, ...	Mrs. A. E. de Montmorency,	Broughillstown,
	776	George James, ...	Sir Clement J. Wolseley, Bt.,	Williamstown, ...
	777	Thomas Molloy, ...	do.	do. ...
R. Reeves, Q.C. (Legal). T. A. Dillon. T. Davidson.	778	Catherine Joyce, ...	John Corcoran, ...	Kilcolman, ...
	779	Pierce Joyce, ...	do.	do. ...
	780	John Kirwan, ...	P. J. Newton, ...	Knockroe, ...
	781	Thomas Hickey, ...	do.	do. ...
	782	Christopher Hughes, ...	Charles M. Doyne, ...	Kilballyhue, ...
	783	Thomas Lennon, ...	do.	do. ...
	784	Patrick Hayden, ...	do.	do. ...
	785	Catherine Kavanagh, ...	do.	do. ...
	786	Bridget Doyle, ...	Earl of Courtown, ...	Slievebawn, ...
	787	Patrick Maher, ...	do.	Ballyhacket, ...
	788	Bryan Long, ...	Rt. Hon. A. McM. Kavanagh,	[illegible],
	789	Ellen Dalton, ...	do.	Mullinagown, ...
	790	Michael Flood, ...	do.	[illegible],
	791	Thomas Murphy, ...	do.	do. ...
	792	Daniel Kavanagh, ...	do.	do. ...
	793	John Kane, ...	do.	Ballyglisheen, ...
	794	Do., ...	do.	Mullinagown, ...
	795	James Ryan, ...	do.	Drumagh, ...
	796	Do., ...	do.	Drummond, ...
	797	Mogue Byrne, ...	do.	Drumagh, ...
	798	Mary Cullen, ...	do.	do. ...
	799	Terence Dalton, ...	do.	do. ...
	800	Thomas Byrne, ...	do.	Mullinagown, ...
	801	James Farrell, ...	do.	do. ...
	802	Michael Doyle, ...	do.	do. ...
	803	Do., ...	do.	Ballyglisheen, ...
	804	Thomas Byrne, ...	do.	do. ...
	805	James Brohan, ...	do.	Templenaboe, ...
	806	James Dunphy, ...	do.	St. Mullins & others
				Total, ...

CARLOW—*continued.*

Extent of Holding, Statute.	Poor Law Valuation.	Former Rent.	Judicial Rent.	Observations.
A. R. P.	£ s. d.	£ s. d.	£ s. d.	
45 0 7	34 0 0	34 0 0	25 0 0	
36 2 21	25 0 0	28 9 0	23 0 0	
40 0 11	27 18 9	35 17 5	25 0 0	
30 0 4	10 10 0	15 5 0	8 5 0	
20 0 4	11 13 0	15 5 0	9 18 0	
9 3 10	3 10 0	6 0 0	5 18 0	
4 0 7	unascertained.	2 10 10	1 5 0	
15 2 7	14 0 0	18 10 0	13 10 0	
11 1 28	10 5 0	11 7 0	7 0 0	
4 3 15	5 0 0	6 0 0	4 5 0	
34 2 21	15 0 0	18 2 0	14 0 0	
0 2 20	0 15 0	1 0 0	0 10 0	
31 2 21	15 10 0	16 0 0	18 10 0	
11 3 8	4 15 0	4 0 0	3 15 0	
13 [illegible] 33	5 5 0	5 5 6	5 13 6	
47 3 25	10 15 0	11 0 0	8 0 0	
25 3 18	10 15 0	15 10 0	12 10 0	
45 0 17	10 5 0	10 5 0	12 5 0	
26 1 7	unascertained.	10 0 0	8 18 0	
25 0 20	16 15 0	12 0 0	10 0 0	
1 2 30	unascertained.	0 15 0	0 5 0	
78 0 25	33 5 0	35 5 0	28 0 0	
34 1 15	18 10 0	16 10 0	11 10 0	
25 2 25	9 15 0	10 0 0	7 18 0	
8 0 3	3 5 0	8 10 6	7 5 0	
11 1 7	5 10 0	5 4 8	4 0 0	
30 0 2	19 0 0	13 3 0	10 0 0	
25 0 0	17 18 0	13 15 0	10 15 6	
5 0 35	2 13 0	3 3 10	2 10 0	
17 1 25	4 5 0	5 0 0	4 0 0	
16 0 37	18 5 0	10 15 4	8 8 0	

COUNTY OF

Names of Assistant Commissioners by whom Cases were decided	No.	Name of Tenant.	Name of Landlord.	Townland.
Assistant Commissioners—				
R. Reeves, Q.C. (Legal). J. J. Gorey. H. G. Hare.	1516	Roger Colclough, ...	Arthur St. George, ...	Tulrid Upper, ...
	1517	Patrick Lambert, ...	Edward L. Warren, ...	Graiguenamanagh, ...
	1518	Edward Phelan, ...	do.	Loughstown, ...
	1519	James Griffith, ...	Captain St. George, ...	Barna, ...
	1520	George H. Colclough, ...	do.	do. ...
	1521	Joseph Julian, ...	do.	Kyle, ...
	1522	Patrick Butler, ...	Miss Sophia Walsh, ...	Cloppagh, ...
	1523	Denis Dunne, ...	Latitia R. G. Brady and others, Reps. of R. G. Brady.	Drumhaystown, ...
	1524	Edmond Butler, ...	Major William G. Thomas,	Knockabeadally,
	1525	Michael Tobin, ...	Mrs. Henry Flood, ...	Conversetown and another.
	1526	John Phelan, ...	John Ryan, ...	Scatteraugh, ...
	1527	William Dunphy, ...	Sir J. Coghill, Bart., ...	Kingsland, West,
	1528	Nicholas Farrell, ...	William Lawler, ...	Clonmore, ...
	1529	Michael Gibbons, ...	Sir John St. George, ...	Graiguenatagh, Upr.
	1530	Mary Kennedy, Rep. of Richard Kennedy.	T. St. George, ...	Lower Tulrid, ...
	1531	Edmond Leahy, Rep. of Mary Leahy.	do.	do. ...
	1532	Andw Butler, Lgl. Admor. of Michael Butler, jun.	Major William G. Thomas, ...	Tullabin, ...
	1533	Murtagh Dowling, Lgl. Admor. of Cathl. Fitzpatrick.	Thomas Eyre, ...	Tobernapeiste and another.
	1534	Nicholas Power, ...	Sir J. J. Coghill, Bart., ...	Gorting, ...
	1535	John Brennan, Lgl. Admr. of James Brennan, decd.	Right Rev. M. F. Day and ors., Trustees of Bellows's Charity.	Clohogue, ...
	1536	Edmond Rochford, ...	George Haly, ...	Drumaghmore and another.
	1537	John Robinson, ...	Michael Dan Kenealy, ...	Foxhill, ...
	1538	Anne Nugent, ...	do. ...	do. ...
	1539	Bridget Bergin, ...	do. ...	do. ...
R. Reeves, Q.C. (Legal). T. A. Dillon. T. Davidson.	1540	James Dooley, ...	Major Edward O'Brien, ...	Tinnakilly, Big,
	1541	Patrick Egan and anor.,	Bellingham Gunnet and ors., Trusts. of M. T. L. Murphy, a minor.	Curraghmore, ...
	1542	James Stanchfield, ...	Richard M. Greene, ...	Smithstown, ...
	1543	Richard Greer, ...	Dorothea Smith and another,	Glenpipe, ...
	1544	Peter Walsh, ...	do.	Mullenakill, ...
	1545	Do., ...	do.	Garranborough ...
	1546	William Tracy, ...	do.	Glenpipe, ...
	1547	Michael Cody, Lgl. Admor. of Patrick Cody.	do.	do. ...
				Total, ...

KILKENNY.

Extent of Holding. Statute.	Poor Law Valuation.	Former Rent.	Judicial Rent.	Observations.	Value of Tenancy.
A. R. P.	£ s. d.	£ s. d.	£ s. d.		£ s. d.
16 0 8	13 0 0	8 8 8	7 10 0		
7 2 25	5 15 0	6 17 8	5 12 0		
53 3 9	31 18 0	34 15 0	26 11 0		
27 1 30	19 0 0	20 0 0	14 0 0		
67 2 8	37 10 0	35 5 8	32 0 0		
142 2 30	unascertained.	61 14 8	54 0 0		
11 1 23	3 10 0	8 0 0	4 10 0		
67 1 18	25 0 0	31 13 6	23 0 0		
14 0 21	3 5 0	8 3 8	4 10 0		
156 2 10	106 0 0	100 0 0	80 0 0		
9 2 18	7 16 0	10 0 0	6 0 0		
78 2 32	23 10 0	33 14 10	28 14 10		
17 2 16	3 5 0	7 18 3	6 10 0		
31 0 32	18 10 0	23 12 0	17 0 0		
36 1 0	13 0 0	23 11 3	16 0 0		
16 2 15	10 0 0	11 18 0	10 0 0		
24 3 27	10 10 0	16 17 0	10 0 0		
27 0 39	24 5 0	30 2 6	28 0 0		
23 2 0	18 10 0	19 3 4	16 0 0		
33 2 37	19 10 0	20 16 5	14 0 0		
147 0 0	94 0 0	81 3 0	65 0 0	By consent.	
7 2 24	3 10 0	4 5 8	3 16 0		
34 2 11	21 0 0	19 14 0	16 16 0		
13 0 16	31 10 0	10 15 0	9 0 0		
19 0 32	10 15 0	10 13 1	9 8 0		
73 0 32	16 0 0	25 10 0	17 10 0		
47 0 31	27 10 0	21 10 0	18 0 0		
17 1 27	8 10 0	8 10 0	8 13 0		
73 3 21	15 0 0	16 0 0	11 10 0		
27 2 13	8 10 0	9 0 0	7 10 0		
1 1 0	1 5 0	1 5 0	1 0 0		

COUNTY OF

Names of Assistant Commissioners by whom Cases were decided.	No.	Name of Tenant.	Name of Landlord.	Townland.
Assistant Commissioners—				
R. R. Kane (Legal). T. Rowan. W. B. Hope.	1734	Edward Flanagan,	Colonel Wentworth H. King-Harman,	Derrinlurg,
	1735	James Flanagan,	do.	Lyanna,
	1736	Mrs. Mary Kenny,	Miss Emily Robinson,	Knockagh,
	1737	Miles Magrath,	Lord Annaly,	Toneymoney,
	1738	Do.,	W. T. Norris,	Lisnacreevagh and another,
	1739	Daniel Rourke,	Miss Frances A. King-Harman,	Derrygeel,
	1740	James Glynn,	do.	Gallowsmoney,
	1741	Dominick Sweeney,	do.	Derrygowna,
	1742	Mathew Ledwith,	Jacques J. Brown,	Ballynahoughton,
	1743	Dominick Quain,	do.	do.
	1744	Mary Garrigy,	do.	Ballynakey, Lower,
	1745	Anne Keenan,	Henry G. Grady,	Curryroe,
	1746	Michael Gilleny,	do.	do.
	1747	Patrick Gannon,	Mrs. Emily Fox and another,	Corrigeen,
	1748	Ellen Flood,	Edward Murray,	Aghamore,
	1749	John Dunne,	Colonel E. R. King-Harman, continued in name of W. H. King-Harman,	Killashee,
	1750	John Carey,	Colonel A. Brodie,	Glenmore,
	1751	Honor Gallen,	Captain John Shuldham,	Corraghmore,
	1752	John Conlan,	do.	Corraghboy,
	1753	James Reilly,	do.	do.
	1754	Philip Doyle,	Dr. Thomas R. Scott,	Fargarty,
	1755	Mary Moran,	T. A. Gamble, Trustee of the Will of Mrs. E. Jessop,	Cloughan,
	1756	Michael McGarry,	do.	Cornhill Mountain,
	1757	Ann Cunningham,	do.	do.
	1758	John Lenehan, junior,	do.	do.
	1759	Mary Moran,	do.	Cloughan,
	1760	Andrew Nolan,	John H. Reid,	Loughsheedan,
	1761	John Shelly,	Captain William Reid,	Clare,
	1762	James Martin,	Colonel E. R. King-Harman, continued in name of W. H. King-Harman,	Lyanna,
	1763	James Glynn,	do.	Derrygowna,
	1764	Bridget Rowan,	do.	do.
	1765	Patrick Farrell,	do.	Derrygeel,
	1766	Thomas Farrell,	Thomas Kennedy,	Derryoghil,

LONGFORD.

Extent of Holding Statute.	Poor Law Valuation.	Former Rent.	Judicial Rent.	Observations.	Value of Tenancy.
A. R. P.	£ s. d.	£ s. d.	£ s. d.	£ s. d.	£ s. d.
26 3 28	unascertained.	5 0 0	7 10 0		
145 3 27	74 18 0	70 0 0	70 0 0	Rent changed in 1867 from 48 5 0	
106 [illegible] 8	64 16 0	63 [illegible] 0	67 0 0		
81 1 21	33 18 0	40 0 0	65 0 0		
60 0 12	41 5 0	60 [illegible] 0	54 10 0	1864 40 0 10	
26 1 16	16 10 0	22 0 0	15 0 0	1880 14 0 0	
25 0 20	12 0 0	14 14 8	11 [illegible] 0		
27 3 4	11 0 0	17 0 0	18 0 0	1878 18 [illegible] 4	
68 0 11	22 6 0	21 6 10	14 0 0	1877 20 13 4	
30 3 24	13 [illegible] 0	14 [illegible] [illegible]	10 1 6	do. 14 0 0	
47 1 29	25 [illegible] 0	34 18 10	22 12 [illegible]	1871 32 18 10	
23 1 10	15 10 0	13 [illegible] 8	9 0 0		
14 [illegible] [illegible]	8 0 0	8 3 10	7 [illegible] 0		
50 1 7	30 15 0	64 10 0	37 10 0		
29 0 16	19 15 0	24 10 0	18 10 0	1881 20 0 0	
47 [illegible] 27	21 10 0	43 7 0	30 0 0		
16 1 14	6 10 0	8 13 0	5 0 0	1883 10 0 0	
49 1 14	20 [illegible] 0	55 0 0	35 0 0	1882 47 10 0	
35 0 [illegible]	17 18 0	20 0 0	17 10 0	1883 28 [illegible] [illegible]	
20 [illegible] 0	12 [illegible] 0	18 4 0	8 [illegible] [illegible]	do. 17 [illegible] 6	
4 1 13	3 10 0	4 10 0	2 18 0	1878 3 10 0	
34 [illegible] 11	unascertained.	6 4 0	6 [illegible] 0		
29 [illegible] 17	11 4 0	11 17 6	7 15 [illegible]		
33 1 [illegible]	14 0 0	16 7 4	10 15 0		
14 0 34	4 15 0	6 1 4	4 10 0		
26 3 30	unascertained.	6 18 0	5 [illegible] 0		
25 [illegible] [illegible]	9 0 0	8 0 0	6 0 0	1882 [illegible] 0 0	
37 0 0	17 18 0	17 0 0	15 0 0	do. 23 15 0	
9 3 [illegible]	3 10 0	[illegible] [illegible] 10	[illegible] 0 0		
30 0 16	9 10 0	18 0 [illegible]	10 0 0	1871 [illegible] 3 11	
37 3 31	10 0 0	13 10 0	10 10 0		
17 0 1	6 16 0	10 12 0	7 14 0	1880 6 [illegible] 0	
31 [illegible] 0	10 [illegible] 0	20 0 0	7 10 0	1882 15 0 0	
10 [illegible] 0	3 10 0	3 10 0	[illegible] 0 0	do. 4 3 0	

COUNTY OF

Names of Assistant Commissioners by whom Cases were decided.	No.	Name of Tenant.	Name of Landlord.	Townland.
Assistant Commissioners—				
R. R. Kane (Legal). T. [illegible]. W. S. Butt.	1768	Thomas McHugh, ...	Thomas Kennedy, ...	Derryhill, ...
	1769	Peter Mullany, ...	William Bond, ...	Charle, ...
	1770	Patrick Hatton, ...	Henry G. Grady, ...	Garryowen, ...
	1771	Eliza McCormick, ...	do.	do. ...
	1772	James Mullany, ...	do.	do. ...
	1773	Patrick Kenny, ...	Lord Annaly, ...	Carne, ...
	1774	Patrick Farrell, ...	do.	Tashinny, ...
	1775	Christopher Mulvihill,	do.	Carrowdongh, ...
	1776	James Hopkins, ...	do.	do. ...
	1777	Bridget Smith, ...	do.	do. ...
	1778	Michael Brennan, ...	do.	do. ...
	1779	Patrick Brennan, ...	do.	do. ...
	1780	John Kenny, ...	do.	Tomlough, ...
	1781	Bryan Fleming, ...	Edwin O'Brien and others, ...	Kilshrewly, ...
	1782	John Kelly, ...	Rev. Thomas Moore, ...	Tonrae, ...
	1783	James Healy, ...	Robert Armstrong, continued in name of W. H. King-Harman.	Creagh, ...
	1784	John Mannion, ...	Edwin O'Brien and others, ...	Kilshrewly, ...
	1785	James Mannion, ...	do.	do. ...
	1786	James Cleary, ...	do.	do. ...
	1787	Catherine Atkinson, ...	Thomas R. Isaac, ...	Forgney, ...
	1788	Patrick Killmeade, ...	do.	Forgney & anm.,
	1789	Do., ...	do.	do. ...
	1790	Bryan Keegan, ...	Captain John Shuldham, ...	Grovelang, ...
	1791	Mary Kelly, ...	do.	Moygh, ...
	1792	Sarah Curry, ...	Colonel E. R. King-Harman, continued in name of W. H. King-Harman.	Kenl, ...
	1793	Thomas Dennigan, ...	do.	Cloonmilon, ...
	1794	Sarah Curry, Rep. of T. Curry,	do.	Kenl, ...
	1795	Alexander Mills, ...	do.	Pallasbeg, ...
	1796	John Morris, ...	do.	Abbeyshrule, ...
	1797	William Robins, ...	do.	Lyneen, ...
	1798	James Ward, ...	do.	Derryart, ...
	1799	Patrick Kane, ...	do.	do. ...
	1800	Anne Cotton, ...	do.	Killeenatoolan, ...
	1801	Michael Murphy, ...	do.	Coolcaldeemh, ...

LONGFORD—continued.

Extent of Holding. Statute.	Poor Law Valuation.	Former Rent.	Judicial Rent.	Observations.	Value of Tenancy.
A. R. P.	£ s. d.	£ s. d.	£ s. d.	£ s. d.	£ s. d.
[illegible] 1 6	11 0 0	10 10 0	8 15 0	Rent changed in 18[illegible] from . . . 14 0 0	
8 1 20	6 10 0	8 0 0	4 0 0	do. 8 17 0	
2 0 16	1 6 0	1 10 0	1 0 0		
15 0 31	8 15 0	7 0 0	6 11 0		
[illegible] 1 17	12 15 0	11 6 0	9 18 0		
[illegible] 0 24	19 15 0	15 10 0	12 10 0		
43 0 [illegible]	[illegible] 0 0	[illegible] 0 0	26 0 0		
[illegible] 3 [illegible]	15 5 0	11 11 5	10 5 10		
[illegible] 3 34	19 10 0	16 1 2	15 0 6		
30 0 6	21 10 0	19 0 0	16 0 0		
27 1 12	[illegible] 5 0	15 15 4	14 0 0		
25 1 36	17 15 0	14 0 0	12 15 0	1875 18 16 0	
18 2 4	17 10 0	[illegible] 10 0	19 0 0	do. 20 0 10	
24 1 14	15 10 0	15 10 8	13 10 0	1879 12 0 0	
8 0 16	3 5 0	3 15 7	2 10 0		
15 3 [illegible]	15 5 0	12 0 0	11 0 0		
16 0 27	11 5 0	10 0 0	6 0 0	do. 8 7 0	
14 1 35	10 5 0	6 16 2	8 10 0	do. 7 8 4	
15 3 27	18 0 0	9 9 0	7 0 0		
19 0 [illegible]	10 0 0	11 0 0	8 0 0	18[illegible] 16 5 0	
21 0 0	[illegible] 10 0	20 0 0	15 10 0		
31 2 17	[illegible] 10 0	15 17 6	14 7 8	1881 20 5 6	
[illegible] 0 14	21 5 0	[illegible] 0 0	11 0 0	1828 29 0 0	
30 0 12	37 0 0	19 0 0	15 10 0	18[illegible] [illegible] 10 0	
43 3 34	34 0 0	36 0 0	30 0 0	1863 [illegible] 13 6	
34 2 [illegible]	8 15 0	11 0 0	8 0 0	1854 15 0 0	
[illegible] 3 18	[illegible] 0 0	17 19 5	[illegible] 0 0		
46 0 0	30 0 0	31 4 4	23 0 0		
[illegible] 1 8	34 0 0	42 0 6	[illegible] 0 0	1866 20 0 0	
27 3 27	29 10 0	[illegible] 0 0	[illegible] 4 0	1854 40 0 0	
27 0 6	14 0 0	17 0 10	12 10 0	1856 14 0 6	
4 0 13	3 10 0	2 4 0	1 18 0		
21 0 17	14 5 0	13 10 0	8 10 0	1866 8 1 0	
[illegible] 0 37	9 5 0	8 0 8	7 10 0		

COUNTY OF

Names of Assistant Commissioners by whom Cases were decided.	No.	Name of Tenant.	Name of Landlord.	Townland.
Assistant Commissioners—				
E. R. Kane (Legal). F. Roberts. W. S. Hunt.	1802	Ellen Mulvihill,	Colonel E. R. King-Harman, continued in name of W. H. King-Harman.	Fragha,
	1803	James McCormack,	do.	Carrowkeel,
	1804	James Carr,	do.	Kilmacrinan,
	1805	Martin Malia,	do.	Derryart,
	1806	John Higgins,	do.	Abbeyderrig,
	1807	Patrick Connor,	do.	Cooleshamroch,
	1808	Thomas Howard,	do.	Aughamore,
	1809	Margaret Farrell, Limtd. Admix. of Thos. Farrell.	do.	do.
	1810	John York,	do.	Barry,
	1811	Ellen Farrell,	do.	do.
	1812	Patrick Mulligan,	do.	Cross,
	1813	John F. Allen,	do.	Carnan, Little,
	1814	Bernard McGivney, Ltd. Admor. of Bernard McGivney.	Rev. Francis Dopping,	Kilrea,
	1820	Elizabeth Quinn,	Major Robert Blackall,	Aughnacliffe,
				Total,

COUNTY OF

Names of Assistant Commissioners by whom Cases were decided.	No.	Name of Tenant.	Name of Landlord.	Townland.
Head Commissioner.	1091	Thomas Gleeson,	Heads of J. A. Mooney and others, Assignees of Sir W. Nugent, a Bankrupt.	Carrowmore,
Assistant Commissioners—	1092	Patrick Boyle,	Rev. George H. Martin,	Balgill,
E. R. Kane (Legal). J. S. Fenton. J. Byrne.	1093	John F. Garnett,	Earl of Howth,	Balmer,
	1094	Thomas Murray,	Heads of J. A. Mooney and others, Assignees of Sir W. Nugent, a Bankrupt.	Ballyhon,
	1095	Christopher Conlan,	W. F. Garnett,	Drumlusky,
	1096	Patrick Murphy,	Richard J. Smith,	Summerhill, Upr.,
	1097	James Doherty,	do.	do.
	1098	Ann Fitzpatrick,	do.	do.
	1099	Thomas Cassidy,	do.	do.
	1100	Bridget Hickey, Ltd. Admix. of Thos. Hickey.	do.	Summerhill, Lr.,
	1101	Patrick Caffrey,	do.	do.
	1102	Kate Davis,	Henry G. Singleton,	Drumcondra,
	1103	Do.,	do.	do.
	1104	Mary Tighe,	William P. Garnett,	Drumsheble,
				Total,

LONGFORD—*continued.*

Extent of Holding, Statute.	Poor Law Valuation.	Former Rent.	Judicial Rent.	Observations.	Value of Tenancy.
A. R. P.	£ s. d.	£ s. d.	£ s. d.	£ s. d.	£ s. d.
60 1 20	15 18 0	19 4 6	18 10 0		
24 3 7	17 10 0	20 0 0	16 10 0		
16 0 12	8 10 0	7 10 0	4 5 0	Rent changed in 1856 from . . . 5 10 0	
3 1 12	1 15 0	1 14 6	1 10 0		
33 0 8	21 0 0	25 0 0	18 0 0		
17 0 0	8 0 0	8 0 0	5 10 0		
60 1 6	56 0 0	60 0 0	40 0 0		
22 3 0	15 0 0	20 0 0	15 5 0		
6 2 31	8 5 0	10 10 0	7 6 0	1866 9 0 0	
17 0 28	14 10 0	11 0 0	13 0 0		
27 2 0	14 0 0	15 8 10	10 10 0	By consent.	
57 3 10	56 0 0	39 12 8	27 0 0	By consent. Rent changed in 1851 from . £40 18s. 10d.	
11 2 10	3 10 0	4 0 0	4 0 0		
28 0 0	22 8 0	21 1 4	17 10 0		
2,316 2 23	1,401 5 0	1,836 6 4	1,272 16 10		

MEATH.

21 2 15	24 8 0	24 7 6	18 7 8		
28 0 12	21 5 0	25 15 7	18 0 0		
189 1 37	190 10 0	290 1 0	225 0 0		
11 0 26	6 0 0	13 17 6	8 10 0		
63 0 9	63 10 0	56 18 0	39 0 0	Rent changed in 1867 from . . . £ 48 0 0	
3 2 2	2 15 0	6 0 0	3 10 0		
8 0 8	1 18 0	3 0 0	2 2 0		
15 2 2	12 0 0	16 6 5	10 0 0		
5 0 34	2 18 0	3 5 0	3 5 0		
3 0 25	2 10 0	4 0 0	2 10 0		
3 3 26	3 4 0	5 18 0	3 15 0		
5 0 14	4 8 0	5 2 0	4 12 0		
50 3 15	71 10 0	104 9 8	80 0 0		
55 0 5	40 0 0	58 0 0	40 0 0	do. 65 4 4	
463 2 20	417 3 0	582 3 8	450 2 8		

COUNTY OF

Names of Assistant Commissioners by whom Cases were decided.	No.	Name of Tenant.	Name of Landlord.	Townland.
Head Commission	1234	Patrick Healy, ...	J. A. Macready and others, Assignees of Sir W. Nugent, a Bankrupt.	Ballinderry, ...
Assistant Commissioners—	1239	Michael Farrell, ...	Thomas H. Mulloch, ...	Knockdoney, ...
R. B. Kane (Legal). J. F. Bompas. J. Gardiner.	1240	Thomas Ledwith, ...	Jonathan Cuffe Reilly, ...	Dunlom, West,
	1241	Margaret Allen, ...	do.	Ballydougan, ...
	1242	Laurence Cunningham,	do.	Dunlom, West,
	1243	Mary Kennedy, ...	do.	do. ...
	1244	Thomas Dalton, ...	do.	do. ...
	1245	Mathew Brennan, ...	John Egan, ...	Coolrush, ...
	1246	Laurence Kilcoby, ...	do.	do. ...
	1247	John Larkin, ...	do.	do. ...
	1248	Tim Curley, ...	do.	do. ...
	1249	John Smyth, ...	George W. Marsh, ...	Crowe, ...
	1250	John Conlon, ...	do.	do. ...
	1251	John Duffy, ...	do.	do. ...
	1252	Thomas Murphy, ...	do.	do. ...
R. B. Kane (Legal). J. F. Bomford.	1253	James Connolly, ...	P. J. Healy, ...	Rathcahill, ...
	1254	Ellen M. Delamer, ...	Lord Greville, ...	Ballyglassed and another.
	1255	Julia Murray, ...	Charles J. Tisdall, ...	Rodanstown,
	1256	William Brabazon and another, Exors. of James Brabazon and another.	W. M. Boyd, ...	Jamestown, ...
	1257	William Longworth, ...	William R. Digby, ...	Moranstown, ...
	1258	Thomas Finn, ...	do.	do. ...
				Total, ...

COUNTY OF

Assistant Commissioners—	1545	John Murray, ...	F. A. Leigh, ...	Clongowes and another.
R. Reeves, Q.C. (Legal). T. A. Dillon. T. Davidson.	1547	Catherine Given, ...	G. A. Jameson, Trustee for sale of Lord Rathdonnell's Estate.	Glencarran, ...
	1548	John Rossiter, ...	do.	Waddington and another.

WESTMEATH.

Extent of Holding. Statute.	Poor Law Valuation.	Former Rent.	Judicial Rent.	Observations.	Value of Tenancy.
A. R. P.	£ s. d.	£ s. d.	£ s. d.		£ s. d.
45 0 0	59 10 0	52 0 0	39 10 0	The rent in this case was fixed by consent of the parties at the sitting of the Court in Dublin.	
30 0 36	21 10 0	30 16 0	18 0 0	By consent.	
38 1 37	23 16 0	27 4 8	21 16 4	do.	
3 1 7	8 10 0	3 5 0	1 15 0	do.	
9 5 8	5 10 0	5 8 3	4 0 0	do.	
1 3 25	1 10 0	1 10 0	1 4 0	do.	
13 2 10	7 10 0	8 3 3	6 6 8	do.	
1 0 30	1 0 0	2 0 0	1 0 0	do.	
4 3 0	8 0 0	3 0 0	2 0 0	do.	
1 3 30	0 15 0	1 0 0	0 16 0	do.	
0 3 10	0 15 0	1 0 0	0 15 0	do.	
4 1 0	8 0 0	3 17 0	2 10 0	do.	
5 2 [illegible]	4 10 0	4 5 0	3 0 0	do.	
57 8 0	29 15 0	[illegible] 0 0	21 0 0	do.	
8 1 6	1 10 0	4 0 0	2 10 0	do.	
6 1 2	unascertained,	3 18 0	8 5 0		
53 1 0	44 10 0	[illegible] 9 6	49 9 8		
61 2 4	24 0 0	30 1 5	22 5 0		
150 1 3	173 0 0	190 0 0	155 0 0		
16 3 18	14 0 0	15 16 6	18 0 0		
15 2 24	12 0 0	14 0 0	11 10 0		
537 3 22	408 10 0	478 7 4	374 11 6		

WEXFORD.

COUNTY OF

Names of Assistant Commissioners by whom Cases were decided.	No.	Name of Tenant.	Name of Landlord.	Townland.
Assistant Commissioners—				
B. Reeves, esq. (Legal). T. A. Dillon. T. Davidson.	1549	Moses Daly, ...	G. A. Jameson, Trustee for sale of Lord Rathdowne's Estate.	Waddington, ...
	1550	John Cheney, ...	do.	do. ...
	1551	Patrick Day, ...	do.	Moortown, ...
	1552	Ellen Malloy, ...	do.	Waddingtown, ...
	1553	Patrick Hore, ...	Lord Carew, ...	Mount Pill, ...
	1554	Benjamin Gabbert, ...	John B. Barwick and another,	Ballyvoon, ...
	1555	Do., ...	do.	Ballyvoon Bar Carew.
	1556	Patrick Clinch, ...	Harvey Boxwell, ...	Lingstown, Lr.,
	1557	James Murnagh, ...	Mrs. Frideswid Roddy and others,	Coolnamain, ...
	1558	Moses Leary, ...	do.	Ballybrigan, ...
	1559	James Walsh, ...	Mrs. Elizabeth Winder and another,	Tincone, ...
	1560	Thomas Rowe, ...	Ebenezer H. Rowe, ...	Grahormick, ...
	1561	Ellen Whitty, ...	do.	Moortown, Great,
	1562	Francis Furlong, ...	do.	do. ...
	1563	Nicholas Rossiter, ...	Earl of Donoughmore, ...	Ballindinas, ...
	1564	Nicholas Molane, ...	do.	Coolcotts, ...
	1565	Patrick Keegan, ...	John Rossiter, ...	Ballinagale, ...
	1566	James Banks, deceased, continued in name of John Banks.	Ebenezer H. Rowe, ...	Littletown, ...
				Total, ...

COUNTY OF

WEXFORD—*continued.*

Extent of Holding. Statute.	Poor Law Valuation.	Former Rent.	Judicial Rent.	Observations.	Value of Tenancy.
A. R. P.	£ s. d.	£ s. d.	£ s. d.		£ s. d.
28 3 4	18 5 0	23 13 2	18 0 0		
9 3 0	3 10 0	6 0 0	8 0 0		
2 2 13	1 10 0	1 18 4	1 6 0		
1 3 6	1 10 0	1 16 8	1 4 0		
68 2 3	47 0 0	60 12 10	48 0 0		
3 0 24	1 15 0	3 0 0	1 18 0		
4 3 30	unascertained,	3 16 0	3 0 0		
1 2 13	2 0 0	3 0 0	2 10 0		
10 2 4	10 10 0	16 18 0	14 0 0		
24 2 13	16 0 0	21 0 0	16 0 0		
29 1 37	10 0 0	16 0 0	10 0 0		
88 0 31	73 0 0	92 4 8	[illegible] 0 0		
12 3 20	9 15 0	10 2 4	7 7 0		
19 3 10	6 10 0	8 19 0	6 10 0		
19 2 39	7 0 0	7 3 3	6 0 0		
33 0 23	31 10 0	28 4 4	23 4 4		
18 1 10	6 6 0	7 4 0	6 0 0		
16 3 19	9 0 0	14 1 6½	9 16 0		
455 1 4	272 19 0	416 0 0½	310 1 4		

WICKLOW.

Extent of Holding. Statute.	Poor Law Valuation.	Former Rent.	Judicial Rent.	Observations.	Value of Tenancy.
12 0 13	18 0 0	16 7 0	16 7 0		
23 1 12	11 18 0	14 11 10	8 10 0	And right of three collops on mountain.	
80 2 34	25 5 0	33 7 8	23 15 0	And right of nine collops on Rostyduff Mountain.	
104 0 18	52 0 0	65 0 0	64 0 0		
20 2 19	11 6 0	16 0 0	13 0 0		
43 1 24	46 18 0	49 3 0	18 3 0		
303 2 22	165 0 0	195 4 6	158 15 0		

PROVINCE OF

COUNTY OF

Names of Assistant Commissioners by whom Cases were decided.	No.	Name of Tenant.	Name of Landlord.	Townland.
Assistant Commissioners—				
M. T. Cusack (Legal). E. McCabe. W. Whelan.	7411	James Bohan,	Colonel M. F. Blake,	Shanbally,
	7412	Anthony Dervan,	do.	[illegible]
	7413	James Bohan.	do.	Newtown[illegible]lagh.
	7414	Michael Larkin,	Burton W. Persse,	[illegible]
	7415	Anne Coen,	do.	[illegible]
	7416	Thomas Lowry,	E. J. McKay and another,	[illegible]
	7417	Jerome Donnelly,	Michael J. Lynch,	Killeen,
	7418	Michael Gorman,	Mary Scanlan and others,	[illegible]
	7419	Edward Thornberry,	do.	Birchpark,
	7420	Richard Hanrahan,	Lady [illegible],	[illegible]
	7421	James Bohan,	do.	do.
	7422	Michael Hanrahan,	Sir Henry Burke, Bart.,	[illegible]
	7423	Michael Kelly,	do.	do.
	7424	John Cassidy,	Lord Clanricarde,	Moorfield,
	7425	Patrick Staunton,	do.	do.
	7426	Michael McGrath,	do.	do.
	7427	Thomas Manion,	do.	[illegible]
	7428	Stephen Manion,	do.	Gortnahy,
	7429	John Keighry,	do.	Fairyhill,
	7430	John Neville,	do.	[illegible] and another.
	7431	John Mannion,	do.	Gort[illegible]aky,
	7432	Winifred Mannion,	do.	[illegible]
	7433	Bridget Tarpey,	do.	Rossmore,
	7434	Thomas Fahy,	do.	[illegible]
	7435	Denis Mooney,	do.	[illegible] and another.
	7436	John Lynch, Ltd. Admor. of Michael Lynch.	do.	Moorfield,
	7437	Michael J. Martin,	do.	[illegible]
	7438	Patrick Hogan, Limited Admor. of Mary Hogan.	John F. George,	[illegible]
	7439	Patrick Mulgannon,	do.	do.
	7440	Ellen McNamara,	do.	[illegible]

CONNAUGHT.

GALWAY.

Extent of Holding. Statute.	Poor Law Valuation.	Former Rent.	Judicial Rent.	Observations.
A. R. P.	£ s. d.	£ s. d.	£ s. d.	£ s.
7 0 3	—	1 3 4	1 3 4	
8 0 6	9 5 0	4 10 0	9 0 0	
15 1 5	8 15 0	7 0 0	3 5 0	
85 0 15	88 5 0	85 12 6	34 10 0	
8 2 8	10 5 0	18 15 8	11 10 0	
31 0 0	14 15 0	19 0 0	10 15 0	
40 5 6	21 5 0	30 0 0	23 0 0	
18 3 1	8 8 0	7 0 0	5 0 0	
3 2 20	1 8 0	2 0 0	1 14 0	
67 3 18	48 15 0	37 11 10	37 0 0	
11 0 37	8 15 0	8 0 0	8 15 0	Rent changed in 1863 from . . . 9 10
13 0 0	8 15 0	10 6 0	6 5 0	
30 3 30	6 0 0	8 13 8	5 15 0	1853 6 0
14 2 13	6 15 0	10 1 10	7 10 0	
23 1 37	16 0 0	18 0 0	12 0 0	
20 3 20	18 5 0	13 0 0	11 5 0	1877 11 10
8 1 33	5 5 0	5 0 0	6 0 0	
8 3 28	3 15 0	4 0 0	3 10 0	do. 3 15
7 3 8	1 15 0	3 0 0	2 10 0	
51 0 23	18 15 0	19 0 0	15 0 0	
10 1 10	4 10 0	4 18 0	6 2 0	
6 0 0	4 15 0	5 0 0	1 5 0	
9 2 35	4 15 0	4 0 0	3 5 0	
4 0 23	1 15 0	3 0 0	2 7 6	
11 3 30	5 5 0	7 7 8	6 0 0	
15 0 17	8 0 0	5 10 0	5 15 0	do. 7 5
7 2 18	3 10 0	4 0 0	4 0 0	
18 0 9	6 15 0	8 15 0	5 15 0	
15 3 20	2 15 0	9 15 0	7 15 0	
28 0 35	7 10 0	7 10 0	7 10 0	

COUNTY OF

Names of Assistant Commissioners by whom Case was decided.	No.	Name of Tenant.	Name of Landlord.	Townland.
Assistant Commissioners—				
M. T. Crean (Legal). R. McCrea. W. Williams.	7441	Thomas Begley, —	John F. George, — —	Kilclaren, Lower,
	7442	James Begley, —	do. — —	do. —
	7443	Thomas Shannon, —	do. — —	Middleline, —
	7444	Daniel McMahon, —	do. — —	do. —
	7445	William Tuohy, —	do. — —	Derlane, —
	7446	Margaret Keane, —	do. — —	Glenmarta, —
	7447	Ellen Minogue, —	do. — ...	Derryvaun, Upper,
	7448	Thady Minogue, —	do. — —	Mountshannon, —
	7449	John Halloran, —	do. — —	Cloonlea, North,
	7450	Margaret Dixon, Limited Admix. of John Dixon.	do. — —	Derryvaun, —
	7451	John Rourke, —	do. — —	do. —
M. T. Crean (Legal). F. O'Callaghan. J. Walsh.	7452	Michael Collins, —	Sir John Bradstreet, Bart., —	Carrowduff, —
	7453	Thomas Lyons, —	do. — —	do. —
	7454	Thomas Graham, —	do. — —	do. —
	7455	Bryan Cunningham, ...	do. — —	do. —
	7456	Thomas Connaughton, —	do. — —	do. —
	7457	Thomas Mannion, —	do. — —	do. —
	7458	Mary Collins, Ltd. Admix. of John Collins, deceased.	do. — —	do. —
	7459	Catherine Morrissey, Ltd. Admix. of Thomas Morrissey, deceased.	do. — —	do. —
	7460	Patrick Cunningham, —	do. — —	do. —
	7461	John Donnelly, —	do. — —	do. —
	7462	Edward Donnelly, —	do. — —	do. —
				Total, —

COUNTY OF

GALWAY—*continued.*

Extent of Holding (Statute).	Poor Law Valuation.	Former Rent.	Judicial Rent.	Observations.	Value of Tenancy.
A. R. P.	£ s. d.	£ s. d.	£ s. d.		£ s. d.
100 0 26	26 13 0	28 13 0	26 13 0		
78 1 23½	24 10 0	26 10 0	25 10 0		
29 1 26	9 16 0	9 10 0	8 10 0		
36 0 0	13 8 0	13 0 0	11 0 0		
33 2 16	11 13 0	11 15 0	8 10 0	And the right of grazing one-third of 180a. 1r. 11p. commonage.	
26 3 8	8 10 0	8 10 0	8 10 0		
16 3 11	5 18 0	8 16 0	7 5 0	And the right of grazing one-fourth of 180a. 1r. 11p.	
60 3 3	9 10 0	9 10 0	8 5 0		
22 3 3	5 0 0	6 0 0	5 10 0		
34 3 2	2 10 0	2 10 0	2 0 0		
38 1 23	11 15 0	11 16 0	6 10 0	do.	
6 2 7	5 0 0	3 12 0	3 0 0	£ s. d.	
17 3 33	8 0 0	7 12 0	6 0 0	Rent changed in 1880 from 8 17 6	
14 2 13	6 10 0	6 14 0	4 15 0		
8 1 1	4 10 0	5 9 0	3 5 0	do. 4 17 2	
16 0 16	7 8 0	7 4 0	6 5 0	do. 9 16 9	
6 2 20	5 3 0	5 1 0	4 3 0	do. 6 9 2	
10 1 30	4 10 0	4 7 0	3 3 0	do. 6 17 2	
9 0 16	4 13 0	4 16 0	3 8 0		
10 0 19	5 13 0	4 16 0	3 8 0	do. 5 1 7	
18 0 20	8 4 0	8 15 0	6 5 0		
14 2 10	6 12 0	8 1 0	6 10 0	do. 8 16 6	
1,231 3 9½	480 6 0	541 13 4	473 5 10		

MAYO.

7 3 18	unascertained,	6 6 4	4 5 0	By consent.	
13 1 33	7 15 0	6 10 0	6 10 0	do.	
8 1 30	7 0 0	6 6 0	5 0 0	By consent. With right of grazing in common with ten others.	
17 1 30	unascertained,	5 0 0	4 0 0	By consent.	
6 1 34	4 0 0	4 0 0	4 0 0	do.	

COUNTY OF

Names of Assistant Commissioners by whom Cases were decided.	No.	Name of Tenant.	Name of Landlord.	Townland.
Assistant Commissioners—				
E. O. MacDermott (Legal). T. Hall. J. Martin.	7858	Anne Walsh,	Marquess of Sligo,	Carrowkeel,
	7859	Do.,	do.	Lisnalara,
	7860	Mary Neary,	John N. Farrell,	Culnacleha,
	7861	Ellen Coolfield,	do.	do.
	7862	Catherine Greene,	Viscount Dillon,	Ardcorry,
	7863	Pat Lyons,	do.	Brackloon,
	7864	Cecilia Flatley, Ltd. Admix. of Pat Flatley.	do.	Treenaglearaun,
	7865	Bridget Fitzmaurice,	do.	do.
	7866	Pat Finn (Catherine),	do.	do.
	7867	John Moran,	do.	do.
	7868	James Waldron,	do.	do.
	7869	Pat Finn (Pat),	do.	do.
	7870	Martin Waldron,	do.	do.
	7871	John Fitzmaurice,	do.	Derrynacong,
	7872	Pat Fitzmaurice,	do.	do.
	7873	Bridget Ford,	do.	do.
	7874	Thomas Boyle,	do.	Carrowreagh,
	7875	Michael Connolly,	do.	Killeaden,
	7876	Bridget Hunt, Ltd. Admix. of Thomas Hunt.	do.	do.
	7877	John Doory,	do.	do.
	7878	Pat Regan,	do.	do.
	7879	Thomas Boyle,	do.	do.
	7880	Pat Combat,	do.	do.
	7881	Thomas Kelly,	do.	do.
	7882	John Humphreys',	do.	do.
	7883	Pat Kelly,	do.	do.
	7884	Michael Regan,	do.	do.
	7885	John Grogan (Mary),	do.	do.
	7886	Thomas Regan, Ltd. Admr. of John M. Grogan.	do.	do.
	7887	Bridget Brown, Ltd. Admix. of Pat Brown.	do.	do.
	7888	Andrew Moran, Ltd. Admr. of Andrew Caddy.	do.	do.
	7889	Thomas Murphy, Ltd. Admr. of William Grogan.	do.	do.
	7890	Catherine Greally, Ltd. Admix. of Pat Greally.	do.	do.
	7891	James Boyle,	do.	do.
	7892	Pat Costello,	do.	Brackloon, South,

AYO—*continued.*

…tent of Holding. Statute.	Poor Law Valuation.	Former Rent.	Judicial Rent.	Observations.
A. R. P.	£ s. d.	£ s. d.	£ s. d.	
18 0 18	4 15 0	5 0 0	5 10 0	By consent.
8 1 18	3 8 0	8 10 0	2 10 0	do.
5 1 34	3 16 0	4 3 4	3 0 0	
10 3 6	3 10 0	5 13 0	3 0 0	
11 0 0	3 7 0	3 18 0	1 5 0	
23 0 20	5 13 0	8 10 0	5 10 0	
13 3 36	3 7 0	5 7 0	3 13 0	
20 3 0	8 4 0	5 18 8	2 15 0	
12 0 18	8 7 0	3 13 0	3 18 0	
23 3 14	4 8 0	4 16 4	3 15 0	
28 2 8	3 11 0	8 4 0	2 11 0	
20 2 0	2 16 0	6 7 0	2 15 0	
21 3 30	4 8 0	4 15 0	4 0 0	
30 0 0	4 15 0	8 14 0	4 10 0	
18 0 15	8 10 0	2 5 0	8 0 0	
17 3 26	4 0 0	4 8 8	2 15 0	
19 1 20	2 15 0	4 8 6	3 0 0	
21 0 0	4 3 0	6 0 10	3 0 0	
4 3 37	3 0 0	2 6 8	1 15 0	
26 1 34	7 10 0	8 5 9	4 15 0	
28 3 8	5 6 0	7 10 6	5 5 0	
15 1 20	4 18 0	5 10 10	4 15 0	
6 8 37	2 7 0	2 5 10	2 0 0	
8 3 2	3 18 0	2 0 8	2 0 0	
34 2 15	3 17 6	6 19 4	2 12 0	
6 2 16	2 0 0	1 19 6	1 15 0	
20 2 24	3 5 0	6 12 4	4 15 0	
13 0 0	2 7 0	3 12 10	3 0 0	
16 2 23	2 17 0	3 12 4	2 15 0	
11 3 37	6 8 0	3 13 6	2 10 0	
16 0 0	7 18 0	5 5 8	3 3 6	
16 2 16	3 2 0	5 7 0	5 0 0	
14 1 18	2 7 0	3 7 10	3 0 0	
10 3 37	6 3 0	5 5 8	3 15 0	
4 0 5	1 5 0	1 11 8	1 4 0	

COUNTY OF

Names of Assistant Commissioners by whom Cases were decided.	No.	Name of Tenant.	Name of Landlord.	Townland.
Assistant Commissioners—				
E. O. MacDevitt (Legal). T. Hall. J. Martin.	7893	Mathew Maguire,	Viscount Dillon,	Brackloon, South,
	7894	Michael Dyer,	do.	do.
	7895	Pat Higgins,	do.	do.
	7896	Patt Dyer (Edmund),	do.	do.
	7897	Mary McHugh Ltd. Admix. of Pat Dyer,	do.	do.
	7898	Mary Murphy, Ltd. Admix. of Tim Murphy,	do.	Largan,
	7899	John Keilan,	do.	Moneymore,
	7900	Mark Hunt,	do.	do.
	7901	Maria Waldron, Ltd. Admix. of Andrew Waldron,	do.	do.
	7902	Patt Nolan,	do.	Mountain,
	7903	Winifred Finn, Ltd. Admix. of John Finn,	do.	do.
	7904	Michael Nolan, Ltd. Admor. of Owen Nolan,	do.	do.
	7905	Patt Finn, Ltd. Admon. of Barnley Finn,	do.	do.
	7906	Ellen Nolan, Ltd. Admix. of Dominick Nolan,	do.	do.
	7907	Thomas Murphy,	do.	Graffagh,
	7908	Michael Waldron,	do.	do.
	7909	Bridget Reilly, Rep. of James Reilly,	do.	do.
	7910	Thomas Lofton,	do.	do.
	7911	John Lofton,	do.	do.
	7912	John Reilly, Rep. of Pat Reilly,	do.	do.
	7913	Charles Kelly,	do.	do.
	7914	Pat Fitzmaurice, Limited Admor. of James Dwyer,	do.	Gurteen Bog,
	7915	Anne Finlay, Ltd. Admix. of Thomas Killeen,	do.	Largan,
	7916	Michael Finn, Rep. of James Finn,	do.	Lisheen, West,
	7917	John Moran,	do.	Cashelgarran,
	7918	James Moran,	do.	Scregg,
	7919	Patrick Freehilly,	do.	do.
	7920	Thomas Freehilly,	do.	do.
	7921	Pat Lyons,	do.	Ballinphuill,
	7922	Catherine Parkes, Ltd. Admix. of Pat Parkes,	do.	Tartaghmore,
	7923	Hugh Lyons,	do.	Knockbrack,
	7924	Thomas Flanagan,	do.	do.
	7925	Andrew Bailey (Patt),	do.	Bargarriff,
	7926	Timothy Cummins,	do.	Knockbrack,
	7927	John Coyne, junior,	do.	Bargarriff,

MAYO—*continued.*

Extent of Holding. Statute.	Poor Law Valuation.	Tenancy Rent.	Judicial Rent.	Observations.	Value of Tenancy.
A. R. P.	£ s. d.	£ s. d.	£ s. d.		£ s. d.
13 3 1	2 0 0	2 0 0	8 0 0		
21 3 25	3 10 0	4 3 6	5 10 0		
15 1 23	2 5 0	6 3 0	2 10 0		
23 0 9	3 16 0	4 18 0	3 8 0		
15 1 8	2 5 0	8 7 0	1 15 0		
19 0 0	5 5 0	4 0 0	2 10 0		
48 1 17	8 10 0	5 13 8	4 8 0		
23 0 15	5 0 0	3 0 0	2 15 0		
63 0 30	8 15 0	5 15 0	5 17 6		
14 3 9	8 7 0	4 9 8	3 0 0		
13 1 24	2 11 0	8 2 4	3 0 0		
30 2 6	4 2 0	6 8 6	5 10 0		
18 5 25	2 17 0	3 18 2	8 10 0		
60 3 25	8 16 0	7 11 10	4 18 0		
4 3 18	8 6 0	9 11 0	3 0 0		
30 2 19	15 5 0	16 16 0	10 10 0		
67 1 28	19 15 0	19 19 4	24 0 0		
5 0 26	2 17 0	2 9 0	2 0 0		
7 0 13	2 16 0	2 6 6	2 0 0		
7 3 13	3 17 0	2 8 4	2 0 0		
9 2 30	3 18 0	2 11 5	2 11 8		
30 0 22	4 18 0	8 18 5	4 7 0		
15 0 25	2 17 0	2 19 10	3 0 0		
6 2 16	2 18 0	3 0 8	2 5 0		
67 0 32	25 17 0	28 4 0	25 0 0		
13 3 6	3 10 0	4 11 0	3 10 0		
30 0 21	5 15 0	4 12 0	8 5 0		
18 0 31	2 0 0	2 18 0	3 0 0		
8 3 20	3 8 0	5 1 8	5 0 0		
34 2 31	3 7 0	4 0 0	4 0 0		
14 1 20	4 3 0	5 10 0	3 10 0		
18 1 0	5 10 0	4 11 0	3 0 0		
16 0 15	4 15 0	4 18 9	3 10 0		
15 0 0	4 15 0	5 18 0	4 10 0		
15 5 22	4 2 0	8 17 10	3 5 0		

COUNTY OF

Names of Assistant Commissioners by whom Cases were decided.	No.	Name of Tenant.	Name of Landlord.	Townland.
Assistant Commissioners—				
E. O. MacDevitt (Legal). T. Hall. J. Martin.	7928	Pat Bailey, ...	Viscount Dillon, ...	Sragarriff, ...
	7929	Andrew Bailey (John),	do. ...	do. ...
	7930	William Waldron (Simon), Limited Admon. of Simon Waldron.	do. ...	Sragh, ...
	7931	Margaret Beaty, Limited Admix. of Owen Beaty,	do. ...	do. ...
	7932	William Frehilly, ...	do. ...	do. ...
	7933	James Hunt, ...	do. ...	do. ...
	7934	Mary Frehilly, Limited Admix. of Jas. Frehilly,	do. ...	do. ...
	7935	David Waldron, Rep. of Michael Waldron.	do. ...	do. ...
	7936	Pat Flanagan, ...	do. ...	Lurgan, ...
	7937	John Higgins, ...	do. ...	Cloonkeelaun, ...
	7938	Mary Finn, ...	do. ...	Fortaghmore, ...
	7939	Pat Tully, ...	do. ...	Brackloon, South,
	7940	Pat Grogan (Margaret),	do. ...	Killinlaw, ...
	7941	M. McGarry, Limited Admon. of P. Horkan.	do. ...	do. ...
	7942	Austin Healy, junior, ...	do. ...	do. ...
	7943	Michael Glynn, ...	do. ...	Feraghmore, ...
	7944	Ellen Grogan, Limited Admix. of Pat Grogan.	do. ...	Cloonagleave, ...
	7945	Pat Higgins, ...	do. ...	Lurgan, ...
E. O. MacDevitt (Legal). A. R. Montgomery.	7946	Thomas McGowan, ...	Sir R. W. Palmer, Bart., ...	Aughaward, ...
J. Martin. T. Hall.	7947	Patrick Phillips, ...	Viscount Dillon, ...	Cloonacurrane, ...
	7948	Thomas Commons, ...	do. ...	do. ...
	7949	Michael Jordan, Rep. of Martin Jordan.	do. ...	do. ...
	7950	Mark Hyland, ...	do. ...	Caldrough, ...
	7951	Pat Finn, ...	do. ...	Lisheen, West,
	7952	Thomas Lyons, Rep. of Peter Lyons.	do. ...	Carrowrea, ...
	7953	Michael Higgins, ...	do. ...	do. ...
	7954	David Mulkeen, ...	do. ...	Cloontamper, ...
	7955	Andrew Ford, Rep. of John Kilbrany.	do. ...	do. ...
	7956	James Mullaly, ...	do. ...	do. ...

MAYO—*continued.*

Extent of Holding, Statute.	Poor Law Valuation.	Former Rent.	Judicial Rent.	Observations.	Value of Tenancy.
A. R. P.	£ s. d.	£ s. d.	£ s. d.		£ s. d.
23 2 5	5 0 0	9 0 0	6 0 0		
18 0 9	4 18 0	4 17 0	4 0 0		
26 2 11	3 0 0	5 18 0	5 7 0		
23 1 31	5 5 0	4 5 0	3 2 0		
29 6 3	2 5 0	3 19 0	2 0 0		
60 2 36	5 0 0	7 19 0	8 10 0		
40 1 17	5 10 0	6 7 6	5 10 0		
31 3 19	5 0 0	5 10 0	4 5 0		
43 1 21	6 2 6	5 15 6	4 17 6		
17 0 37	5 3 6	5 18 8	4 5 0		
83 1 25	3 7 0	4 5 6	5 0 0		
15 1 33	3 5 0	4 7 0	3 0 0		
43 1 37	1 15 0	3 10 10	3 14 10		
11 0 0	1 8 0	1 16 10	1 5 0		
20 0 0	3 0 0	2 1 10	1 16 0		
10 0 35	1 15 0	2 1 8	1 15 0		
60 3 15	11 6 8	18 7 0	14 0 0		
16 2 30	4 2 0	3 5 10	3 10 0		
13 3 21	6 8 0	4 5 0	3 5 0		
61 0 36	15 15 0	16 6 0	13 0 0		
14 1 35	8 0 0	9 0 0	6 10 0		
10 3 5	6 15 0	7 5 0	6 10 0		
30 3 25	10 0 0	12 4 0	10 15 0		
9 3 3	6 17 0	4 17 0	3 17 0		
14 6 25	6 5 0	6 14 4	5 10 0		
13 1 37	5 4 0	6 14 0	6 0 0		
10 3 30	6 10 0	5 14 0	6 0 0		
9 3 33	5 5 0	5 9 0	4 0 0		
13 3 9	6 10 0	7 13 0	6 0 0		

COUNTY OF

Names of Assistant Commissioners by whom Cases were decided.	No.	Name of Tenant.	Name of Landlord.	Townland.
Assistant Commissioners—				
J. Martin (Legal). T. Hall.	7957	Margaret Cribbin, ...	Viscount Dillon, ...	Cloontumper, ...
	7958	Thomas Cox, ...	do.	do. ...
	7959	Martin McGarry, ...	do.	do. ...
	7960	Pat Henry, ...	do.	do. ...
	7961	Thomas Kane, ...	do.	[illegible], ...
	7962	James Morris, ...	do.	do. ...
	7963	Patrick Mulrenin, ...	do.	do. ...
	7964	John Kane, ...	do.	do. ...
	7965	Philip Grimes, ...	do.	do. ...
	7966	Michael Mullen, ...	do.	Cloonshallon, ...
	7967	Bridget Kavanagh, ...	do.	do. ...
	7968	James Lyons, ...	do.	Oralleagh, ...
				Total, ...

COUNTY OF

Assistant Commissioners—	4094	Owen Healy, ...	William G. Molloy, ...	Ballyfermoyle, ...
M. F. Cullen (Legal). H. C. Gregory. W. N. Hamill.	4095	John McCabe, ...	Colonel W. H. Molloy, ...	Derrymannan, ...
	4096	James Connaughton and another.	Mrs. Mary A. Townsend and another.	Kingsland, ...
	4097	Pat Beirne, ...	Colonel E. R. King-Harman, continued in name of F. A. King-Harman.	[illegible], ...
	4098	Pat Nancy, ...	do.	Towran, ...
	4099	Laurence Mulrooney, ...	do.	do. ...
	4100	Bartley Sharkell, ...	do.	do. ...
	4101	John King, ...	do.	do. ...
	4102	Catherine Reilly, ...	do.	do. ...
	4103	Thomas Cregg, ...	do.	do. ...
	4104	Laurence Morris, ...	do.	do. ...
	4105	Bryan Gryan, ...	do.	Eskullaragh, ...
	4106	Neal Ward, ...	do.	Tawnagh, ...
	4107	Patrick Lee, ...	do.	Ballyhean, ...
	4108	James Gray, ...	do.	Orangebeg, ...

MAYO—*continued.*

Extent of Holding in Statute.	Poor Law Valuation.	Former Rent.	Judicial Rent.	Observations.
A. R. P.	£ s. d.	£ s. d.	£ s. d.	
13 3 7	6 5 0	7 9 0	5 0 0	
6 1 15	4 8 0	4 6 0	5 0 0	
8 1 20	6 10 0	5 13 0	4 5 0	
10 2 20	6 0 0	6 11 0	2 15 0	
27 3 36	7 0 0	6 0 0	6 13 0	
20 1 7	8 5 0	9 14 10	5 0 0	
41 0 7	10 5 0	11 13 8	10 0 0	
24 0 30	7 10 0	9 0 4	7 15 0	
21 3 25	6 15 0	8 0 0	6 13 0	
11 1 31	5 18 0	5 17 10	4 5 0	

Names of Assistant Commissioners by whom Cases were decided.	No.	Name of Tenant.	Name of Landlord.	Townland.
Assistant Commissioners— M. T. Crean (Legal). H. C. [illegible]. W. H. [illegible].	4109	Anne Skeffington, ...	Colonel E. R. King-Harman, continued in name of F. A. King-Harman.	Aughnaskeagh,
	4110	Patrick Connolly, ...	do.	do. ...
	4111	Pat McLoughlin, ...	do.	do. ...
	4112	Michael McGreevy, ...	do.	Tirarragh, ...
	4113	John Moran, ...	do.	Flaugh, ...
	4114	Martin Finnerty, ...	do.	do. ...
	4115	Anne Sheeran, ...	do.	Warren, ...
	4116	Do., ...	do.	Warren and another,
	4117	Do., ...	do.	Derrynock, ...
	4118	Do., ...	do.	Tawnytaskin, ...
	4119	James Drury, jun., ...	do.	Derryvoragh, ...
	4120	Do., ...	do.	do. ...
	4121	Mary Ford, ...	do.	do. ...
	4122	Owen Ford and another,	do.	Derryvoragh and another.
	4123	Alfred Ford, ...	do.	do. ...
	4124	John Drury, ...	do.	Portnacroagh, ...
	4125	Winifred Kelly, ...	do.	do. ...
	4126	Mary Kelly, ...	do.	do. ...
	4127	Catherine Drury, ...	do.	Derryvoragh and another.
	4128	Edward Sharkey, ...	do.	Tawnagh and another.
	4129	Patrick Murray and ors.,	do.	Kingsland, ...
	4130	Mary Harrington, ...	do.	do. ...
	4131	Patt Beirne, ...	do.	do. ...
	4132	Michael Shannon, ...	do.	Carrowkeel, ...
	4133	Michael Flanagan, ...	do.	do. ...
	4134	Lewis Ward, ...	do.	Kingsland, ...
	4135	Patrick Butler and anor.,	do.	do. ...
	4136	Mary Kelly, ...	do.	Shelagh, ...
	4137	Edward Harrington, ...	do.	Portnacroagh,
				Total, ...

ROSCOMMON—*continued.*

Extent of Holding Statute.			Poor Law Valuation.			Former Rent.			Judicial Rent.			Observations.	Value of Tenancy.		
A.	R.	P.	£	s.	d.	£	s.	d.	£	s.	d.		£	s.	d.
10	0	19	5	0	0	4	4	8	8	15	0				
18	3	20	9	0	0	10	18	4	8	0	0				
9	2	26	6	10	0	5	15	10	7	17	6				
40	0	15	24	10	0	29	17	0	20	0	0				
16	3	20	10	5	0	11	10	0	9	0	0				
19	3	4	18	10	0	13	14	0	10	10	0				
2	2	9	4	0	0	4	18	4	3	15	0				
0	3	36	0	5	0	0	18	0	0	10	0				
9	0	6	8	10	0	6	12	0	5	17	6				
4	1	0	3	0	0	3	7	0	3	7	0				
14	0	18	7	3	0	7	5	6	6	7	6				
14	0	30	5	9	0	6	16	5	6	11	9				
14	1	29	6	5	0	6	18	8	6	18	5				
28	1	20	16	10	0	15	16	8	13	0	0				
13	1	0	5	0	0	8	1	10	4	15	0				
19	3	1	19	5	0	12	18	4	11	15	0				
11	1	23	5	15	0	5	16	6	5	5	0				
18	3	9	8	10	0	8	15	8	8	5	0				
16	3	23	7	19	0	10	1	3	8	10	0				
23	0	35	12	4	0	12	14	4	10	15	0				
21	3	37	12	10	0	18	14	8	10	5	0				
17	3	10	8	10	0	4	8	10	6	10	0				
15	0	29	4	4	0	5	4	4	5	4	4				
30	3	29	18	0	0	13	16	8	13	5	0				
18	1	33	11	5	0	16	1	4	11	0	0				
28	3	27	17	0	0	17	9	5	17	8	6				
19	3	38	11	5	0	12	0	8	10	3	0				
11	3	35	7	15	0	7	11	3	6	10	0				
34	0	9	8	8	0	8	11	4	5	11	4				
768	3	34	407	4	0	441	16	5	365	18	1				

COUNTY OF

Names of Assistant Commissioners by whom Cases were decided.	No.	Name of Tenant.	Name of Landlord.	Townland.
Assistant Commissioners—				
E. O. MacDevitt (Legal). M. Kelly.	3766	Patrick Hawley,	Colonel Richard Philbin,	Curry,
	3767	Anthony Irwin,	Captain James W. Armstrong,	[illegible],
	3768	Alexander Mullarkey,	Miss Georgina Philbin,	Tullaville,
	3769	Bridget Marren,	John H. Brett and others,	Carrowlagh,
	3770	Michael Durcan,	Colonel Richard Knox and ors.,	Rathmagurry,
	3771	Patrick Cafferty (Peter),	do.	[illegible],
	3772	Pat McGowan,	do.	do.
	3773	James Gallagher,	do.	Bunnacranagh,
	3774	Mary Peyton,	do.	do.
	3775	Timothy [illegible],	do.	do.
	3776	John Feehily,	do.	do.
	3777	Bridget Vesey,	do.	do.
	3778	William Durcan,	do.	Ballincurry,
	3779	Thomas McVann,	Colonel E. H. Cooper,	Kilcummin,
	3780	Luke Kilcoyne,	do.	Oughambrown,
	3781	Michael Battle,	Rev. John M. Young,	[illegible],
	3782	Thomas Loftus,	do.	do.
	3783	Michael Kivlehan,	Charles W. O'Hara,	Shancrough,
	3784	James Leviston,	do.	do.
	3785	Anne Brennan,	Lord Harlech,	Goldfield,
	3786	Patrick [illegible],	do.	[illegible],
	3787	Anthony Horan,	do.	[illegible] and another,
	3788	Thomas Hawley,	do.	do.
	3789	John O'Hara,	do.	[illegible],
	3790	Michael Dunlogan,	do.	do.
	3791	Michael O'Donnell,	do.	Dawros,
	3792	Dominick O'Donnell,	do.	do.
	3793	Andrew McCoy,	do.	do.
	3794	William Durcan,	do.	do.
	3795	James May,	do.	do.
	3796	Mary Marren,	do.	do.
	3797	Thomas Walsh,	do.	do.
	3798	Bridget Marren, Ind. Admix. of Thomas Marren.	do.	do.
	3799	James Walsh,	do.	do.
	3800	Michael Marren,	do.	do.

SLIGO.

Extent of Holding. Statute.	Poor Law Valuation.	Former Rent.	Judicial Rent.	Observations.	Value of Tenancy.
A. R. P.	£ s. d.	£ s. d.	£ s. d.		£ s. d.
6 3 20	5 8 0	5 1 6	4 10 0		
47 1 20	29 10 0	34 6 6	24 10 0		
54 0 0	11 0 0	12 10 0	8 5 0	With right of commonage of grazing as heretofore.	
12 0 0	5 5 0	6 6 3	5 17 6		
17 1 3	10 0 0	11 5 0	7 10 0		
43 0 15	10 0 0	8 10 0	6 15 0		
10 3 27	6 15 0	7 0 0	6 15 0		
10 2 4	5 5 0	5 7 0	4 5 0		
18 3 7	8 15 0	10 3 6	8 5 0		
13 2 10	7 5 0	7 1 6	5 5 0		
12 3 34	5 10 0	5 5 0	5 7 6		
5 2 22	3 10 0	5 14 6	3 10 0		
17 1 0	8 0 0	11 13 6	7 10 0		
8 0 15	6 0 0	5 10 0	1 5 0		
60 3 17	28 15 0	24 19 8	19 0 0		
17 2 26	6 0 0	4 5 0	3 15 0	With right of grazing over 779a. 2r. 14p. with nine others.	
20 0 19	6 5 0	6 9 0	3 19 0	do.	
20 3 17	6 0 0	6 0 0	6 5 0		
23 0 0	16 0 0	10 0 0	6 0 0		
6 0 16	4 5 0	5 5 0	4 0 0		
5 6 13	5 5 0	3 18 6	3 15 0		
24 1 33	5 10 0	6 0 0	5 0 0		
4 3 36	3 0 0	3 10 0	2 15 0		
11 3 14	6 10 0	4 5 0	3 5 0		
11 2 14	5 10 0	4 5 0	3 5 0		
21 1 4	5 5 0	5 18 0	5 10 0		
22 2 20	6 0 0	6 10 0	6 5 0		
14 0 0	6 5 0	6 10 0	5 5 0		
22 0 0	6 15 0	7 0 0	6 17 6		
25 3 18	5 16 6	5 10 0	5 15 0		
21 0 9	5 0 0	7 10 0	6 12 6		
16 0 0	6 0 0	6 10 0	5 5 0		
29 0 0	5 5 0	5 0 0	5 16 0		
13 0 0	5 14 0	4 0 0	3 5 0		
13 1 20	7 5 0	6 0 0	6 17 6		

COUNTY OF

Names of Assistant Commissioners by whom Cases were decided.	No.	Name of Tenant.	Name of Landlord.	Townland.
Assistant Commissioners—				
R. O. MacDevitt (Legal). E. Kelly.	3801	John Commons, ...	Lord Harlech, ...	Belclare, ...
	3802	Peter Goldrick, ...	do.	do. ...
	3803	Martin Quinn, ...	do.	do. ...
	3804	Michael Goldrick, ...	do.	do. ...
	3805	James Battle, ...	do.	do. ...
	3806	John Goldrick, ...	do.	do. ...
	3807	Daniel Carey, ...	do.	Oughaval, ...
	3808	Thomas Maher, ...	do.	do. ...
	3809	Michael Boland, ...	do.	Letterbrone, ...
	3810	Stephen Maxwell, ...	do.	Ros, ...
	3811	James O'Hara, ...	do.	Kinnadilea, ...
	3812	Patk. O'Connor, Lgl. Admor. of Thos. O'Connor,	Colonel H. H. Cooper, ...	Barnas Garry, ...
	3813	Philip Durcan, ...	Lord Harlech, ...	Dawros, ...
	3814	Thomas Morran, ...	do.	do. ...
	3815	John Goldrick, ...	do.	Belclare, ...
	3816	William Haggarty, ...	do.	do. ...
	3817	Charles Commons, ...	do.	do. ...
				Total, ...

PROVINCE OF

COUNTY OF

Assistant Commissioners—	4506	Michael Rooney, ...	Colonel J. O'Callaghan, ...	Milltown, ...
J. S. Greer (Legal). R. B. Hervey. J. Rice.	4507	John Murphy, ...	Sir A. Fitzgerald, Bart., ...	Silver Grove, ...
	4508	Patrick Culligan, ...	Marquis Conyngham, ...	Drumdoonan, ...
	4509	Thomas Glesson, ...	C. W. Smith, ...	Kilburn, ...
	4510	Thomas Reidy, ...	Captain R. G. O'Callaghan, ...	Garraragh, ...
	4511	James McInerney, ...	Daniel O'Connell, ...	Cloonconry, ...
	4512	James McGrath, ...	Mrs. Jane Callaghan, ...	Clonaloam, ...
	4513	Patrick Hennessy, ...	Arthur G. Jodd, ...	Tooreagh, ...
	4514	Patrick McNamara, jun.,	Major Roger Hall, ...	Knocknahinesy, ...
	4515	John Hehir, ...	John Scott, ...	Craigahenan, ...

SLIGO—*continued.*

Extent of Holding. Statute.	Poor Law Valuation.	Former Rent.	Judicial Rent.	Observations.	Value of Tenancy.
A. R. P.	£ s. d.	£ s. d.	£ s. d.		£ s. d.
45 2 20	5 10 0	5 0 0	3 15 0		
30 0 20	4 15 0	3 0 0	2 7 6		
10 1 17	4 5 0	4 0 0	3 0 0		
16 0 0	5 10 0	3 10 0	3 5 0		
18 0 0	3 10 0	3 15 0	3 15 0		
17 0 0	4 5 0	4 3 0	3 5 0		
13 1 10	4 10 0	3 12 6	3 0 0		
15 0 22	5 15 0	5 5 0	4 7 6		
160 0 0	18 0 0	8 0 0	9 0 0	With right of commons of grazing [illegible].	
41 1 10	38 0 0	23 0 0	18 10 0		
6 0 23½	3 5 0	3 13 4	2 13 0		
49 1 34	5 18 0	6 0 0	4 7 6		
27 2 25	4 12 0	6 10 0	4 17 6		
30 3 9	8 0 0	7 10 0	6 5 0		
18 0 0	4 0 0	3 0 0	2 7 6		
18 0 0	3 15 0	3 5 0	3 12 6		
6 1 3	4 10 0	3 3 0	2 18 0	With right of commons of grazing with two others over 52 acres.	
1,156 0 31½	374 2 0	329 5 3	290 13 6		

MUNSTER.

CLARE.

COUNTY OF

Names of Assistant Commissioners by whom Cases were decided.	No.	Name of Tenant.	Name of Landlord.	Townland.
Assistant Commissioners—				
J. S. Green (Legal). R. B. Hampson. J. Sale.	4516	Michael Flynn,	Mrs. Ellen Byrne,	A[illegible],
	4517	John McNamara, Junr.,	Rev. C. O'D. Boyles,	Keogh, North, and another.
	4518	Martin Liddy,	do.	Killeenan,
	4519	Patrick Keogh,	Sophia M. Massy and another,	Knockanean,
	4520	Catherine Grady,	do.	[illegible],
	4521	Mary Broderick, Rep. of James Broderick.	Nicholas Butler,	Killeeneen,
	4522	Honora Brady,	do.	do.
	4523	Martin Maloney,	do.	do.
	4524	James Brady,	do.	do.
	4525	Anastatia Clune,	Anne F. Butler and others,	Ballymarkham,
	4526	Michael Casey,	William M. Maloney,	Gortown[illegible],
	4527	Thomas Dooley,	do.	Drumgh, Middle,
	4528	Patrick McInerney,	do.	do.
	4529	Michael Ryan,	do.	do.
	4530	Pat Moroney,	Thomas B. Browne,	Ballycasey,
	4531	Bartholomew Rogers,	do.	Lee,
	4532	Patrick Ryan,	do.	Loughnasteen and another.
	4533	Mary Ryan,	do.	do.
	4534	Margaret Mageen,	do.	Lee,
	4535	Michael McTea,	Susanna Boyles, continued in name of Rev. C. O'D. Boyles.	Keogh, North.
	4536	Margaret Ahern, Limtd. Admix. of Pat Ahern.	do.	do.
	4537	John Mullins,	do.	do.
	4538	Patrick Collins,	do.	do.
	4539	John Donnellan,	do.	Clonloaf,
	4540	John Ryan,	Lord Limerick,	do.
	4541	Connor Donnellan,	do.	do.
	4542	John Lenihan, Rep. of Daniel Lenihan.	Lord Fitzgerald,	Lakyle,
	4543	Margaret Hogan and another.	do.	Cappalaheen,
J. S. Green (Legal). J. Armstrong. J. Carr.	4544	Peter Donnellan,	Thomas Crowe,	Maleasky,
	4545	Francis Curry,	Mathew Kelly,	Clonmadrum,
	4546	Anthony Curry,	Charles F. Bolton,	Knockroskilleg,
	4547	David O'Keeffe,	W. F. Crowe,	Clongarrane,

CLARE—*continued.*

Area of Holding. Statute.	Poor Law Valuation.	Former Rent.	Judicial Rent.	Observations.	Value of Tenancy.
A. R. P.	£ s. d.	£ s. d.	£ s. d.		£ s. d.
92 1 20	48 15 0	50 0 0	35 0 0		
68 0 32	65 10 0	48 10 7	52 10 0		
6 3 14	5 15 0	8 8 0	4 5 0		
80 0 31	13 15 0	16 0 0	12 0 0		
51 0 0	14 0 0	17 4 6	18 10 0		
126 0 3	8 0 0	35 2 4	31 0 0		
17 3 0	5 10 0	10 0 0	15 10 0	And an undivided moiety of 160 acres.	
104 3 26	7 12 0	38 0 0	8 0 0		
104 1 33	65 15 0	48 7 5	30 15 0		
30 0 0	21 0 0	25 8 8	17 0 0		
11 5 5	6 10 0	5 0 0	4 10 0		
28 0 0	7 0 0	8 0 0	5 5 0		
31 2 36	11 0 0	10 0 0	8 5 0		
49 2 0	5 7 0	7 18 0	5 8 0		
29 1 38	9 10 0	9 8 0	7 0 0		
65 1 37	23 10 0	73 10 0	19 0 0		
69 3 16	19 7 0	15 16 0	24 5 0		
84 2 0	18 12 0	11 5 0	10 15 0		
30 1 8	15 5 0	16 5 0	11 10 0		
14 3 36	10 15 0	19 0 0	8 10 0		
8 1 18	7 18 0	7 14 10	4 0 0		
84 1 0	16 12 0	31 8 0	18 10 0		
7 3 1	3 5 0	8 6 8	4 5 0		
70 2 0	28 10 0	27 0 0	23 10 0		
21 0 5	7 15 0	8 0 0	9 10 0		
27 3 13	17 5 0	13 8 0	18 10 0		
65 3 25	60 0 0	*31 3 0	20 0 0	*Including drainage charge of £3 9s.	
31 0 8	15 0 0	18 10 0	9 10 0		
41 3 16	17 0 0	21 5 0	17 0 0		
40 1 0	20 5 0	25 0 0	18 18 0		
18 0 0	8 5 0	7 0 0	5 0 0		
14 8 28	6 8 0	7 15 5	8 15 0		

COUNTY OF

Names of Assistant Commissioners by whom Case was decided.	No.	Name of Tenant.	Name of Landlord.	Townland.
Assistant Commissioners—				
J. S. Gaynor (Legal). J. Armstrong. J. Carr.	4548	Denis Foran, ...	Randal Borough, ...	Querrin and ...,
	4549	Patrick Carmody, ...	William C. V. Barton, ...	Crom, ...
	4550	William O'Dwyer, ...	Richard Bishop and another,	Quilty, East, ...
	4551	James Carmody, ...	do.	do. ...
	4552	James O'Gorman, ...	Mrs. Jane Collins, ...	Ballymakealag, ...
	4553	James Doyle, ...	do.	Ballymaken, ...
	4554	Francis Keane, ...	do.	Ballymakealag, ...
	4555	Thomas Marrin, ...	do.	do. ...
	4556	Daniel Scanlan, ...	do.	do. ...
	4557	Timothy McCarthy, ...	do.	do. ...
	4558	Bernard Keating, ...	W. H. W. Fitzgerald, ...	Cloheenmovrane, ...
	4559	John Crowe, ...	Mrs. Margaret Crowe, ...	Leitrim, ...
	4560	Michael Killeen, ...	do.	do. ...
	4561	Daniel Murphy, ...	Richard Griffith, ...	Clonlahan, East,
	4562	Bernard Keating, ...	Miss B. Goldwyn and another,	Cloheenmovrane, ...
	4563	Do., ...	Mrs. J. G. Molder, ...	do. ...
	4564	Mary Foran, ...	Lord Leconfield, ...	Glenlaun, ...
	4565	Bernard Keating, ...	Captain A. Morgan, ...	Cloheenmovrane, ...
	4566	Michael O'Gorman, ...	Thomas Mahon, ...	Craggaun, ...
	4567	Michael Ryan, ...	do.	do. ...
	4568	Bernard Keating, ...	James Sheehan, ...	Cloheenmovrane, ...
	4569	John O'Neill, ...	Richard Stacpoole, ...	Tullaher, ...
	4570	Bernard Keating, ...	Rev. F. Tymons and another,	Cloheenmovrane, ...
	4571	Francis Walsh, ...	Colonel B. Vandeleur, ...	Quilty, East, ...
	4572	Michael Hassett (Matt),	Hector S. Vandeleur, ...	Moyne, ...
	4573	Richard O'Dwyer, ...	do.	Ballyvoe, West,
	4574	Do., ...	do.	Ballyvoe, ...
	4575	Augustus Warren, ...	do.	do. ...
	4576	John Hollingsworth, ...	do.	Ballynoe, West,
	4577	John Keane, ...	John G. Scott, ...	Shanakinnane, ...
	4578	Denis McInerney, ...	do.	Killadysert, ...
	4579	Mortimer Keane, ...	Hector S. Vandeleur, ...	Moyasta, ...
	4580	Timothy Killeen, ...	Michael Studdert, ...	Carrowlagan, ...
	4581	Bridget Fitzsimons, Ltd. Admix. of Thos. Fitzsimons,	Francis Healy, ...	Tarmon, ...
	4582	Timothy Flynn, ...	Richard Stacpoole, ...	Armagh, ...

CLARE—*continued.*

Extent of Holding, Statute.	Poor Law Valuation.	Former Rent.	Judicial Rent.	Observations.	Value of Tenancy.
A. R. P.	£ s. d.	£ s. d.	£ s. d.		£ s. d.
37 1 0	23 10 0	28 0 0	31 10 0		
11 1 14	9 12 0	6 1 0	8 5 0		
17 0 0	7 8 0	8 9 7	8 0 0		
1 3 19	1 6 0	1 0 0	0 12 0		
6 1 0	1 0 0	3 7 6	2 2 0		
7 3 37	6 0 0	8 18 8	4 5 0		
12 2 10	5 10 0	11 5 0	7 10 0		
16 0 0	5 10 0	11 9 6	7 10 0		
37 0 16	15 8 0	21 16 4	20 0 0		
19 3 0	8 10 0	24 16 6	10 12 0		
19 3 35	—	9 13 0	6 8 0		
34 0 29	11 5 0	13 8 0	10 6 0		
16 1 29	8 10 0	6 18 0	5 5 0		
43 1 8	6 0 0	6 10 0	5 10 0		
9 3 8	unascertained,	6 3 0	5 3 0		
8 2 0	do.	1 18 6	1 0 0		
84 1 7	9 10 0	21 8 8	10 0 0		
1 3 39	unascertained,	1 8 0	1 0 0		
8 2 16	6 0 0	8 0 0	4 5 0		
0 2 19	6 10 0	9 0 0	3 15 0		
19 2 37	unascertained,	9 9 0	6 10 0		
42 3 27	9 16 0	17 5 0	11 0 0		
10 3 20	unascertained,	8 12 6	5 0 0		
25 1 16	14 0 0	17 0 0	12 15 0		
33 3 0	16 0 0	23 0 0	18 10 0		
8 0 0	8 18 0	14 10 0	9 18 0		
8 2 0	15 0 0	16 10 0	11 10 0		
22 3 39	28 5 0	40 0 0	33 0 0		
14 3 19	17 10 0	27 0 0	18 10 0		
6 2 0	unascertained,	2 0 0	1 1 0	By consent.	
2 2 20	2 10 0	4 16 0	3 0 0	do.	
18 0 31	7 16 0	9 13 0	8 0 0		
20 1 7	10 16 0	14 8 0	9 10 0		
11 3 35	7 8 0	7 16 0	5 0 0		
16 3 28	7 10 0	8 7 8	6 12 0		

COUNTY OF

Names of Assistant Commissioners by whom Cases were decided.	No.	Name of Tenant.	Name of Landlord.	Townland.
Assistant Commissioners—				
J. S. Greene (Legal) J. A[illegible] J. Carr	4583	Michael Curry, ...	Thomas Crowe, ...	Mulkerry, ...
	4584	Michael Killeen, ...	do.	Cragaknock, East,
	4585	Michael Curry, ...	do.	Mulkerry, ...
	4586	Michael O'Gorman, ...	do.	do. ...
	4587	Patrick Morrissey (Pat),	W. F. Crowe, ...	Ballynakenure & another.
	4588	Patrick J. Morrissey, ...	do.	Ballynakenure,
	4589	James Morrissey, ...	do.	do. ...
	4590	Thomas Nugent, ...	do.	Cloongaunam, ...
				Total ...

COUNTY OF

Head Commissioner.	4703	William W. Mahony, ...	Elizabeth Mary Clarke, ...	Upper Leitra, ...
Assistant Commissioners—	4704	Peter Clancy, ...	Richard Longfield, ...	Farnanagala, ...
L. Doyle (Legal). E. O'Neill. J. Geraghty.	4705	Jeremiah Field, ...	John Murphy, ...	Curraheenvarig, ...
	4706	Catherine Sullivan, Ld. Admix. of John Sullivan.	Albin R. Aldworth, ...	Stockham, ...
	4707	William Winters, ...	Colonel R. W. Aldworth, ...	Knocanm, ...
	4708	John M. Curtin, ...	Arthur Longford, ...	Dowel Longford, North, and another.
	4709	Kate Anne Harding, ...	Lord Plunkett, ...	Shanaugh, ...
	4710	Denis Lehane, ...	James M. Creagh and others,	Tureen, ...
	4711	Patrick McAuliffe, ...	William N. Leader, ...	Mountinfel, ...
	4712	Eugene Sullivan, ...	Sir Henry W. Becher, Bart.,	Clonguel, ...
	4713	Daniel McCarthy, ...	do.	Gneeves, ...
	4714	Jeremiah Lyons, ...	Alice Irwin and another, ...	Clogeenen, ...
	4715	Daniel Callaghan, ...	Edward O'Callaghan, ...	Knocknanagh, ...
	4716	John Hickey, ...	do.	do. ...
	4717	Cornelius Galvin, ...	do.	do. ...
	4718	Michael Connors, ...	Godfrey T. Baker, ...	Knockduhig, ...
	4719	John Rossiter, ...	do.	do. ...
	4720	John Boyce, ...	do.	do. ...
	4721	Ellen Barry, ...	do.	do. ...

CLARE—*continued.*

Extent of Holding. Statute.	Poor Law Valuation.	Former Rent.	Judicial Rent.	Observations.	Value of Tenancy.
A. R. P.	£ s. d.	£ s. d.	£ s. d.		£ s. d.
28 3 16	18 0 0	18 15 0	16 0 0		
19 3 0	7 10 0	9 7 8	8 0 0		
31 3 19	unascertained.	14 10 0	13 10 0		
53 2 8	19 5 0	25 0 0	20 10 0		
18 0 4	15 4 0	18 11 8	12 10 0		
16 0 16	11 3 0	14 8 0	10 10 0		
16 0 16	11 8 0	14 8 9	10 10 0		
26 0 31	7 17 0	10 0 0	6 15 0		
1,518 3 33	894 0 0	1,395 10 4	956 14 0		

CORK.

12 3 30	3 0 0	3 0 0	1 10 0	The rent in this case was fixed by consent of the parties at the sitting of the Court in Dublin.	
87 3 8	34 10 0	40 0 0	27 0 0		180 0 0
40 1 10½	21 13 0	36 16 2	24 16 9		130 0 0
39 0 20	17 15 0	19 4 0	19 4 0		
105 0 0	60 0 0	74 15 8	66 0 0		300 0 0
201 2 33	51 1 0	64 0 0	38 0 0	With free turbary.	100 0 0
83 0 5	30 10 0	33 19 4	27 10 0		
97 1 37	14 8 0	37 0 0	20 0 0		
30 0 30	4 0 0	9 1 1	6 5 0		
23 3 28	13 14 0	18 9 8	15 10 0		
180 2 35	79 16 0	110 0 0	82 0 0		
45 2 37	30 4 0	30 0 0	30 0 0		
21 1 32	8 10 0	19 19 11	12 0 0		
64 2 4	24 10 0	46 18 0	34 0 0		
41 1 19	18 10 0	41 4 0	30 10 0		
16 0 0	6 5 0	8 17 0	6 13 4		
14 3 7	5 18 0	8 10 0	7 0 0		
78 3 30	33 10 0	48 0 0	37 0 0		
11 2 0	5 10 0	9 10 0	6 15 0		

COUNTY OF

Names of Assistant Commissioners by whom Cases were decided.	No.	Name of Tenant.	Name of Landlord.	Townland.
Assistant Commissioners—				
L. Doyle (Legal). R. O'Keeffe. J. Gorham.	4722	John Lyons, ...	Godfrey T. Baker, ...	[illegible], ...
	4723	Edmund Murphy, ...	Colonel B. W. Aldworth, ...	[illegible], ...
	4724	John Shea, ...	Ellen Cleary and others, ...	[illegible], &c.,
	4725	John Daly, ...	David Coughlan, ...	Tullodeel, ...
	4726	Denis Fitzpatrick, ...	Sir John St. J. Colthurst, Bt.,	[illegible], ...
	4727	John Herlihy, ...	Joseph V. Carpenter & anor.,	[illegible]-taugh.
	4728	Cornelius Crowley, ...	do.	do. ...
	4729	Johanna Leary, ...	Mrs. Elizabeth Massy and others,	Ardnageeha, ...
	4730	Ellen Connell, ...	Michael Nash, ...	Clash, ...
	4731	James Wall, ...	R. Murrough Bernard, ...	Ballintlea, ...
	4732	Michael Fitzgerald, ...	John O'Brien, ...	Ardmore, ...
	4733	Denis Callaghan, ...	Louisa O'Keeffe and others, minors, by Wilhelmina O'Keeffe, their Guardian, and another,	Knocknaloo, ...
L. Doyle (Legal). W. Walpole. W. J. Gorman.	4734	Patrick O'Leary, ...	James Lambkin and others,	Inchideraugh, ...
	4735	Timothy Riordan, ...	do.	do. ...
	4736	Patrick Hurley, ...	Robert Hedges Eyre White,	Maulawaddig, ...
	4737	John Sullivan (Dan) and another.	do.	Carrigles, ...
	4738	Cornelius Ryan, ...	do.	[illegible], ...
	4739	Jeremiah Leary, ...	do.	Inchigeera, ...
	4740	Daniel [illegible], ...	Earl of Bantry, ...	Tramain, ...
	4741	John Crimmen, ...	do.	Gorrain, ...
	4742	Richard Hennessy, ...	Earl of Bandon, ...	Brohalish, ...
	4743	Jeremiah Brien, ...	Michael M. Morris and anor.,	Murragh, ...
	4744	John Begun, ...	Mrs. Ellen Wright, ...	[illegible], ...
	4745	John McCarthy and anor.,	Samuel N. Hutchins and ors.,	Scartbawn, ...
	4746	John Ross, ...	Sir Henry W. Becher, Bt.,	Glaniart, ...
	4747	Michael Daly, ...	Earl of Bandon, ...	Dromaleigh, ...
	4748	Daniel Daly, ...	do.	do. ...
	4749	Catherine Crowle, Ld. Admix. of William Crowle, deceased.	do.	do. ...
	4750	Richard Nicholas, ...	do.	do. ...
	4751	John Crowley, ...	Mrs. O'Donovan, ...	Curlisheen, ...
	4752	Johanna Kingston, ...	do.	do. ...
	4753	Michael Hurley, ...	do.	do. ...

CORK—*continued.*

Extent of Holding.	Poor Law Valuation.	Former Rent.	Judicial Rent.	Observations.
A. R. P.	£ s. d.	£ s. d.	£ s. d.	
40 0 0	18 0 0	30 0 0	22 0 0	
63 2 12	37 0 0	45 0 0	37 10 0	
17 0 0	6 15 0	8 0 0	7 10 0	
13 0 30	7 5 0	12 4 0	7 0 0	
16 1 25	5 10 0	8 10 0	8 10 0	
180 0 0	9 0 0	16 0 0	12 0 0	
175 0 0	15 15 0	36 0 0	24 15 0	
7 0 0	6 15 0	8 10 0	6 7 6	
3 2 18	2 15 0	8 10 0	6 7 4	
21 0 0	19 0 0	25 5 8	21 0 0	By consent.
1 0 0	—	4 0 0	6 0 0	do.
43 3 16	34 5 0	37 0 0	28 0 0	
84 0 6	53 10 0	80 0 0	67 18 6	
17 1 9	13 10 0	14 10 0	13 9 0	
10 1 6	no separate valuation.	5 5 0	6 10 0	
64 0 0	do.	14 0 0	13 0 0	
14 2 10	6 0 0	5 0 0	5 0 0	
32 1 7	6 10 0	10 10 0	7 10 0	
30 3 25	11 15 0	16 18 6	14 17 9	
13 3 38	5 0 0	8 10 0	7 0 0	
85 0 0	24 0 0	22 19 8	25 0 0	With right of grazing and turbary on mountain.
44 2 0	7 15 0	15 0 0	10 5 0	
18 0 0	5 15 0	9 0 0	7 5 0	do.
48 2 28	10 15 0	25 11 0	20 0 0	
117 1 5	23 10 0	35 0 0	27 0 0	
46 0 11	13 5 0	19 13 0	19 18 0	do.
35 3 20	8 15 0	11 13 9	10 10 0	do.
43 1 28	14 15 0	19 13 0	17 7 8	do.
25 3 10	8 10 0	0 11 1	5 12 4	do.
86 0 0	18 0 0	30 0 0	20 0 0	do.
30 0 0	16 5 0	26 10 0	20 5 0	do.
36 0 0	10 0 0	17 0 0	14 7 0	do.

COUNTY OF

Names of Assistant Commissioners by whom Cases were decided.	No.	Name of Tenant.	Name of Landlord.	Townland.
Assistant Commissioners—				
L. Doyle (Legal). W. Walpole W. J. Coughlan.	4734	Cornelius Keohane, ...	Earl of Bantry, ...	Tooreennadree, ...
	4735	James Goggin, ...	do.	Garrane, ...
	4736	Anne Atteridge, ...	Jane H. Swanton and anor.,	Ballydehob, ...
L. Doyle (Legal). W. Walpole J. J. Grier.	4737	Jeremiah Donovan, ...	James Welply, ...	Cahergal, ...
				Total, ...

COUNTY OF

Assistant Commissioners—	3314	William Ryan, ...	George Hewson, ...	Gortnaskehy, ...
J. G. Oakes (Legal). J. Harrington. J. J. O'Shaughnessy.	3315	Thomas Quill, ...	Sophia Chambers, ...	Tarrama, ...
	3316	Jeremiah Brennan, ...	do.	do. ...
	3317	Margaret O'Connor, Limited, Admix. of Michael O'Connor.	do.	do. ...
	3318	John Hanrahan, ...	do.	do. ...
	3319	John Wallace, ...	Charles O'B. Gough & anor. Trustees of John Gough, decd.	do. ...
				Total, ...

CORK—*continued.*

Extent of Holding. Statute.	Poor Law Valuation.	Former Rent.	Judicial Rent.	Observations.	Value of Tenancy.
A. R. P.	£ s. d.	£ s. d.	£ s. d.		£ s. d.
204 1 30	55 0 0	70 0 0	60 0 0		
34 0 17	13 0 0	21 0 0	16 18 0		
6 3 6	3 10 0	6 0 0	6 0 0	By consent.	
11 1 0	10 0 0	18 0 0	12 7 6		
3,629 2 7½	957 11 0	1,363 2 3	1,110 13 3		

KERRY.

8 0 0	8 0 0	5 0 0	4 0 0		
27 3 8	7 5 0	12 15 0	6 0 0		
16 0 37	5 15 0	10 0 0	5 10 0		
18 3 1	7 5 0	12 0 0	8 0 0		
80 3 31	7 6 0	11 0 0	8 10 0		
20 2 9	10 10 0	15 5 0	13 5 0		
113 0 6	41 6 0	66 0 0	45 5 0		

LIMERICK.

112 2 19	77 16 0	100 0 0	86 0 0		
3 1 0	3 10 0	3 10 0	3 17 0		
14 3 11	6 0 0	11 0 0	8 0 0		
8 0 0	18 15 0	12 10 0	9 10 0	By consent.	
79 3 0	34 15 0	44 0 8	34 0 0	do.	
15 1 29	18 0 0	18 0 0	15 0 0		
27 1 22	15 10 0	41 19 8	11 0 0		

COUNTY OF

Names of Assistant Commissioners by whom Cases were decided.	No.	Name of Tenant.	Name of Landlord.	Townland.
Assistant Commissioners— J. H. Edge (Legal). F. M. Gardiner. J. T. Davys.				
	1913	Henry Shea,	Thomas R. D. Atkinson,	Ballinacourty,
	1914	Thomas Reidy,	do.	Cloonteraple
	1915	James Linehan,	do.	Gurteen,
	1916	Patrick Burke,	do.	do.
	1917	Michael Houlihan,	Mrs. Eleanor Goodwin,	Kilmore,
	1918	John Fahill,	Edward White,	Derrivile,
	1919	Mary A. Connolly,	Lord Sackville and others,	Cloongra,
	1920	John Quirk,	R. W. H. Moreland and anor.,	Ballingarane,
	1921	Maurice Walsh,	Dean Skelton,	Croghtenan,
	1922	Cornelius O'Brien,	Richard Harte,	[illegible]
	1923	Patrick Barry,	Mrs. Elizabeth Heffernan Considine,	Lisheenagh,
	1924	John O'Shaughnessy,	John F. Heffernan Considine, a minor, by Capt. Williamson.	Manister,
	1925	Daniel Madden,	do.	do.
	1926	Daniel Mangan,	do.	do.
	1927	Edmond Cahill,	do.	do.
	1928	James Walsh,	Frederick Maurice and others, Legatees of Col. Hamilton.	Dromore, Upper,
	1929	Do.,	do.	do.
	1930	Arthur O'Leary,	Charles Conyers,	Castletown,
	1931	Patrick C. Madigan,	Robert E. Conyers and anor.,	Graigue,
	1932	John O'Leary and anor.,	do.	do.
	1933	Patrick Donegan,	Edward White,	Cappaninane,
	1934	Patrick Riordan,	do.	Derrivile,
	1935	Benjamin Daly,	do.	Cappaninane,
	1936	John Culhane,	Major William Cox,	Upr. Dromdough,
	1937	Michael Fitzgibbon,	do.	Lr. Dromdough.
				Total,

COUNTY OF

Assistant Commissioners— J. H. Edge (Legal). M. F. Lynch. W. H. Browning.	2569	Thomas O'Meara,	George Holmes,	Lisdeal
	2570	John Kennedy,	Henry J. Lloyd,	Barrinamahony.
	2571	James Hewson,	Joseph Griffith,	Balaghan,
	2572	James Russell,	William Lloyd,	Kyleballyhanlon,

LIMERICK—*continued.*

Extent of Holding. Statute.	Poor Law Valuation.	Former Rent.	Judicial Rent.
A. R. P.	£ s. d.	£ s. d.	£ s. d.
65 1 10	19 10 0	28 0 0	25 0 0
8 0 22	8 0 0	5 10 0	3 10 0
126 3 30	72 0 0	32 18 0	22 5 0
9 1 25	7 5 0	9 15 6	8 0 0
11 0 0	6 5 0	10 9 4	8 10 0
1 3 24	unascertained,	1 16 0	1 0 0
64 2 20	19 10 0	30 15 0	23 0 0
17 0 0	8 0 0	11 15 0	7 10 0
21 0 5	8 10 0	22 0 0	14 0 0
8 1 36	3 15 0	4 4 0	4 4 0
8 2 10	unascertained,	5 0 0	4 0 0
13 3 23	10 10 0	13 10 0	10 0 0
17 0 33	15 0 0	17 0 0	13 0 0
18 2 15	10 0 0	12 10 0	10 0 0
14 0 9	15 0 0	16 15 4	10 0 0
18 2 37	14 15 0	18 6 4	13 0 0
12 0 0	8 0 0	9 0 0	7 0 0
12 0 13	6 0 0	8 0 0	5 10 0
30 0 8	19 0 0	25 14 6	19 0 0
34 2 1	18 15 0	21 0 0	18 0 0
1 2 26	unascertained,	2 5 0	0 15 0
1 0 30	0 15 0	2 0 0	1 5 0
8 0 39	unascertained,	3 10 0	1 10 0
10 1 25	4 15 0	7 13 4	3 0 0
15 2 22	8 16 8	12 11 7	10 0 0
522 3 18	285 6 6	341 9 3	262 12 0

TIPPERARY.

COUNTY OF

Names of Assistant Commissioners by whom Cases were decided.	No.	Name of Tenant.	Name of Landlord.	Townland.
Assistant Commissioners—				
J. H. Rane (Legal). M. P. Lynch. W. H. Browning.	2873	Daniel Creed, ...	Miss Kate Lloyd, ...	Kyleunaddy, ...
	2874	Denis Vaughan, ...	Major Lidwell, ...	Dromard, ...
	2875	John Phelan, ...	do.	do. ...
	2876	Thomas Ryan, ...	Dixon O'Keeffe, ...	Clonmore, ...
	2877	John Maher, ...	Count De Salis and another,	Shanakill, ...
	2878	Thomas Hayes, ...	Hon. Otway Toler, ...	Spruce Hill, ...
	2879	William Kennelly, ...	Joseph Griffiths, ...	Killea, ...
				Total, ...

COUNTY OF

Names of Assistant Commissioners by whom Cases were decided.	No.	Name of Tenant.	Name of Landlord.	Townland.
Assistant Commissioners—				
L. Doyle (Legal). C. R. Butler. R. B. Bayly.	1103	Garrett Nugent, ...	Earl of Huntingdon, a minor, by Countess of Huntingdon, his Guardian.	Rossmore and another.
	1104	Michael Tobin, ...	Pierce English, ...	Garrane, Upper,
	1105	James Fogg, ...	Godfrey J. Smith, ...	Curriera, ...
	1106	William Power, ...	Thomas Hennigan, ...	Glenagort, ...
	1107	John Nugent, ...	John H. Barton, ...	Lefanta, ...
	1108	John Hickey, ...	Duke of Devonshire, ...	Ballyrandrough,
	1109	Michael R. Hynes, ...	do.	Townparks, ...
	1110	Cornelius Hurley, ...	Emily F. O'Donnell, by Mary O'Donnell, his Mother, and another,	Killowen, East, ...
	1111	Allen Callander, ...	George R. Poer, a minor, by Mary Poer, his Guardian.	Mogeely, ...
	1112	Walter Callander, ...	do.	Clashnagarrane,
	1113	Patrick Brown, ...	Arthur B. Ussher, ...	Barranagappul, ...
	1114	John Lowham, ...	do.	Carrigane, ...
	1115	Thomas Cunningham, ...	do.	Carrigane, and another.
	1116	do.	do.	Camphire, ...
	1117	John Cuffe, ...	Lieut.-Col. George R. Hillier,	Tubbernabolla, ...
	1118	Mary Downes, ...	do.	Knockyoolahan.
	1119	Ellen Buckley, ...	do.	do. ...
	1120	Patrick Carroll, ...	Sir Richard F. Keane, ...	Knockboy and another.
	1121	Patrick Brien, ...	do.	Tooraneena, ...
	1122	John Connors, ...	do.	Chilaldine, ...

TIPPERARY—continued.

Extent of Holding. Statute.	Poor Law Valuation.	Former Rent.	Judicial Rent.	Observations.	Value of Tenancy.
A. R. P.	£ s. d.	£ s. d.	£ s. d.		£ s. d.
16 0 0	8 0 0	12 0 0	8 0 0		
6 0 7	1 10 0	2 0 0	1 10 0		
5 2 18	1 15 0	7 0 0	3 0 0		
48 3 10	34 0 0	35 0 0	27 0 0		
31 0 6	11 10 0	13 0 0	9 5 0		
111 2 2	70 0 0	73 5 1	66 0 0		
9 1 12	4 10 0	7 0 0	3 10 0		
611 3 37	374 15 0	396 5 1	300 3 6		

WATERFORD.

Extent of Holding. Statute.	Poor Law Valuation.	Former Rent.	Judicial Rent.	Observations.	Value of Tenancy.
30 0 20	12 5 0	20 5 8	19 2 6	With right of grazing three two year old cattle on mountain of [illegible].	
98 1 12	30 0 0	35 0 0	29 10 0		
180 2 4	144 15 0	215 7 3	180 0 0		
8 2 0	8 5 0	3 10 0	2 6 0		
3 1 27	3 0 0	4 0 0	3 10 0		
66 2 34	60 15 0	75 12 0	63 7 6		
48 3 16	63 0 0	63 10 0	45 10 0		
37 0 17	41 0 0	43 0 0	30 10 0		
125 0 25	79 0 0	104 0 0	78 0 0		
46 1 16	38 0 0	60 0 0	39 13 6		
27 3 5	9 10 0	11 0 0	6 12 6		
6 0 7	4 0 0	4 13 0	3 0 0		
71 0 23	34 10 0	40 0 0	31 0 0		
17 0 0	16 10 0	25 16 0	17 0 0		
31 0 9	6 6 0	8 0 0	5 0 0		
35 0 13	18 10 0	26 15 8	17 0 0		
30 2 8	21 0 0	34 2 10	17 8 0		
15 3 10	3 6 0	3 6 0	2 3 0		
15 0 35	3 0 0	3 10 0	3 0 0		
90 0 0	21 10 0	25 0 0	19 0 0		

COUNTY OF

Names of Assistant Commissioners by whom Cases were decided.	No.	Name of Tenant.	Name of Landlord.	Townland.
ssistant Commissioners—				
L. Doyle (Legal). C. R. Butler. E. R. Bayly.	1123	William Ahern, ...	Sir Richard F. Keane, Bart.,	Tinure, ...
	1124	Mary Connor, ...	do.	Cooleagarraine, ...
	1125	John Coleman, ...	do.	Tournamraine, ...
	1126	James Mansfield, ...	do.	do. ...
L. Doyle (Legal). E. B. Bayly.	1127	James Prendergast, ...	Earl of Huntingdon, a minor, by Guardians of Huntingdon.	Whitechurch, ...
	1128	John J. Costin, ...	Cecilia Cahill and others, ...	Ballynamrane and another, .
				Total, ...

Rents fixed upon the Reports of Valuers appointed by the Irish Land

PROVINCE OF

COUNTY OF

Number.	Name of Tenant.	Name of Landlord.	Townland.
[illegible]	George Quin and others, ...	George Quin and others, ...	Burleigh, ...

PROVINCE OF

WATERFORD—*continued.*

Extent of Holding. Statute.	Poor Law Valuation.	Former Rent.	Judicial Rent.	Observations.	Value of Tenancy.
A. R. P.	£ s. d.	£ s. d.	£ s. d.		£ s. d.
83 3 30	45 5 0	63 0 0	45 10 0		
[illegible] 0 18	6 13 0	6 16 0	5 5 0		
12 3 33	3 16 0	1 0 0	[illegible]		
[illegible]	2 10 0	[illegible] 0 0	[illegible] 0		
15 1 20	13 15 9	22 0 0	11 15 0		
156 0 7	58 0 0	56 0 0	[illegible] 0 0		
1,161 0 13	738 17 9	959 6 4	610 8 0		

Commission on the Joint Applications of Landlords and Tenants.

LEINSTER.

WEXFORD.

Extent of Holding. Statute.	Poor Law Valuation.	Former Rent.	Judicial Rent.	Observations.
A. R. P.	£ s. d.	£ s. d.	£ s. d.	
45 0 0	33 0 0	31 19 1	21 0 0	

MUNSTER.

CORK.

10 1 30	4 10 0	7 0 0	4 10 0	
4 2 10	2 0 0	2 0 0	1 10 0	
99 3 11	13 18 0	[illegible] 0 0	16 0 0	
206 3 27	67 0 0	150 13 0	93 0 0	
37 0 0	16 0 0	59 0 0	36 0 0	

LAND LAW (IRELAND) ACT, 1887.

LEASEHOLDERS.

PROVINCE OF

COUNTY OF

Names of Assistant Commissioners by whom Cases were decided.	No.	Name of Tenant.	Name of Landlord.	Townland.
Head Commission.	471	John Young, ...	William Moore, ...	Cabbinshall, ...
	472	Thomas Patton, ...	do.	Livery, Upper,
	473	William Hemphill, ...	do.	Cabbinshall, ...
	474	William Patton, ...	do.	Livery, Upper,
	475	William J. Sayers, ...	do.	Cabbinshall, ...
	476	Do., ...	do.	do. ...
	477	Archibald Libby, ...	do.	do. ...
	478	Andrew Bradshaw, ...	Colonel Alexander Murray,	Craigfield, ...
	479	William Gregg and anor.,	do.	Gabbanagh, ...
	480	Sarah Boyd, Admix. of John Boyd, deceased.	George Smith and others, Trustees and Exors. of late Sir E. Cary, and continued in the names of E. Cary.	Ballyscoley and another.
	481	Rev. W. J. McCreadye and another, Exors. of late Thomas Kelly.	Mrs. Sarah H. Torrens, ...	Ballyhamage, ...
	482	Do., ...	do.	Dough, ...
	483	Samuel A. Nixon, ...	Gilbert McIlveen, ...	Ballygianiff, ...
	484	Charles Quinn, ...	do.	do. ...
	485	Samuel Whiteside, ...	do.	do. ...
	486	Samuel A. Nixon, ...	do.	do. ...
	487	Henry Boyd, ...	William Moore, ...	Mullinsallagh, ...
	488	Hugh Walker, ...	Countess of Shaftesbury, ...	Carndoff, ...
	489	Robert Mitchell, ...	Sir Charles Lanyon, ...	Tannybrack, ...
	490	Andrew Harper and anor.,	Mrs. Sarah H. Torrens, ...	Ballyhamage, ...
	491	Alexander Baillie, ...	John Armstrong, ...	Ballynabe, ...
	492	Thomas B. Hill, ...	John J. Rowan, ...	Killane, ...
	493	Charles Johnston, ...	John Wardlow, ...	Ballylummin, ...
	494	Margaret Rankin, ...	do.	Lisnisky, ...

ULSTER.

ANTRIM.

Extent of Holding. Statute.	Poor Law Valuation.	Former Rent.	Judicial Rent.	Observations.	Value of Tenancy.
A. R. P.	£ s. d.	£ s. d.	£ s. d.		£ s. d.
65 3 10	56 0 0	80 0 0	54 10 0	The rent in this case was fixed by consent of the parties at the sitting of the Court in Dublin.	
[illegible] 2 [illegible]	15 0 0	23 0 0	13 18 0	do.	
34 0 4	25 5 0	31 10 0	21 10 0	do.	
[illegible] 3 12	17 5 0	25 0 0	15 10 0	do.	
[illegible] 0 0	[illegible] 5 0	57 10 0	[illegible] 17 8	do.	
[illegible] 0 30	35 5 0	40 0 0	27 18 4	do.	
[illegible] 3 27	17 0 0	[illegible] 5 0	15 1 0	do.	
15 0 21	13 0 0	11 1 6	10 0 0	do.	
30 1 27	no separate valuation.	13 13 0	14 6 0	do.	
64 2 37	65 0 0	100 0 0	80 0 0	do.	
18 1 [illegible]	20 0 0	[illegible] 0 0	18 15 0	do.	
17 0 [illegible]	61 10 0	[illegible] 8 6	16 5 0	do.	
14 0 34	unascertained.	24 0 10	10 10 0	do.	
17 2 5	19 0 0	27 16 8	13 15 0	do.	
13 2 34	20 0 0	19 17 8	14 15 0	do.	
64 1 [illegible]	unascertained.	56 18 6½	44 7 0	do.	
64 3 12	35 0 0	[illegible] 14 10	30 0 0	do.	
9 2 0	18 10 0	15 0 0	11 0 0	do.	
48 3 38	23 5 0	[illegible] 0 0	19 18 0	do.	
79 3 4	[illegible] 15 0	40 6 6	38 0 0	do.	
[illegible] 1 0	24 18 0	31 0 0	[illegible] 0 0	do.	
[illegible] 3 30	107 0 0	100 0 0	78 0 0	do.	
8 0 [illegible]	8 10 0	8 10 0	4 10 0	do.	
6 1 4	6 5 0	6 18 0	4 15 0	do.	

Names of Assistant Commissioners by whom Cases were decided.	No.	Name of Tenant.	Name of Landlord.
Assistant Commissioners—			
E. Greene (Legal). J. M. Weir. R. Sproule.	495	Samuel Hamilton, ...	Andrew Lowther,
	496	William B. Erskine, ...	Frederick H. Henry, in place of Frederick Henry.
	497	James McCauley, ...	Sir Richard Wallace,
	498	Michael P. Armstrong,	do. ...
	499	Isaac Green, ...	do. ...
	500	Thomas Spence, ...	do. ...

Names of Assistant Commissioners by whom Cases were decided.	No.	Name of Tenant.	Name of Landlord.
Head Commissioner.	171	Joseph McKinney, ...	James G. Reid, ...
	172	James Cardoner, ...	do. ...
	173	Ralph James, ...	do. ...
	174	William McCreery, ...	do. ...
	175	Do., ...	do. ...
	176	Do., ...	do. ...
	177	Patrick McNeilly, ...	Edward S. O'Brien
Assistant Commissioners—			
D. Tierney (Legal). R. E. Senior. H. Johnston.	178	William Moffett, ...	Earl of Charlemont,
	179	Henry Clougher, ...	do. ...
	180	John Ruddell, ...	George W. Francis,
	181	Bernard McConnell, ...	Earl of Gosford, ...
	182	W. H. Brown, ...	do. ...
	183	Andrew Jenkins, ...	do. ...
	184	Eliza Farley, ...	do. ...
	185	Elizabeth Stevenson, ...	Miss J. B. Molyneux,
	186	David Purdy, ...	Duke of Manchester,
	187	Benjamin Mullagh, ...	do. ...

ANTRIM—*continued.*

Extent of Holding. Statute.	Poor Law Valuation.	Former Rent.	Judicial Rent.	Observations.	Value of Tenancy.
A. R. P.	£ s. d.	£ s. d.	£ s. d.		£ s. d.
84 0 0	35 0 0	46 0 0	32 0 0		
71 1 8	74 10 0	55 0 0	58 0 0		
43 0 29	46 0 0	54 11 0	35 10 0		
15 1 35	unascertained.	14 8 9	9 5 0		
15 1 17	17 0 0	11 7 0	10 0 0		
34 2 23	18 5 0	29 4 0	24 10 0		
1,039 2 20	878 5 0	1,038 17 3½	769 10 0		

ARMAGH.

11 3 1	10 0 0	11 0 0	6 15 0	The rent in this case was fixed by consent of the parties at the sitting of the Court in Dublin.	
6 3 25	4 5 0	7 12 0	5 12 8	do.	
6 1 12	6 0 0	7 0 5	6 0 0	do.	
8 3 13	5 10 0	9 18 5	8 0 0	do.	
4 0 0	4 0 0	5 1 6	3 11 8	do.	
10 3 20	9 0 0	11 9 4	8 8 4	do.	
5 1 24	6 15 0	6 0 11	4 15 0	do.	
6 0 24	9 0 0	5 15 0	4 10 0		
5 0 33	—	4 13 10	3 15 0		
36 1 38	44 10 0	73 16 1	50 0 0		
18 2 1	15 0 0	14 6 8	10 15 0		
19 0 14	—	22 10 4	17 0 0		
18 2 5	20 10 0	19 18 7	15 0 0		
10 0 0	13 10 0	10 15 6	7 0 0		
74 0 7	87 0 0	60 14 0	63 10 0		
17 2 10	17 10 0	15 0 10	13 0 0		
15 3 30	27 10 0	15 18 10	14 0 0		
32 1 24	—	33 17 6	21 0 0		
25 2 0	—	44 5 6	34 0 0	By consent.	
14 0 0	10 0 0	19 18 6	12 5 0		
29 3 30	35 10 0	31 2 8	25 10 0		

Names of Assistant Commissioners by whom Cases were heard.	No.	Name of Tenant.		Name of Landlord.
Assistant Commissioners—				
D. [illegible] (Legal). H. K. [illegible] H. [illegible]	192	Patrick Kinney,	...	John T. Burgess,
	193	Joseph McKee,	...	Earl of Charlemont,
	194	James Dunlop,	...	Angle A. D'Arcy,

ARMAGH—*continued.*

Extent of Holding Statute.	Poor Law Valuation.	Former Rent.	Judicial Rent.	Observations.	Value of Tenancy.
A. R. P.	£ s. d.	£ s. d.	£ s. d.		£ s. d.
20 3 33	25 0 0	21 10 0	16 10 0	By consent.	
84 3 36	20 5 0	17 6 0	13 0 0		
81 0 0	84 10 0	125 0 0	100 0 0		
13 0 15	16 15 0	18 9 10	21 0 0		
8 2 20	12 0 0	13 3 2	8 10 0	do.	
18 2 21	30 0 0	30 17 5	25 0 0	do.	
8 2 0	13 15 0	13 7 0	9 15 0	do.	
6 0 0	9 0 0	15 0 0	10 0 0		
13 3 30	7 15 0	30 15 0	25 0 0	do.	
15 0 0	10 0 0	23 1 8	18 5 0		
348 0 35	284 10 0	760 15 1	561 5 6		

CAVAN.

COUNTY OF

Names of Assistant Commissioners by whom Cases were decided.	No.	Name of Tenant.	Name of Landlord.	Townland.
HEAD COMMISSIONER.	255	John Brown,	John J. Whyte,	Dunghery,
	256	Hugh Martin,	Mrs. Mary A. Watson,	Longham,
	257	James Hunter,	Rev. Edward J. Smyth,	Ballytinel,
	258	James O'Gilrian,	Colonel Alexander Crozy,	Ballyorgan (part of).
Assistant Commissioners— R. Gibson (Legal). J. Cunningham. T. Smith.	259	James and Hugh Stone, Reps. of Henry and James Stone.	John Q. Henry,	Dunevan,
	260	Bernard Lynas,	Charles Symmott,	Lisnaran,
	261	Patrick Adolphus McGivern,	do.	do.
	262	Thomas McGee,	do.	do.
	263	Thomas Colgan,	do.	do.
	264	Daniel Kinney,	do.	do.
	265	James White,	do.	do.
R. Gibson (Legal). R. Garrett. A. Chambers.	266	Theophilus Legate, Exor. of James Redel.	Viscount Bridport and anor., Trustees of Marquis of Downshire.	Drumaniskey,
	267	William A. Campbell,	Sir David Taylor,	Ballyguran and another.
	268	Lowry Carlisle,	James Robinson,	Ballymaguirick,
	269	Robert Dorman, junior,	Robert N. Batt,	Drumbo,
	270	Andrew Kennedy,	George A. Hume, and others, Reps of the Misses Kilmurry.	Gilhamkirk,
	271	Thomas Morrow,	do.	do.
	272	Robert Smith,	James C. Price,	Tullywest,
	273	James Kirkpatrick,	do.	Drumgooland, West.
	274	Jonathan Turner,	Viscount Bridport and anor., Trustees of Marquis of Downshire.	Ballykeelartifinny
	275	Finlo A. Graham,	Alexander Allen and another,	Dundady,
	276	David Lindsay,	do.	do.
				Total.

DOWN.

Extent of Holding. Statute.	Poor Law Valuation.	Former Rent.	Judicial Rent.	Observations.	Value of Tenancy.
A. R. P.	£ s. d.	£ s. d.	£ s. d.		£ s. d.
38 3 30	30 5 0	43 1 8	30 0 0	The rent in this case was fixed by consent of the parties at the sitting of the Court in Dublin.	
10 0 38	9 5 0	13 18 0	8 8 0	do.	
14 1 18	—	13 18 11	9 0 0	do.	
80 3 23	100 10 0	100 6 8	75 0 0	do.	
3 0 35	3 6 0	4 1 0	3 0 0		
9 3 17	7 5 0	9 4 1	6 0 0		
10 0 25	14 10 0	9 5 4	7 0 0		
5 1 1	5 0 0	5 11 1	4 15 0		
16 3 35	17 10 0	18 8 8	15 0 0		
6 1 30	4 10 0	4 3 9	5 0 0		
18 2 15	6 15 0	7 5 8	5 5 0		
93 3 31	115 0 0	104 16 0	78 0 0		
33 1 32	30 0 0	43 9 8	40 0 0		
6 1 0	5 5 0	8 10 0	4 12 0		
13 3 26	17 3 0	16 15 3	12 11 0		
3 3 1	4 3 0	7 3 4	3 0 0		
15 2 17	18 15 0	23 14 6	17 10 0		
16 1 34	13 10 0	18 7 6	10 10 0		
18 0 0	10 10 0	16 5 5	11 5 0		
17 10 0	—	14 9 3	18 0 0		
38 1 11	84 0 0	80 11 0	63 0 0		
31 2 17	25 0 0	34 2 8	26 0 0		
488 2 30	481 3 0	559 0 10	400 17 0		

COUNTY OF

Names of Assistant Commissioners by whom Cases were decided.	No.	Name of Tenant.	Name of Landlord.	Townland.
Head Commission.	341	John Murray, ...	The Hon. The Irish Society,	Ballynagowan, ...
	342	James Browne, ...	do.	do. ...
	343	Robert McConnell, ...	do.	do. ...
	344	Elizabeth Doak, ...	do.	do. ...
	345	Robert J. McAdam, ...	do.	Bogbill, ...
				Total, ...

COUNTY OF

Assistant Commissioners— W. F. Bailey (Legal). J. D. Ball. W. S. Buchanan.	76	Thomas Gillanders, ...	Mrs. Catherine Leavy,	Broghlarton, ...
	77	Mary Adams, ...	do.	do. ...
				Total, ...

COUNTY OF

Head Commission.	291	William McFarland, ...	William Knox, ...	Kilclean, ...
	292	Do., ...	do.	do. ...
	293	John Milton, ...	John G. Whiteside, ...	Gortin, ...
Assistant Commissioners— D. Tierney (Legal). A. S. Drake. A. Lucas.	294	Charles Bradley, ...	Rev. James Hamilton, ...	Corit, ...
	295	Francis Boyd, ...	Francis A. Eblin, ...	Carrickaneddin
	296	Michael McQuaide, ...	Major Thomas Auchinleck, ...	do. ...
	297	Dennis O'Neill, ...	Rev. John P. Maguire, ...	Glenabill, ...
	298	Patrick McCanny, ...	do.	Murrock, ...
	299	James Hoynes, ...	R. S. Mansfield, ...	Cavanalliagh, ...
	300	Pat McMenamin, ...	do.	Curraghmacall, ...
	301	Patrick Gilleese, ...	do.	Glenghan, ...
	302	Mary Curran, ...	Samuel Leary, M.D., and others,	Coolnaboro, ...
	303	Robert Walker, ...	R. S. Mansfield, ...	Willmount, ...
	304	George Montgomery, ...	do.	Billany, ...
	305	Annie M. Fleming, ...	Henry De C. Stuart, ...	Dovene, ...
				Total, ...

LONDONDERRY.

Extent of Holding, Statute.	Poor Law Valuation.	Former Rent.	Judicial Rent.	Observations.	Value of Tenancy.
a. r. p.	£ s. d.	£ s. d.	£ s. d.		£ s. d.
13 0 14	8 0 0	13 4 8	6 8 0	The rent in this case was fixed by consent of the parties at the sitting of the Court in Dublin.	
3 1 16	3 5 0	4 1 5	3 0 0	do.	
18 0 30	Not known,	7 7 1	5 10 0	do.	
5 0 23	3 10 0	4 1 6	3 1 0	do.	
37 3 35	13 10 0	26 0 0	16 14 4	do.	
71 0 36	33 5 0	55 14 10	35 7 4		

MONAGHAN.

16 3 30	13 10 0	14 18 8	10 0 0		
15 3 20	12 10 0	16 13 4	9 0 0		
31 3 10	26 0 0	30 12 0	19 0 0		

TYRONE.

143 1 18	81 10 0	45 0 0	60 15 0	The rent in this case was fixed by consent of the parties at the sitting of the Court in Dublin.	
85 0 25	43 15 0	43 10 0			
8 1 20	6 0 0	13 8 10	6 3 5	do.	
16 0 20	15 10 0	10 13 7	10 0 0		
17 3 20	10 15 0	10 0 0	7 4 0		
67 1 26	23 5 0	84 0 0	17 0 0		
14 1 20	5 0 0	5 0 0	4 10 0		
19 0 0	6 13 0	8 0 0	5 0 0		
11 1 20	6 15 0	6 0 0	4 10 0		
25 1 0	8 15 0	9 11 4	7 0 6		
25 2 30	8 15 0	5 13 3	3 5 0		
31 1 0	35 10 0	30 0 0	25 0 0		
15 0 0	6 5 0	8 0 0	4 0 0		
13 2 20	4 0 0	5 0 0	4 7 5		
81 0 17	38 15 0	47 3 5	37 10 6	By consent.	
580 0 31	278 15 0	256 1 4	209 1 5		

PROVINCE OF

COUNTY OF

Names of Assistant Commissioners by whom Cases were decided.	No.	Name of Tenant.	Name of Landlord.	Townland.
Head Commission.	172	William Watchorn, ...	Sir Thomas P. Butler, Bart.,	Aughnarta, ...
	173	Joseph Smith, ...	do.	Lumsy, ...
	174	Timothy Foulon, ...	Anne Garrett, ...	Ballintrain, ...
	175	Robert Little, ...	Right Hon. Henry Bruen, ...	Ballyloo, ...
	176	William Semple, ...	do.	Kilree, ...
	177	Catherine Murphy, ...	do.	Ballymurphy, ...
	178	Do., ...	do.	do. ...
Assistant Commissioners— R. Reeves, Q.C. (Legal). S. Mowbray. F. V. Jeffers.	179	Thomas Agar, ...	Sir Thomas Butler, Bart., ...	Coolnakisha, ...
	180	Thomas Lyons, ...	do.	Ballintemple, ...
	181	Thomas Agar, ...	do.	Coolnakisha, ...
	182	Thomas Lyons, ...	do.	Ballintemple, ...
	183	Alexander McDonald, ...	do.	Coolnakisha, ...
	184	John Tharp, ...	do.	Lumsy, ...
	185	Mrs. Maria Mahon, ...	do.	Rathvinden, ...
	186	Jane Cundell, Rep. of Thomas Cundell.	do.	Aughnarta, ...
	187	Joseph Daly, Rep. of H. Daly.	do.	do. ...
	188	Lawrence Neill, ...	Right Hon. Henry Bruen,	Coolasnaghta,
	189	Ellen Byrne, ...	Cecilia W. Harvey, ...	Ballinakillen, ...
	190	Michael Byrne, ...	do.	do. ...
	191	Robert Hagarty, senior,	Sarah A. Ryan, ...	Barrahill, ...
	192	Michael Brien, ...	Sir Clement Wolseley, Bt., ...	Williamstown,
	193	Mary Brady, ...	John M. Fitzmaurice, Trustee of J. Wingfield Stratford's Estate.	Mangan, ...
	194	James Earl, ...	Rev. Samuel Quinton and ors.,	Baugh, ...
	195	Alice Hendy, ...	do.	do. ...
	196	Laurence Kelly, ...	Sir Clement Wolseley, Bt., ...	Williamstown,
	197	Charles Byrne, ...	do.	do. ...

LEINSTER.

CARLOW.

Extent of Holdings.			Poor Law Valuation.			Present Rent.			Judicial Rent.			
A.	R.	P.	£	s.	d.	£	s.	d.	£	s.	d.	
87	1	0	25	15	0	30	0	0	25	0	0	The ren… renew… adjoin…
80	0	0	34	5	0	57	6	2	32	0	0	
61	3	33	55	5	0	47	0	0	47	0	0	
134	0	30	204	10	0	372	12	10	284	18	10	
60	1	30	37	5	0	48	13	4	31	0	0	
14	3	38	13	5	0	23	15	6	18	0	0	
5	3	31	7	0	0	5	10	0	4	0	0	
110	0	26	unascertained.			78	15	0	60	0	0	By cons…
17	0	0	do.			15	5	0	13	0	0	do.
36	0	27	do.			23	19	1	18	0	0	do.
79	1	18	do.			61	7	3	60	0	0	do.
50	0	13	17	0	0	28	3	0	20	0	0	do.
90	2	6	48	10	0	55	0	0	50	0	0	do.
17	3	20	18	15	0	25	0	0	10	0	0	do.
84	2	26	16	0	0	22	0	6	18	0	0	do.
34	0	0	6	10	0	13	0	0	4	15	0	do.
61	1	5	29	10	0	65	0	0	35	0	0	do.
18	0	20	18	10	0	13	8	10	11	0	0	do.
89	0	10	49	10	0	80	5	0	40	0	0	do.
21	1	11	10	18	0	31	0	0	15	0	0	
17	3	10	4	15	0	10	18	0	8	15	0	
70	0	0	28	0	0	31	14	2	24	0	0	
20	1	15	19	15	0	25	3	7	20	0	0	
60	1	5	unascertained.			82	17	6	65	0	0	
75	0	6	31	0	0	20	8	5	16	0	0	
25	0	31	31	0	0	42	19	8	25	0	0	

COUNTY OF

Names of Assistant Commissioners by whom Cases were decided.	No.	Name of Tenant.	Name of Landlord.	Townland.
Assistant Commissioners—				
R. R. Reeves, Q.C. (Legal). T. A. Dillon. T. Davenport.	198	John Murphy and anor.,	John Corcoran, ...	K[illegible], ...
	199	Michael Nowlan, ...	P. J. Newton, ...	[illegible], ...
	200	David Nolan, ...	do.	do. ...
	201	Mary Jane Horrick, ...	Earl of Courtown, ...	[illegible], ...
R. Reeves, Q.C. (Legal). M. P. Lynch. A. [illegible]	202	Michael Baggot, ...	Rev. A. W. [illegible], ...	[illegible], ...
				Total, ...

COUNTY OF

Head Commission.	139	Michael Jordan, ...	Sir William McMahon, Bart.,	Oldtown, ...
	140	Do., ...	do.	do. ...
	141	Mrs. Elizabeth Magrath,	Countess of Kingston, ...	[illegible], ...
				Total, ...

COUNTY OF

Head Commission.	184	Christopher Miley, ...	Sarah A. Walsh, ...	[illegible], ...
	185	William Murphy, ...	J. P. Murphy, ...	[illegible], ...
				Total, ...

COUNTY OF

CARLOW—continued.

Extent of Holding. Statute.			Poor Law Valuation.			Former Rent.		
a.	r.	p.	£	s.	d.	£	s.	d.
77	1	23	unascertained.			19	1	9
78	0	10	7	13	0	15	15	6
[illegible]	0	11	7	10	0	18	0	10
39	1	6	17	0	0	19	16	6
42	1	17	10	15	0	15	0	0
1,311	1	[illegible]	[illegible]	10	0	1,[illegible]	6	0

DUBLIN.

51	0	[illegible]	71	5	0	124	0	0
8	0	16	10	10	0	80	0	0
184	2	15	176	15	0	220	7	6
243	3	[illegible]	[illegible]	10	0	424	8	6

KILDARE.

COUNTY OF

Names of Assistant Commissioners by whom Cases were decided.	No.	Name of Tenant.	Name of Landlord.	Townland.
Assistant Commissioners—				
R. Reeves, Q.C. (Legal). J. J. Gwynn. H. G. Nash.	96	Anastatia Cleary, Admix. of William Cleary, and Guardian of Thomas Cleary, a minor.	Major Edward Gilbertson, ...	Tinnahilly, ...
	97	Pierce Maloney, ...	Davenport Smith and another,	Garranslarragh, ...
	98	Anthony E. Graves, ...	Hon. Julia Bell, ...	Annefield, ...
	99	Edward Campion, ...	Robert Tyndall, ...	Inchacorse, ...
	100	Paul Murphy, junior, ...	Augustus Hartford, ...	Smithstown, ...
	101	Martin Moroney, ...	Sir James H. Ramsay, Bart., and another, Trustees of F. M. Harold and another.	Clara, Upper, ...
	102	John Dowling, ...	Captain A. E. St. George, ...	Cappanagh and another.
	103	Patrick Dowling, ...	do.	Kevarava, ...
	104	John Dowling, ...	do.	Kilrush, ...
	105	Margaret Campion, ...	do.	Tubrid, Upper, ...
	106	James Shortal, ...	do.	do. ...
	107	William Maher, ...	J. W. Tunkin, ...	Shellumsrath, ...
	108	Mrs. Susan Colclough, ...	Captain St. George, ...	Clomanto, ...
	109	Samuel Miller, ...	Michael Des Kenting, ...	Darby's Hill, ...
	110	William Dowling, ...	do.	Darbystown, ...
	111	Patrick Dunne, ...	do.	Darby's Hill, ...
	112	James Carroll, ...	do.	Kilderlough, ...
	113	John Bowden, ...	do.	do. ...
	114	Richard Purcell, ...	do.	do. ...
	115	Margaret Phelan, Rep. of James Phelan,	do.	Upr. Kilderlough,
	116	Michael Butler, ...	do.	Kilderlough, ...
	117	William Leahy and anor.,	do.	Craiguenakeerna & another.
	118	John Bowe, ...	do.	do. ...
	119	John Phelan and others, Reps. of James Phelan.	do.	Kilderlough, ...
	120	Martin Joyce, tenant in possession under judgment mortgage of Patrick Leahy.	do.	Craiguekeatown,
	121	Bridget Kennedy, Rep. of William Kennedy.	Mrs. Dorothea Butler, ...	Bawnmore, ...
	122	Margaret Murphy, Rep. of John Murphy.	Major John Otway Wemyss,	Longwell, ...
R. Reeves, Q.C. (Legal). T. A. Dillon. T. Davidson.	123	Edmund Rochford, ...	George Hely, ...	Garryghmore, Upper and Lower.
				Total, ...

TABLE OF JUDICIAL RENTS.

KILKENNY—*continued*.

Extent of Holding. Statute.	Poor Law Valuation.	Former Rent.	Judicial Rent.	Observations.
A. R. P.	£ s. d.	£ s. d.	£ s. d.	£ s. d.
11 0 13	11 5 0	13 0 0	10 0 0	
64 3 35	31 0 0	43 7 1	30 0 0	
73 3 23	117 10 0	150 0 0	105 0 0	
116 0 21	93 10 0	105 10 0	71 0 0	Rent changed in 1877 from . . . 66 12 0
66 3 0	33 15 0	43 10 0	30 0 0	
103 1 10	114 0 0	130 10 0	110 0 0	
100 0 3	61 5 0	63 0 0	57 10 0	
4 1 30	6 0 0	7 10 0	5 5 0	
74 1 10	45 10 0	54 15 0	40 0 0	
35 0 0	23 0 0	31 4 10	22 10 0	
120 1 22	45 10 0	60 15 0	43 0 0	
15 3 6	14 15 0	19 0 0	12 10 0	
116 0 13	80 0 0	105 0 0	77 0 0	
4 1 34	6 0 0	6 11 0	4 10 0	
46 1 0	33 5 0	37 0 0	33 0 0	
2 1 20	1 15 0	3 0 0	1 0 0	
150 0 7	43 0 0	60 0 0	28 10 0	
6 0 3	3 0 0	3 15 0	3 5 6	
1 1 11	1 15 0	3 5 0	1 0 0	
16 0 17	9 10 0	11 0 0	6 10 0	
7 0 21	1 16 0	2 0 0	1 5 0	
110 0 3	64 15 0	73 0 0	63 0 0	
36 0 4	16 0 0	23 15 0	13 0 0	
170 3 0	115 10 0	167 3 9	150 0 0	
49 1 34	30 0 0	40 15 1	36 0 0	
53 3 6	27 5 0	34 0 0	22 0 0	
86 3 7	71 0 0	41 0 0	46 0 0	
67 0 5	40 0 0	53 5 0	45 0 0	By consent.

COUNTY OF

Names of Assistant Commissioners by whom Cases were decided.	No.	Name of Tenant.	Name of Landlord.	Townland.
Assistant Commissioners—				
R. R. Kane (Legal). T. Baldwin? W. S. Hutt?	85	Palmer Neeley?,	William Reed?,	Clarin?,
	86	Michael Mullin,	Robert Barlow?,	Rathurney?,
	87	James Ross,	Mrs. Emily Fox and others, Trustees of Richard Fox, decd.	Newport?,
	88	Robert McCormack,	Mrs. Jane Guy,	Kilcurry,
	89	Maria Mulvihill, Ad. Admix. of Peter Mulvihill	Kate J. Hanley?, a minor, by Mrs. Ellen Mulvihill and another, her Guardians.	Ardoghill,
	90	Thomas Reilly,	Rev. Francis Dopping,	Kilcon?,
	91	David Harris,	A. E. Edgeworth,	Drumderrig,
	92	James Martin,	Earl of Granard,	Bryanstown?,
	93	Denis Rivers,	Mrs. Jane Guy,	Kilcurry,
				Total,

COUNTY OF

Head Commission.	80	James Ferguson & another,	Alexander M. Bruce?,	Castletownmoyley?,

COUNTY OF

Head Commission.	160	Michael Rogers,	William E. Cairnes,	Moneymore? and another.
	161	Patrick P. Murray,	do.	do.
	162	James Meade,	James W. Murland?,	Hopkinstown,
	163	Margaret Rourke?,	Luke A. I. Norman,	Rathbeallan?,
	164	Michael Rochford?,	Alderman A. W. Harris,	Newtownmoyaghy?,
	165	Cornelius Lynch,	Anne Mansfield? and another,	Bobbs?, Great,
	166	Nicholas Walsh,	Robert G. Dunville,	Waterside?, Great,
	167	William Crosby,	Constance Beaufort?, Widow of late Francis T. Beaufort,	Balrathboyne Glebe,
	168	Thomas Fitzharris,	John T. Madden,	Kennastown?,
	169	Matthew Hopkins,	P. S. Ireland?,	Kilcarnbane?,
	170	John Clarke,	George P. Lynch,	Tullaghanoge?,

6 10

14 8

[illegible] 12

COUNTY OF

Names of Assistant Commissioners by whom Cases were decided.	No.	Name of Tenant.	Name of Landlord.	Townland.
Assistant Commissioners—				
R. R. Kane (Legal). T. Purvis. J. Dove.	171	William McKeown, ...	William M. Longfield, ...	Knock, ...
	172	Henry Shekleton, ...	Mrs. Emily M. Paton, ...	Ballyban, ...
	173	Owen McGahan, ...	do.	do. ...
	174	George Miles, ...	Lord [illegible] and Farrard,	Ballyhaggan, ...
	175	Thomas Hickey, ...	Richard J. Smith, ...	Summerhill, Up.,
	176	Robert Ellery, ...	do.	Summerhill, Lr.,
	177	James McDonnell, ...	do.	do. ...
	178	Ellen Farrell, ...	do.	Summerhill, Up.,
	179	Thomas Smith and anor.,	Arthur Forbes, ...	Ballymacnaigan & another.
	180	Thomas Smith and anor., Admors. of Wm. Smith.	do.	Ballyfarnah, ...
	181	Catherine Cassidy, ...	John A. McCausland and others, Assignees of W. T. Murray.	Ballyban, ...
				Total, ...

COUNTY OF

Head Commission.	46	[illegible] J. F. Magill, ...	Charlotte Fetherstonhaugh and others.	Ordinstown, ...
	47	James O'Neill, ...	Walter J. Nugent, ...	Clonagunagh, ...
Assistant Commissioners—	48	Andrew Moore, ...	Hon. Arthur E. Harris and [illegible].	Farranagarvant & another.
R. R. Kane (Legal). J. F. Redford. J. Gallagher.	49	John Smyth, ...	George W. Marsh, ...	Craeve, ...
	50	Andrew Keegan, ...	do.	do. ...
	51	James Conlon, ...	do.	do. ...
R. R. Kane (Legal). J. F. Redford.	52	William Kelson, ...	Thomas A. Cusack, ...	Knaper, ...
	53	Michael Dunne, senior,	Hon. Thomas A. [illegible] and others, Trustees of Lord Longford.	Killynure, ...
	54	Garrett Harkin, ...	James Gaynor, ...	Clonsheardin, ...
	55	Thomas Cormack, ...	Major-General W. D. Moore,	Kilgrovey, ...
	56	John Prendergast, ...	do.	Balrath, ...
	57	George Moorman and anor.,	James Lane, ...	Tubbercurraich &

MEATH—*continued.*

Extent of Holding. Statute.			Poor Law Valuation.			Present Rent.			Judicial Rent.			Observations.	Value of Tenancy.
A.	R.	P.	£	s.	d.	£	s.	d.	£	s.	d.	£ s. d.	£ s. d.
17	1	[illegible]	17	5	0	[illegible]	5	0	47	10	0		
67	2	9	31	5	0	[illegible]	0	0	37	10	0		
[illegible]	0	19	72	5	0	30	0	0	23	10	0		
213	1	36	110	10	0	170	0	0	140	0	0	Rent changed in 18[illegible] from 220 0 0	
61	1	9	35	0	0	48	17	9	34	0	0		
[illegible]	0	0	46	10	0	67	10	0	60	0	0		
23	3	16	19	10	0	23	10	0	17	0	0		
65	1	30	73	0	0	93	0	0	70	0	0		
184	3	36	152	10	0	250	0	0	170	0	0		
138	0	12	123	0	0	140	0	0	120	0	0		
75	2	3	32	5	0	34	0	0	28	0	0		
1,013	1	8	1,846	10	0	3,028	12	3	1,640	0	3		

WESTMEATH.

620	3	0	492	0	0	497	19	11	375	14	11	The rents in this case were fixed by consent of the parties at the sitting of the Court in Dublin.	
214	0	29	143	10	0	120	0	0	110	0	0	do.	
184	0	18	65	0	0	182	10	0	100	0	0	By consent.	
31	2	37	30	5	0	25	15	0	18	10	0	do.	
16	0	17	16	0	0	12	0	0	9	10	0	do.	
31	3	31	21	15	0	26	0	0	15	0	0	do.	
61	0	15	35	7	0	40	14	9	25	0	0		
40	0	6	25	0	0	32	7	10	16	0	0		
72	1	36	26	0	0	31	0	0	23	15	0	£ s. d. Rent changed in 1879 from . . . 30 0 0	
20	3	10	15	0	0	19	10	0	14	10	0	do. 15 0 0	
37	3	23	21	5	0	24	15	5	20	5	0		
116	1	13	56	5	0	60	0	0	70	0	0		
396	0	5	377	10	0	457	15	0	275	0	0		

COUNTY OF

Names of Assistant Commissioners by whom Cases were decided.	No.	Name of Tenant.	Name of Landlord.	Townland.
Assistant Commissioners— R. R. Kane (Legal). J. F. [illegible].	59	Mary Elvers,	Alfred W. Harris and anor.,	[illegible]
	60	Patrick L'Estrange,	Mrs. Mary Hope,	[illegible]
	61	Thomas Moorhead,	William D. Digby,	[illegible]
	62	Catherine Kelly,	Allan Montgomery,	[illegible]
	63	Mathew Ledwith,	Alfred W. Harris and anor.,	[illegible]
	64	Michael Martin,	do.	[illegible]
	65	Edward Nally,	do.	do.
	66	Bernard Mullady,	do.	[illegible]
	67	Bryan Nally,	do.	do.
	68	Hugh O'Neill,	John D. F. Grace,	[illegible]
	69	James Savage,	do.	[illegible]
	70	Lawrence Digman,	Colonel Judge H. Cooper,	[illegible]
	71	Mrs. Anne Downes,	do.	[illegible]
	72	Peter McKeogh,	Mrs. Marcella L'Estrange,	[illegible]
	73	Edward Cahill,	do.	[illegible]
	74	John Murray,	do.	[illegible] and another.
	75	Patrick Garty,	W. E. Lefroy and another,	[illegible]
	76	William Halligan,	Alfred W. Harris and anor.,	[illegible]
	77	John Newburn,	Thomas J. Walsh,	[illegible]
	78	Mary Elvers,	John S. Dyas, a minor, by Marcella E. Barrett and another, his Guardians.	[illegible]
	79	George Little,	Francis E. Fetherstonhaugh, a minor, by E. Fetherstonhaugh & ors., his Guardians.	[illegible]
	80	Do.	do.	do.
	81	Do.	do.	do.
	82	Do.	do.	do.
	83	Thomas Walker,	Dame [illegible],	[illegible]
	84	Stephen Hanvey,	George Marsh,	[illegible]
				Total,

COUNTY OF

WESTMEATH—*continued.*

Quantity of Holding. Statute.	Poor Law Valuation.	Former Rent.	Judicial Rent.	Observations.	Value of Tenancy.
A. R. P.	£ s. d.	£ s. d.	£ s. d.	£ s. d.	£ s. d.
187 3 29	191 0 0	273 3 3	187 0 0	Rent changed in 1869 from . . . 221 0 0	
112 0 26	66 15 0	111 8 0	70 0 0		
84 1 5	68 15 0	80 13 0	46 0 0	1874 61 16 0	
30 1 27	14 10 0	20 0 0	15 10 0		
41 0 25	49 14 0	64 16 0	44 0 0		
83 3 5	91 0 0	103 0 0	76 0 0	1867 116 0 0	
79 0 23	20 0 0	23 4 0	20 0 0		
20 1 16	18 10 0	20 0 0	18 0 0		
49 2 10	35 14 0	50 3 0	34 0 0		
30 3 29	23 16 0	37 0 6	26 0 0		
84 1 31	45 18 0	67 17 6	54 18 0	1879 68 0 0	
179 3 30	160 0 0	254 18 0	181 0 0	1873 219 6 0	
61 1 20	48 10 0	86 0 0	77 0 0		
19 0 31	16 10 0	26 18 3	16 0 0		
8 1 11	6 16 0	13 3 0	7 0 0		
15 3 36	10 10 0	16 3 0	9 5 0		
83 2 28	56 10 0	97 17 0	60 0 0	1872 76 19 5	
26 2 06	17 0 0	16 17 0	16 10 0		
344 3 5	246 10 0	430 0 0	320 0 0		
104 3 36	103 10 0	136 10 0	120 0 0		
133 0 27	94 10 0	133 16 0	100 0 0		
65 3 11	44 10 0	45 3 0	43 10 0		
74 3 24	58 13 0	77 0 0	41 0 0		
183 3 3	106 0 0	160 14 0	123 0 0		
220 0 0	205 0 0	230 15 4	167 0 0		
10 3 30	12 16 0	13 16 0	9 10 0	By consent.	
2,777 0 30	2,816 7 0	4,348 11 8	2,874 4 11		

WEXFORD.

61 0 16	66 5 0	73 11 4	66 0 0	The rent in this case was fixed by consent of the parties at the sitting of the Court in Dublin.	
21 0 20	9 2 0	14 0 0	8 5 0	do.	
71 1 3	41 5 0	40 10 0	35 5 0	do.	

COUNTY OF

Names of Assistant Commissioners by whom Cases were decided.	No.	Name of Tenant.	Name of Landlord.	Townland.
Assistant Commissioners—				
R. Reeves, Q.C. (Legal). T. A. Dillon. T. Davidson.	152	Benjamin Goldsbury, ...	John R. Berwick and another,	Ballyrone, ...
	153	Mary Harper, Devisee of Nicholas Harper.	Rodolphus W. Ryan, ...	Charlestown, Nth.,
	154	Patrick Hearn, ...	Lord Carew, ...	Mount Pill, ...
	155	William Moran, ...	Miss Julia Carey, ...	Grange, ...
	156	Patrick Maddock, continued in name of Maria Maddock.	William Markham, ...	Lorstown, ...
	157	James Kavanagh, ...	Mrs. Ellen M. Barrington, ...	Ballybeggan, ...
	158	Anastasia McDonald, ...	Earl of Donoughmore, ...	Terrywarrick, ...
	159	Patrick Gold, ...	do.	Newtown, ...
	160	Thomas Walsh, ...	Henry J. Cooper, ...	Coolnall Big, ...
	161	Do., ...	do.	do. ...
	162	John Berry, ...	Pierce B. Stafford, ...	Ballymore, ...
	163	Do., ...	do.	do. ...
	164	Laurence Devereux, ...	Harvey Boxwell, ...	Ballymurry, ...
	165	Patrick Clinch, ...	do.	Lingstown, Lower,
				Total, ...

COUNTY OF

Head Commissioners.	117	Daniel Sweeney, ...	Earl of Carysfort, ...	Drummin[illegible], ...
	118	Catherine Byrne, ...	do.	[illegible], ...
	119	Daniel Sweeney, ...	do.	Rossmaleigh, East,
Assistant Commissioners—	120	John Valentine, ...	Sir Edward J. Hutchinson, Bart.	Davidstown, ...
R. Reeves, Q.C. (Legal). S. Murray. F. F. Jervis.	121	James Valentine, ...	do.	Castlemacleigh, ...
	122	Robert Wilson, ...	do.	Ballintruer More,
	123	Margaret Lennon, ...	do.	Dallytonle, ...
	124	Annie Heighington, ...	do.	Ballinrahills, Up.
	125	Christopher Hawkins, ...	do.	Castlemacleigh, ...
				Total, ...

WEXFORD—*continued.*

Extent of Holding. Statute.			Poor Law Valuation.			Former Rent.			Judicial Rent.		
a.	r.	p.	£	s.	d.	£	s.	d.	£	s.	d.
67	1	5	35	5	0	50	0	0	35	15	0
7	2	36	6	5	0	7	0	0	6	10	0
45	3	37	47	10	0	67	2	7	41	0	0
7	3	9	7	0	0	14	3	0	9	0	0
7	1	10	7	13	0	8	8	5	8	8	5
16	0	31	22	0	0	40	0	0	27	10	0
45	0	6	31	5	0	46	10	0	30	0	0
90	0	39	60	0	0	73	17	5	52	10	0
105	3	38	35	0	0	74	0	0	60	0	0
56	3	30	27	0	0	45	14	0	33	0	0
35	0	1	unascertained,			31	10	0	17	10	0
183	2	11	do.			228	10	0	146	0	0
27	2	39	30	10	0	36	10	0	19	0	0
17	0	17	16	10	0	51	5	2	10	0	0
[illegible]	0	23	457	15	0	[illegible]	10	9	586	11	5

WICKLOW.

6	2	8	6	10	0	6	0	0	5	0	0
178	3	18	119	0	0	160	0	0	130	0	0
54	3	0	30	0	0	30	0	0	28	0	0
206	0	17	104	0	0	200	0	0	170	0	0
147	0	16	80	0	0	110	0	0	90	0	0
67	2	18	45	10	0	57	17	0	44	0	0
73	0	6	17	0	0	30	0	0	35	0	0
91	1	26	23	0	0	26	0	0	30	0	0
116	3	30	44	15	0	46	0	0	40	0	0
907	1	15	531	15	0	663	17	0	515	0	0

PROV

Names of Assistant Commissioners by whom Cases were decided.	No.	Name of Tenant.	Name of Landlord.
Assistant Commissioners—			
M. T. Cahan (Legal). R. McClean. W. Williams.	176	Thomas Devine, ...	Colonel M. F. Blake,
	177	Anthony Devine, ...	do. ...

CONNAUGHT.

GALWAY.

Extent of Holding Statute.			Poor Law Valuation.			Former Rent.			Judicial Rent.			Observations.	Value of Tenancy.
a.	r.	p.	£	s.	d.	£	s.	d.	£	s.	d.		£ s. d.
68	1	10	[illegible]	10	0	57	2	4	40	0	0		
65	1	23	57	5	0	43	15	8	35	0	0		
106	1	0	70	10	0	137	5	6	64	0	0		
130	3	17	79	10	0	179	0	0	85	0	0		
[illegible]	6	14	100	0	0	100	0	0	70	0	0		
[illegible]	3	24	[illegible]	15	0	511	1	6	[illegible]	0	0		

MAYO.

COUNTY OF

Names of Assistant Commissioners by whom Cases were decided.	No.	Name of Tenant.	Name of Landlord.	Townland.	
Assistant Commissioners—					
M. T. Cogan (Legal). H. G. [illegible]. W. H. [illegible].	16	John Barry,	Patrick Martin,	Woodfield,	
	17	Mary McKeon,	Colonel E. R. King-Harman, as assignee in name of Frances A. King-Harman.	Smutternagh,	
	18	Mary Cryan,	do.	do.	
	19	John Higgins,	do.	Tarmon,	
	20	James McLoughlin,	do.	Smutternagh,	
	21	Henry Kelly,	do.	Derrymaquirk,	
	22	Patrick Sherman,	do.	do.	
	23	Michael Bruen,	do.	Smutternagh,	
	24	Thomas Sherman,	do.	Derrymaquirk,	
	25	Anne Corcoran and another,	do.	do.	
	26	Laurence McCrann,	do.	Orangeboy,	
	27	Ellen McLoughlin,	do.	Smutternagh,	
	28	James Travers,	do.	do.	
	29	Eliza Walsh,	John G. Young,	[illegible],	
	30	Do.,	do.	Mullaghelmaly,	
	31	James Murray,	Christopher R. [illegible],	[illegible],	
				Total,	

COUNTY OF

ROSCOMMON—*continued.*

Extent of Holdings. Statute.	Poor Law Valuation.	Former Rent.	Judicial Rent.	Observations.	Value of Tenancy.
A. R. P.	£ s. d.	£ s. d.	£ s. d.	£ s. d.	£ s. d.
10 3 0	6 5 0	13 18 6	8 0 0		
10 1 23	4 15 0	6 10 0	5 0 0		
16 1 18	5 10 0	8 9 0	4 7 8		
10 0 38	7 16 0	11 3 6	9 0 0	Rent changed in 1863 from . . . 14 8 8	
10 1 23	5 8 0	0 9 0	6 13 0		
30 3 36	15 5 0	24 11 11	17 16 0		
23 0 16	18 5 0	14 10 6	16 10 0		
10 3 35	0 7 0	6 5 0	4 10 0		
18 0 17	11 0 0	11 7 0	11 10 0		
18 0 10	8 5 0	11 11 10	8 10 0		
30 3 31	17 0 0	19 13 6	18 0 0		
10 5 21	8 5 0	8 5 0	6 10 0		
10 1 28	5 5 0	0 8 0	6 10 0		
13 7 34	6 0 0	8 0 0	6 0 0		
7 1 0	3 0 0	3 15 0	3 0 0		
113 1 4	86 0 0	98 11 0	63 10 0		
408 1 8	315 7 0	349 16 $6\frac{1}{2}$	239 16 0		

PROVINCE OF

COUNTY OF

Names of Assistant Commissioners by whom Cases were decided.	No.	Name of Tenant.	Name of Landlord.	Townland.
Head Commission.	224	Patrick Vaughan, ...	Rev. Henry Bayly, ...	Kilmore, ...
	225	Patrick Hanrahan, junr.,	John O. Brady, ...	Barna, ...
	226	John Longhnane, ...	do.	do. ...
	227	Patrick Hanrahan, ...	do.	do. ...
	228	John Longhnane, ...	do.	do. ...
	229	Patrick Byrne, ...	Rev. C. O'D. Bayley, ...	Keagh, ...
Assistant Commissioners— J. E. Greer (Legal). R. B. Harrison. J. Rice.	230	Patrick Carmody, ...	Susanna Bayley, continued in name of Rev. C. O'D. Bayley	Keagh, East, ...
	231	James Liddy, ...	do.	do. ...
	232	Michael Frost, ...	do.	Emock O'Flynn,
	233	Rody McNamara, ...	do.	Keagh, ...
	234	John Gleeson, ...	do.	Newpark,
	235	Timothy McNamara, ...	do.	Killamona, ...
	236	William Moloney, ...	Thomas R. Browne, ...	Morehill, ...
	237	Do., ...	do.	Tulla, ...
	238	John Considine, ...	do.	Ballyvalentry, ...
	239	John O'Dea, ...	Michael Culligan, ...	Drumbarley, ...
	240	Michael King, Rep. of James King,	Right Hon. Lord Fitzgerald,	Ranaugh, ...
	241	Patrick McInerney, ...	do.	Coolshimane, ...
	242	Thomas O'Brien, ...	do.	do.
	243	John Begley, ...	do.	Cappalaheen, ...
	244	Thomas Fitzgerald, ...	do.	do. ...
	245	Patrick Frawley, ...	do.	do ...
	246	Do., ...	do.	Lakyle, ...
	247	James Culligan, ...	do.	Cappalaheen, ...
	248	John Carroll, ...	do.	Lakyle, ...
	249	Michael Lenihan (James),	do.	Gortnakilla, ...

MUNSTER.

CLARE.

Extent of Holding [illegible]	Poor Law Valuation.	Former Rent.	Judicial Rent.	Observations.	Value of Tenancy
A. R. P.	£ s. d.	£ s. d.	£ s. d.		£ s. d.
[illegible] 0 0	[illegible] 0 0	50 0 0	33 0 0	The rent in this case was fixed by consent of the parties at the sitting of the Court in Dublin.	
64 [illegible] [illegible]	[illegible] 5 0	40 0 0	36 0 0	do.	
16 3 10	4 10 0	18 0 0	3 12 0	do.	
61 [illegible] [illegible]	[illegible] 0 0	58 0 0	30 0 0	do.	
84 0 33	11 10 0	[illegible] 0 0	9 4 0	do.	
7 1 6	5 0 0	6 12 [illegible]	5 0 0	do.	
16 3 16	15 10 0	16 10 [illegible]	11 10 0		
[illegible] 2 30	33 0 0	27 15 0	19 0 0		
41 0 [illegible]	14 5 0	27 5 0	15 0 0		
63 1 7	40 0 0	64 0 0	45 10 0		
9 2 20	4 10 0	10 9 5	7 0 0		
11 1 [illegible]	9 9 0	11 11 10	8 0 0		
67 0 [illegible]	35 0 0	48 10 9	33 0 0		
1 3 24	3 6 0	4 0 0	3 10 0		
[illegible] 0 19	43 10 0	[illegible] 14 5	42 0 0		
49 3 17	19 10 0	[illegible] 9 0	[illegible] 0 0		
19 0 0	6 10 0	9 7 0	5 10 0		
50 0 34	23 10 0	[illegible] 17 0	[illegible] 0 0		
[illegible] 0 0	12 16 0	14 0 [illegible]	10 0 0	And £3 drainage charge.	
45 3 [illegible]	17 5 0	21 [illegible] [illegible]	16 5 0		

COUNTY OF

Names of Assistant Commissioners by whom Cases were decided.	No.	Name of Tenant.	Name of Landlord.	Townland.
Assistant Commissioners—				
J. G. Gibson (Legal). B. B. Hewson. J. Rice.	250	James Callaghan, ...	Lord Fitzgerald, ...	Cappalahane, ...
	251	John Carroll, ...	do.	do. ...
	252	Hannah Tobin, ...	Sir Augustine Fitzgerald, Bart.,	Silvergrove, ...
	253	Bridget Molamney, ...	do.	Tiervarranne, ...
	254	Martin Kelly, ...	do.	do. ...
	255	Patrick Sheehan, ...	John Hogan and another, ...	Knockalla, ...
	256	Rev. Daniel Corbett, ...	Thomas G. S. Mahon, ...	Ballyfinny, ...
	257	Daniel Sullivan, Rep. of Michael Sullivan.	do.	Shraheen & anr.,
	258	Bridget Connellan, ...	do.	Gortnamanagh & another.
	259	Patrick Cunnahan, ...	do.	do. ...
	260	Patrick J. O'Halloran,	Major William M. Molony,	Knockdrumaleague and another.
	261	Bridget McGrath, ...	do.	Clonmoylevery and another.
	262	Thomas Duffy, ...	Edmund J. B. MacMahon, ...	Ballyvraheen Oughter.
	263	Thady Connell and anor.,	Pierce O'Brien, ...	Bryanmore[illegible], ...
	264	Patrick Flynn, ...	Colonel John O'Callaghan, ...	Milltown, ...
	265	Johanna Molony, ...	Edward P. Westby, ...	Sunnyshill, ...
J. S. Gibson (Legal). J. Armstrong. J. Carr.	266	Joseph Curry, ...	Hector S. Vandeleur, ...	Ballymacurtane,
	267	Michael S. Brown, ...	do.	Ballyvarra, ...
	268	Daniel Gregan, ...	James Shannon, ...	Kilcarran, ...
	269	John Griffin, ...	Hodges E. Chesterton, ...	Shandrum, ...
	270	Patrick Donnellan, ...	Richard Griffith, ...	Dunogan, ...
	271	John Hehir, ...	Sir Augustine Fitzgerald, Bart.,	Quilty, East, ...
	272	John Casey, ...	Richard M. Studdert, ...	Mountrivers, ...
	273	James Ryan, ...	William C. V. Burton, ...	Gower, ...
	274	John Halloran, ...	do.	Cross, ...
	275	John Kelly, ...	Thomas Mahon, ...	Craganagh, West.
	276	Michael O'Gorman, ...	do.	Craggaunt, ...
	277	Garrett Doherty, ...	Randal Burrough, ...	Querrin and anr.,
	278	John McMahon, ...	do.	do. ...
	279	Patrick Enright & anor.,	Charles P. Bolton, ...	Carrowlagan, ...
	280	Patrick Ahern, ...	do.	do. ...
	281	Margt. Donnellan & anor.,	do.	do. ...

CLARE—*continued.*

Extent of Holding (statute).	Poor Law Valuation.	Former Rent.	Judicial Rent.	Observations.	Value of Tenancy.
a. r. p.	£ s. d.	£ s. d.	£ s. d.		£ s. d.
37 0 0	8 4 0	8 15 6	7 10 0	And £1 15s. 9d. drainage charge.	
6 3 19	1 15 0	4 7 6	3 7 8		
23 3 7	19 0 0	16 16 6	12 0 0		
85 0 0	32 10 0	45 0 0	33 10 0		
31 0 0	5 16 0	11 0 0	6 0 0		
73 2 14	30 0 0	29 0 0	28 0 0		
79 0 0	46 10 0	80 0 0	60 0 0		
28 1 5	24 0 0	34 0 0	24 0 0		
61 2 0	43 15 0	61 5 0	38 0 0	And right of grazing over ⅓ of 71a. 0r. 12p.	
75 2 31	36 15 0	49 15 0	34 0 0	do.	
80 3 0	71 15 0	86 0 0	60 0 0		
105 1 30	67 5 0	78 10 0	60 0 0		
88 0 34	83 5 0	83 17 6	66 0 0		
61 0 30	43 0 0	63 7 0	44 10 0		
84 3 17	41 10 0	73 2 0	57 0 0		
38 1 10	23 0 0	33 0 0	18 10 0		
23 1 11	16 0 0	23 0 0	22 0 0		
84 3 0	40 15 0	93 0 0	64 0 0		
75 0 15	82 10 0	83 10 6	30 0 0		
23 1 20	10 15 0	14 11 8	10 0 0		
29 3 11	11 5 0	18 0 0	12 0 0		
34 0 8	14 15 0	21 10 0	19 0 0		
68 1 30	45 10 0	80 0 0	65 0 0		
43 3 30	20 17 0	27 6 0	22 0 0		
46 1 30	16 10 0	20 0 0	14 5 0		
157 3 10	63 0 0	77 0 0	50 0 0		
88 2 34	47 10 0	70 0 0	64 10 0		
64 0 30	48 15 0	68 7 10	48 0 0		
28 1 17	6 10 0	15 3 6	11 0 0		
63 3 37	20 0 0	28 0 0	19 18 0		
18 3 8	7 10 0	14 0 0	9 0 0		
14 3 13	5 10 0	9 0 0	8 5 0		

COUNTY OF

Names of Assistant Commissioners by whom Cases were decided.	No.	Name of Tenant.	Name of Landlord.	Townland.
Assistant Commissioners—				
J. S. Greer (Legal). J. Armstrong. J. Carr.	282	Daniel Sexton, ...	Charles F. Balton, ...	Finnoran, ...
	283	Patrick Kelly, ...	do.	do. ...
	284	Michael Donnellan, ...	do.	Carrowlagin, ...
	285	Thady Murphy, ...	do.	do. ...
	286	Anne Murphy, ...	do.	do. ...
	287	Patrick Maloney, ...	do.	Balymee, West, ...
	288	Patrick Kelly, ...	do.	Moyglassing, ...
	289	Michael Tarpey, ...	do.	do. ...
	290	Thomas Downes, ...	do.	do. ...
	291	Thady Scanlon, ...	do.	Finnoran, ...
	292	Michael Behan, ...	Francis Healy, ...	Tarmon, ...
	293	William J. Brew, ...	Hector S. Vandeleur, ...	Lissdoon, East, and another, ...
	294	Patrick O'Loughlin, ...	Charles F. Balton, ...	Moyglassing, ...
	295	Patrick Mullahan, ...	Thomas Mahon, ...	Craggane, ...
	296	Thomas Talty, ...	Mary O'Meara, continued in the name of R. W. C. Reeves,	Dunagregan, ...
				Total, ...

COUNTY OF

Head Commission.	1140	Edmund P. Wallis, ...	Colonel James F. Hickie, ...	Ballyvally, ...
	1141	Michael McCarthy, ...	do.	do. ...
	1142	William P. Clarke, ...	Lord De Vesci, ...	Mantlown and another,
	1143	John Crowley, junr., Rep. of Bridget Crowley.	Henry J. Hungerford, ...	Glanakyrach and another.
	1144	Cornelius Sullivan, ...	do.	do. ...
Assistant Commissioners—				
	1145	Cornelius Flynn, ...	Mrs. Evans, ...	[illegible], ...
J. Doyle (Legal). E. O'Kelly. J. Germaine.	1146	Anthony Barrett, ...	Walter Adams, ...	Kilcorra, ...
	1147	Michael Flynn, ...	Judith E. A. Townsend, ...	Dunrigin, ...
	1148	Daniel O'Callaghan, ...	Denis H. Nunan and another,	Rowel Partnagh,
	1149	Timothy Guiney, ...	David Cagney, ...	[illegible], ...

CLARE—*continued.*

Extent of Holding. Statute.			Poor Law Valuation.			Former Rent.			Judicial Rent.			Observations.	Value of Tenancy.		
A.	R.	P.	£	s.	d.	£	s.	d.	£	s.	d.		£	s.	d.
[illegible]	0	0	[illegible]	0	0	23	0	0	16	0	0				
36	0	9	30	0	0	[illegible]	0	0	18	0	0				
13	0	13	6	5	0	8	0	0	6	0	0				
[illegible]	3	35	81	0	0	83	0	0	81	0	0				
23	0	33	20	5	0	25	0	0	16	4	0				
24	1	10	5	6	0	10	10	0	4	6	0				
35	0	16	9	5	0	17	0	0	10	10	0				
21	0	38	9	0	0	18	0	0	10	6	0				
33	1	13	14	15	0	27	10	0	16	10	0				
67	2	16	16	16	0	23	0	0	18	10	0				
80	1	24	46	5	0	60	5	0	31	0	0				
75	1	0	84	0	0	84	0	0	64	0	0				
21	0	36	9	0	0	16	0	0	10	8	0				
114	0	16	70	0	0	90	0	0	64	10	0				
86	0	0	94	0	0	129	14	7	80	0	0				

COUNTY OF

Names of Assistant Commissioners by whom Cases were decided.	No.	Name of Tenant.	Name of Landlord.	Townland.
Assistant Commissioners— L. Doyle (Legal). E. O'Kelly. J. Gulbraith.	1150	John Rahilly,	Robert E. Gibbings,	Carrigleam,
	1151	Margaret Brown, senior, and another.	Miss Frances Ogilvy,	Drumkeen,
	1152	Susan Brown,	do.	Drumkeen, West,
	1153	John J. Hartstonge,	Lord Plunkett,	Kilmurry,
	1154	Mark Moreton and another,	Captain W. H. Davies and another.	Knockananeal,
	1155	Cornelius R. Mackay,	Thomas Boyce,	Kilbrally,
	1156	Cornelius Sheehan,	Ralph C. Twiss and others, Trustees of George Twiss	Rossduff,
	1157	Margaret Nunan,	A. H. Wards,	Sands,
	1158	Dennis Ahern,	Nora Leahy and another,	Kilmorna,
	1159	John Shine and another,	Denis J. Murphy,	Lisrobin, West,
	1160	Do.,	do.	do.
	1161	Joseph Murphy,	William N. D. Latouche and others, Trustees of Peter D. Latouche.	Millmane,
	1162	James Nunan,	do.	Lisnane,
	1163	Do.,	do.	do.
	1164	Michael Nunan,	do.	Killimane,
	1165	Patrick Egan,	Edward Nash,	Knockaville,
	1166	Cornelius Nunan,	do.	do.
	1167	Daniel Cronin,	Robert K. Sheehy,	Derrigle,
	1168	Florence Shea,	Richard D. Mahony,	Longwarrs,
	1169	Timothy Sullivan,	do.	do.
	1170	Mary Rahilly, Limited Admix. of John Rahilly.	do.	do.
	1171	William Madigan,	Elizabeth Lighthurdy,	Dallige,
	1172	Do.,	do.	do.
	1173	Denis Moynihan,	Thomas H. Crofts and anor.,	Clounghomes,
	1174	Jeremiah Dunnane,	do.	do.
	1175	Edmund Burke,	Colonel William St. L. A. Sewell.	Onakencourage,
	1176	Luke Burke,	do.	do.
	1177	Edmund Burke,	do.	do.
	1178	Owen Lehane,	James N. Creagh and others,	Kilcurry,
	1179	Timothy Lehane,	do.	do.
	1180	Denis Connors,	do.	Turnaway,
	1181	Patrick Connors,	do.	do.

TABLE OF JUDICIAL RENTS.

CORK—*continued.*

Extent of Holding Statute.	Poor Law Valuation.	Former Rent.	Judicial Rent.	Observations.
A. R. P.	£ s. d.	£ s. d.	£ s. d.	
79 1 38	62 5 0	91 17 6	72 0 0	
75 1 8	45 10 0	69 13 0	52 0 0	
75 1 0	53 15 0	87 7 0	64 0 0	
86 2 29	45 10 0	97 0 0	60 0 0	
80 0 0	38 10 0	48 14 2	37 10 0	
136 0 33	242 0 0	300 0 0	241 0 0	
121 2 10	82 0 0	93 19 0	82 5 0	
55 2 0	50 0 0	53 7 4	50 5 0	
114 3 0	65 10 0	74 11 0	61 0 0	
11 1 16	5 5 0	6 0 0	5 0 0	
75 3 35	23 0 0	32 0 0	28 0 0	
45 0 18	24 10 0	40 8 3	34 0 0	
4 3 2	5 0 0	7 0 0	4 17 6	
31 3 8	15 10 0	20 1 7	13 0 0	
72 0 16	37 13 10	47 12 6	40 0 0	
75 1 12	19 10 0	42 0 0	30 0 0	
109 3 0	28 15 0	45 0 0	40 0 0	
83 1 7	31 0 0	81 10 0	34 0 0	
8 1 30	6 5 0	20 5 6	18 15 0	
1 2 0	1 0 0	2 3 6	2 3 6	
9 3 16	7 10 0	15 4 4	15 5 0	
41 3 13	21 10 0	33 13 0	24 0 0	
20 1 0	12 0 0	13 15 6	13 10 8	
15 2 30	9 5 0	10 0 0	8 5 0	
22 1 19	6 0 0	18 10 0	10 10 0	

COUNTY OF

Names of Assistant Commissioners by whom Cases were decided.	No.	Name of Tenant.	Name of Landlord.	Townland.
Assistant Commissioners—				
L. Doyle (Legal). W. Walpole. W. J. Gorman.	1162	John Sullivan, ...	General H. P. Mandy & anor.,	Bawngorm, ...
	1163	John Sullivan and anor.,	Richard A. Orpen, ...	West Lisheens, ...
	1164	Cornelius Lynch, ...	do.	do. ...
	1165	Constantine Hurley and another,	do.	do. ...
	1166	John Casey, ...	do.	East Lisheens, ...
	1167	Owen Riordan, ...	James F. Gough and others,	Kilarey, ...
	1168	Honora Flynn, ...	A. O. Anderson, ...	Lr. Ballyvaster,
	1169	Patrick White, ...	E. E. Evans, ...	Barna, North, ...
	1170	Catherine Mahony, ...	Robert H. E. White, ...	Maulavanig ...
	1171	Daniel Leary and anor., Rep. of Hagure Leary.	do.	Kilnamanagh ...
	1172	Jeremiah Sullivan, ...	do.	Ballymanagh,
	1173	Patrick Hurley, ...	do.	Caheragh, ...
	1174	Patrick Cronin, ...	do.	Gortloughra, ...
	1175	Patrick King, ...	do.	do. ...
	1176	John Cronin, ...	do.	Inchideraille & anor.,
	1177	Do., ...	do.	do. ...
	1178	Patrick Sullivan, ...	do.	Bunkie, ...
	1179	Thomas Dillon, ...	do.	Dromaleigh, ...
	1180	James Collins, ...	Samuel Ingen, ...	Lissanbeg, East,
				Total, ...

COUNTY OF

Assistant Commissioners—	310	Pat Long, ...	George Hewson, ...	Gortnaskehy, ...
J. S. Green (Legal). J. Hawtrey. F. J. O'Shaughnessy.	311	Henry Glaister and anor.,	G. E. Browne and another, ...	Tullig, ...
	312	Thomas Canty, ...	do.	do. ...
	313	Jeremiah Nolan, ...	William F. V. Fitzgerald, ...	Dromartin, ...
	314	Gerald McElligott, ...	Earl of Listowel, ...	Ballygrennan, ...
	315	Annie Raftery, Devisee of Alexander Cruikshank.	George Hewson, ...	Gortnaskehy, ...
	316	Michael J. Wren, ...	Charles O'B. Crosbie and anor.,	Tarmons, ...
	317	Michael B. Wren, ...	do.	do. ...
	318	Cornelius O'Connor, ...	do.	do. ...

CORK—*continued.*

Extent of Holding. Statute.	Poor Law Valuation.	Former Rent.	Judicial Rent.	Observations.	Value of Tenancy.
A. R. P.	£ s. d.	£ s. d.	£ s. d.		£ s. d.
33 2 10	10 5 0	14 0 0	11 15 0		
46 0 0	34 0 0	34 0 0	38 10 0		
33 0 29	31 0 0	30 0 0	25 10 0		
103 3 20	35 10 0	70 0 0	45 10 0		
60 0 0	28 10 0	44 10 0	43 3 4		
38 4 32	15 5 0	23 0 0	24 15 0		
33 3 18	38 15 0	38 0 9	37 15 6	By consent.	
61 1 38	40 15 0	103 4 4	55 5 0	do.	
223 1 20	71 0 0	95 0 0	79 0 0		
145 2 2	83 15 0	84 0 0	37 0 0		
209 1 0	18 5 0	96 0 0	31 13 0	With right of grazing on 273 acres of mountain in common with three other tenants.	
36 3 14	8 0 0	11 0 0	8 0 0		
33 3 21	7 0 0	12 0 0	9 0 0		
74 1 4	19 10 0	13 0 0	11 0 0		
110 0 0	19 15 0	31 0 0	20 0 0		
180 0 0	26 5 0	36 10 0	27 0 0		
19 2 25	33 0 0	24 0 0	21 0 0		
19 0 37	21 0 0	23 10 0	25 10 0		
30 1 0	21 15 0	19 10 0	15 10 0	By consent.	
4,126 3 34	2,125 15 10	3,165 7 4	2,288 5 8		

KERRY.

4 0 27	1 14 0	5 0 0	4 10 0		
63 3 27	54 10 0	63 0 0	48 0 0		
35 0 14	17 15 0	14 0 0	20 0 0		
150 1 7	63 15 0	97 0 0	66 10 0		
176 2 31	69 10 0	164 0 0	110 0 0		
160 1 20	88 10 0	219 11 7	150 0 0		
19 1 30	6 5 0	16 0 0	9 0 0		
43 2 7	12 15 0	65 0 0	22 10 0		
93 2 0	16 10 0	25 0 0	16 10 0		

COUNTY OF

Names of Assistant Commissioners by whom Cases were Decided.	No.	Name of Tenant.	Name of Landlord.	Townland.
Assistant Commissioners—				
J. E. Greer (Legal). J. Harrington. J. J. O'Shaughnessy.	319	Daniel Wren, Ltd. Admor. of Daniel Wren.	Charles O'B. Creagh and anor.,	Tarmons, ...
	320	Michael Kissane, ...	do.	do. ...
	321	James Scanlan, ...	do.	do. ...
	322	Timothy Brandon, ...	do.	do. ...
	323	Mary Stevens and anor.,	do.	do. ...
	324	Thomas Enright, ...	do.	do. ...
	325	William Wren, Rep. of Michael Wren.	do.	do. ...
	326	Mary Nolan, ...	Falkiner C. Sandes, ...	Trushragh, ...
	327	William Joy, ...	do.	do. ...
	328	Bridget Mauds, Admix. of John Mauds.	Sophia Chambers, ...	Tarmons, ...
	329	William Wren, Rep. of Michael Wren.	do.	do. ...
	330	Mary O'Connor, ...	Captain Robert Leslie, ...	Kilpaddogue, ...
	331	John Brazill, ...	do.	Tarmon's Hill,
	332	William Walsh, ...	do.	Doonard, Upper,
	333	David W. Quinlan, ...	do.	do. ...
	334	Margaret Egan, ...	do.	Tarmon Hill, ...
	335	Jeremiah Enright, ...	do.	Doonard, Upper,
	336	Patrick Scanlan, ...	do.	Kilpaddogue, ...
	337	Ellen Egan, ...	John P. Bernhardt, ...	Tarmons, ...
	338	Catherine Shanahan and another.	do.	Tarmon's Cross,
	339	William Barnes and anor.,	do.	do. ...
	340	Thomas Twomey, ...	do.	do. ...
	341	Thomas Moore and anor.,	do.	do. ...
	342	Patrick Carroll, ...	do.	do. ...
	343	Edmond Stack, Rep. of Maurice Stack.	Sophia Chambers, ...	Tarmons, West,
	344	Jeremiah Collins & anor., Reps. of John Collins.	do.	Tarmons, ...
				Total, ...

COUNTY OF

Head Commission.	404	Michael Lyddy, ...	Rev. Charles Hutton, ...	Scart, ...
	405	Michael Russell, ...	James R. Stewart, ...	Thomastown, ...

KERRY—*continued.*

Extent of Holding. Statute.			Poor Law Valuation.			Former Rent.			Judicial Rent.			Observations.	Value of Tenancy.
A.	R.	P.	£	s.	d.	£	s.	d.	£	s.	d.		£ s. d.
14	2	0	6	0	0	16	0	0	9	0	0		
16	1	20	4	0	0	13	0	0	8	10	0		
10	2	30	4	0	0	17	0	0	10	10	0		
7	0	8	1	10	0	6	10	0	2	16	0		
18	0	36	7	10	0	18	0	0	10	10	0		
60	2	15	11	10	0	30	0	0	17	0	0		
19	1	10	12	0	0	30	0	0	16	0	0		
67	0	6	21	0	0	41	0	0	[illegible]	0	0		
44	0	38	20	5	0	67	10	0	30	0	0		
45	2	37	18	0	0	15	0	0	18	0	0		
25	0	16	4	0	0	12	0	0	11	0	0		
62	0	0	18	0	0	30	0	0	22	0	0		
81	0	0	14	0	0	33	0	0	15	10	0		
63	2	07	[illegible]	5	0	78	0	0	62	10	0		
127	1	39	16	0	0	80	0	0	71	0	0		
68	2	14	24	10	0	64	0	0	68	10	0		
65	0	5	33	0	0	84	0	0	40	0	0		
17	1	5	13	0	0	23	0	0	16	10	0		
54	1	39	23	0	0	48	0	0	34	10	0		
0	2	4	0	10	0	3	0	0	1	0	0		
62	3	4	14	14	0	38	0	0	18	5	0		
1	1	0	1	0	0	2	0	0	1	0	0		
60	0	0	14	13	0	60	0	0	16	0	0		
4	0	22	2	0	0	4	10	8	4	0	0		
23	0	0	8	0	0	9	0	0	7	10	0		
86	1	27	37	0	0	47	0	0	32	10	0		
1,630	1	15	644	0	0	1,362	0	0	701	0	0		

Names of Assistant Commissioners by whom Cases were decided.	No.	Name of Tenant.	Name of Landlord.
Assistant Commissioners—			
J. H. Edge (Legal). A. F. Curtis. C. O'Keeffe.	[illegible]	Catherine Ahern, Admix. of James Ahern.	Robert S. Palmer,
	407	William Gorman, ...	Lord Muskerry, ...
	408	John Geary, ...	do. ...
	409	James Dore, ...	do. ...
	410	William Irwin, ...	Jane M. Locke and ot
	411	Honoria Irwin, ...	do. ...
	412	Michael Irwin, ...	Michael Scanlan, ...
	413	David Shanahan, ...	Prendergast Plummer,
	414	James Walsh, ...	John Powers, ...
J. H. Edge (Legal). M. P. Lynch. W. H. Brownrigg.	415	James F. Bannatyne, ...	Arthur W. Vincent,
	416	James Mara, ...	La Marchesa della Ro
	417	Do., ...	Miss F. F. Digby and
	418	John Brennan, ...	Miss J. E. M. Molyn
	419	Henry Hannan, ...	Clifford Lloyd, Esq Chetwood, deceased.
	420	John J. Kelly, ...	Colonel Arthur G. Ju
	421	Michael Ryan, ...	Hon. H. Plunkett and
	422	Thomas Murphy, ...	J. Wilson *Fair*, Tr Estate of Mrs. Plunk
J. H. Edge (Legal). F. M. Cagney. J. T. Davis.	423	James Carey, ...	Joseph Bevan, ...
	424	Daniel Hunt, ...	Jane Russell, ...
	425	Patrick Barry, ...	do. ...
	426	Mrs. Honoria Hickey, ...	George Walsh, ...
	427	Daniel Corkery, ...	Colonel Francis M. D
	428	Michael Dempsey, ...	Edward Dunphy,
	429	Anne Boyen, ...	Thomas Cagney & ors of David Cagney, de
	430	William Power, ...	Mrs. Frances E. D. G
	431	Patrick Callen, ...	do. ...

LIMERICK—*continued.*

Extent of Holding, Statute.	Poor Law Valuation.	Former Rent.	Judicial Rent.	Observations.
A. R. P.	£ s. d.	£ s. d.	£ s. d.	
113 0 16	64 5 0	78 17 9	63 10 0	
41 0 37	17 5 0	[illegible] 0 0	[illegible] 10 0	
67 1 30	[illegible] 10 0	[illegible] 0 0	[illegible] 0 0	
71 1 0	[illegible] 0 0	60 0 0	[illegible] 0 0	
[illegible] 0 [illegible]	[illegible] 15 0	133 5 0	113 0 0	
[illegible] 0 8	[illegible] 0 0	50 7 10	[illegible] 0 0	
[illegible] 0 [illegible]	[illegible] 15 0	97 5 4	[illegible] 0 0	
64 0 0	45 0 0	[illegible] 0 0	43 0 0	
4 3 25	unascertained,	3 0 0	2 5 0	
25 3 10	61 10 0	64 13 9	58 11 9	By consent.
[illegible] 1 [illegible]	60 10 0	84 13 9	67 0 0	do.
[illegible] 2 24	[illegible] 0 0	[illegible] 0 0	31 0 0	do.
17 0 14	17 5 0	[illegible] 7 6	14 0 0	do.
[illegible] 1 [illegible]	25 0 0	[illegible] 17 4	[illegible] 0 0	do.
91 2 1	112 5 0	117 0 0	98 0 0	do.
29 0 [illegible]	14 10 0	33 10 0	[illegible] 10 0	do.
19 0 10	[illegible] 15 0	34 0 0	[illegible] 0 0	do.
[illegible] 0 0	49 15 0	77 15 0	44 0 0	
116 2 [illegible]	118 15 0	148 2 0	140 0 0	
[illegible] 0 [illegible]	44 5 0	116 0 0	[illegible] 0 0	
[illegible] 1 37	17 0 0	64 15 6	[illegible] 0 0	
13 3 7	14 5 0	45 0 0	[illegible] 10 0	
119 0 18	119 0 0	166 0 0	118 0 0	
107 3 [illegible]	45 10 0	98 11 10	[illegible] 0 0	
118 0 14	11 15 0	[illegible] 0 0	25 0 0	
84 0 0	49 5 0	103 0 0	[illegible] 0 0	
162 2 2	95 0 0	145 14 0	110 0 0	
78 1 14	40 10 0	86 0 0	84 0 0	

COUNTY OF

Names of Assistant Commissioners by whom Cases were decided.	No.	Name of Tenant.	Name of Landlord.	Townland.
Assistant Commissioners—				
J. H. Edge (Legal). F. M. Carroll. J. T. Davys.	435	William Lee, —	Francis Crowe, — —	Inchirourke, —
	436	James S. Nagan, —	Thomas Fosberry, —	Ballygullenagh,
	437	James Casey, —	do. — —	Ballygullenagh, —
	438	James S. Nagan, —	do. — ...	Ballygullenagh,
	439	Arthur O'Leary, —	Charles Conyers, — —	Castletown, —
	440	John O'Leary, —	do. — —	do. —
	441	John Higgins, —	do. — —	do. —
	442	Do. — —	do. — —	do. —
				Total, —

COUNTY OF

Head Commission.	349	James J. Geary, Heir-at-Law of Philip Geary.	Mrs. Sarah McCarthy, —	Carrigeen, —
Assistant Commissioners—	350	Tobias E. Burke, —	George J. Minchin, —	Rathsaveragh, —
J. H. Edge (Legal). M. P. Lynch. W. H. Beauchamp.	351	Mary Hennessy, —	Estate of Martin v. Dale and others, Reps. of Hon. General A. Fytche,	Killeenkeen, —
	352	Mathew Donley, Rep. of Patrick Donley.	George A. Mellis, ...	Rockstown, —
	353	Louis S. Maher, —	do. ... —	do. —
	354	John Mullally, —	do. — ...	do. —
	355	Mathew Donley, —	do. — —	do. —
	356	Michael Cahen, —	Mrs. Elizabeth O. Maxwell,	Tullaheagh, —
	357	Georgina M. Lloyd and another, Reps. of Horatio Lloyd.	George A. Mellis, —	Barrington, ...
	358	John Mulhearn, —	William A. Egan, ...	Glengarra, —
	359	Patrick Ryan, —	Count De Boise and another,	Shanakill, —
				Total, —

LIMERICK—*continued.*

Extent of Holding. Statute.	Poor Law Valuation.	Former Rent.	Judicial Rent.	Observations.	Value of Tenancy.
A. R. P.	£ s. d.	£ s. d.	£ s. d.		£ s. d.
75 0 13	45 5 0	80 0 0	67 0 0		
107 1 31	64 0 0	110 0 0	[illegible] 0 0		
[illegible] 2 0	37 10 0	41 0 0	[illegible] 0 0		
41 1 36	37 15 0	41 0 0	31 0 0		
45 0 15	14 5 0	[illegible] 0 0	17 0 0		
[illegible] 0 5	5 0 0	14 0 0	9 0 0		
3 1 13	unascertained.	3 0 0	2 0 0		
8 2 37	do.	7 0 0	6 0 0		
2,420 3 13	1,635 10 0	2,577 11 3	1,846 14 2		

TIPPERARY.

291 3 11	211 0 0	300 0 0	185 0 0	The rent in this case was fixed by consent of the parties at the sitting of the Court in Dublin.	
575 0 20	137 0 0	150 0 0	130 0 0		
[illegible] 3 0	55 5 0	122 0 0	85 0 0		
81 1 36	6 0 0	15 0 0	7 10 0		
125 1 22	[illegible] 16 0	131 0 0	85 0 0		
84 0 19	15 0 0	10 0 0	8 0 0		
10 3 14	8 0 0	9 10 5	6 5 0		
4 0 23	5 0 0	10 0 0	6 15 0		
12 0 24	6 15 0	8 5 9	8 5 9		
55 0 11	34 0 0	37 5 0	31 0 0		

COUNTY OF

Names of Assistant Commissioners by whom Cases were decided.	No.	Name of Tenant.	Name of Landlord.	Townland.
Head Commissioner.	76	Patrick Geary, ...	Lieut.-Col. George E. Hillier,	Lyrenaglogh, ...
Assistant Commissioners— L. Doyle (Legal). E. D. Butler. E. B. Hayes.	77	Thomas Power, ...	Sir Richard J. Musgrave, Bart., and another.	Grange and mm.,
	78	Patrick Griffin, ...	Emily F. O'Donnell, by Mary O'Donnell and another.	Kilbree, West, ...
	79	Michael Hayes and anor.,	John Walsh, ...	Boherawilling, ...
	80	Michael O'Connor, ...	Sir R. J. Musgrave, Bart., ...	Ballydaff, Lower,
	81	John Murray, ...	do.	Ballyvolligan, ...
	82	John Flynn, ...	do.	do. ...
	83	John McGrath, ...	Duke of Devonshire, ...	Garrydoyne and another.
	84	Michael B. Hynes, ...	do.	Townparks, East, and another.
	85	Sarah Flynn, ...	Thomas St. J. Grant, ...	Inchinleamy, West,
	86	Patrick Flynn, ...	do.	do. ...
	87	Nicholas Walsh, ...	Earl of Huntington, a minor, by Countess of Huntington.	Farrows, ...
	88	Michael Healy, ...	do.	Curradonn, ...
	89	Michael Morrissy, ...	do.	Farrane, Lower,
	90	Thomas Keating, ...	Thomas O'G. Ussher, ...	Mountain Res, ...
	91	James Whelan, ...	do.	Curraghavaz, ...
	92	Thomas Keating, ...	do.	Mountain Res, ...
	93	William Smyth, ...	do.	Abeanand others,
	94	James Feeney, ...	do.	Curraghmore, ...
	95	John McGrath, ...	Lieut.-Col. G. E. Hillier, ...	Drumana, ...
	96	Patrick Condon, ...	do.	Knocklarn, ...
	97	John Flynn, ...	do.	Ballyhane, ...
	98	Mary Dennis, ...	do.	Ballyhane and another.
	99	Michael Mulcahy, ...	Sir Richard F. Keane, Bart.,	Knocknamanah and another.
	100	Catherine Walsh, ...	do.	Kildarriheen, ...
	101	Thomas Scanlan, ...	do.	Clashganniff and another.
	102	Thomas Griffin, ...	do.	Clashgarriff, ...
	103	Maurice Lane, ...	Lieut.-Col. George E. Hillier,	Tubbermahalla,
	104	William Ahern, ...	Sir Richard F. Keane, Bart.,	Ballynoe, ...
	105	Patrick Healy, ...	do.	Ballynoe, East,
	106	Edmond Walsh, ...	do.	do. ...

WATERFORD.

Extent of Holding. Statute.	Poor Law Valuation.	Former Rent.	Judicial Rent.	Observations.	Value of Tenancy.
A. R. P.	£ s. d.	£ s. d.	£ s. d.		£ s.
77 3 8	23 15 0	44 10 0	31 0 0	The rent in this case was fixed by consent of the parties at the sitting of the Court in Dublin.	
54 0 8	27 10 0	40 0 0	[illegible] 0 0	By consent.	
62 0 [illegible]	17 10 0	23 7 0	16 17 0		
84 3 35	71 0 0	102 0 0	70 0 0		
71 1 30	71 10 0	106 0 0	80 0 0		
54 3 15	35 5 0	47 0 0	37 10 0		
83 2 4	[illegible] 5 0	66 18 0	65 0 0		
105 1 8	145 5 0	109 0 0	175 0 0		
73 0 39	73 0 0	100 10 0	[illegible] 0 0		
[illegible] 0 0	[illegible] 0 0	134 0 0	100 0 0		
35 0 0	41 10 0	50 0 0	41 0 0		
[illegible] 0 1	[illegible] 10 0	62 0 0	47 0 0		
122 0 [illegible]	65 0 0	109 0 0	[illegible] 15 0		
80 0 21	66 10 0	[illegible] 14 8	44 0 0		
80 0 0	4 0 0	16 10 0	7 10 0		
[illegible] 3 15	9 0 0	[illegible] 15 0	15 0 0		
23 0 19	3 5 0	9 0 0	4 10 0		
125 1 5	[illegible] 10 0	207 1 11½	160 0 0		
40 0 0	7 0 0	61 0 0	15 0 0		
94 1 8	80 7 0	80 0 0	80 0 0		
76 0 24	25 10 0	45 0 0	30 0 0		
39 1 37	15 0 0	74 0 0	13 7 6		
130 1 35	75 0 0	116 11 0	84 15 6		
130 0 37	17 5 0	31 0 0	21 0 0		
98 0 15	78 0 0	110 0 0	87 10 0		
94 1 21	17 15 0	[illegible] 0 0	31 15 0		
40 1 14	4 5 0	10 10 0	7 0 0		
45 1 25	12 10 0	[illegible] 0 0	13 5 0		
60 1 30	unascertained.	19 0 0	15 0 0		
56 0 19	18 5 0	55 0 0	31 10 0		
70 0 0	24 15 0	67 0 0	[illegible] 10 0		

COUNTY OF WATERFORD—continued.

[illegible]	No.	[illegible]	[illegible]	[illegible]	[illegible]	[illegible]	[illegible]	[illegible]	[illegible]	[illegible]
					A. R. P.	£ s. d.	£ s. d.	£ s. d.		£ s. d.
[illegible]	[illegible]	[illegible]	[illegible]	[illegible]	[illegible]	[illegible]	[illegible]	[illegible]	[illegible]	
	[illegible]	[illegible]	[illegible]	[illegible]	[illegible]	[illegible]	[illegible]	[illegible]	Do.	
	[illegible]	[illegible]	[illegible]	[illegible]	[illegible]	[illegible]	[illegible]	[illegible]	Do.	
				Total,	[illegible]	[illegible]	[illegible]	[illegible]		

APRIL. 1869.

SUMMARIES FOR APRIL, 1889.

Summary showing, according to Provinces and Counties, the Number of Cases in which Judicial Rents have been Fixed by Sub-Commissions under the Land Law (Ireland) Act, 1881, during the Month of April, 1889; and also the Acreages, Tenement Valuations, Former Rents, and Judicial Rents of the Holdings.

Provinces and County.	Number of Cases in which Judicial Rents have been fixed.	Acreage.	Tenement Valuation.	Former Rent.	Judicial Rent.
		Statute Acres. A. R. P.	£ s. d.	£ s. d.	£ s. d.
ULSTER—					
Antrim, ...	58	1,165 1 10	818 7 0	919 14 8	686 8 8
Armagh, ...	68	886 2 11	850 1 0	301 15 11	491 17 1
Cavan, ...	1	45 1 5	81 15 0	55 0 0	30 0 0
Donegal, ...	125	2,688 3 37	851 4 0	837 18 1½	695 8 11½
Down, ...	95	2,668 3 58	2,503 18 8	1,440 12 11	1,085 13 4
Monaghan, ...	8	18 2 25	18 8 0	17 0 0	13 15 0
Tyrone, ...	68	1,320 3 5	482 10 8	841 10 8	431 7 4
Totals, ...	406	8,095 2 12	4,852 10 8	4,848 6 10½	3,873 15 10½
LEINSTER—					
Carlow, ...	11	650 0 28	325 10 0	387 2 8	345 0 0
Kilkenny, ...	16	760 3 18	115 4 0	461 11 8	336 9 4
Longford, ...	29	665 2 5	320 0 0	391 18 9	279 10 11
Louth, ...	4	58 3 7	89 0 0	87 0 6	82 10 6
Meath, ...	39	768 2 10	565 0 0	748 7 10	600 5 10
Queen's, ...	2	19 0 4	14 6 0	18 8 4	14 8 4
Westmeath, ...	35	1,639 5 7	1,316 0 0	1,499 7 7	1,348 8 8
Wicklow, ...	1	13 5 0	16 8 0	25 10 0	18 19 0
Totals, ...	130	4,297 1 13	2,920 5 0	3,477 9 11	2,760 9 0
CONNAUGHT—					
Galway, ...	88	1,556 2 18	628 3 0	731 18 6	570 18 8
Mayo, ...	99	1,725 3 21	394 1 3	645 13 3	480 18 4
Roscommon, ...	66	737 0 35	460 6 0	505 16 6	412 9 7
Sligo, ...	13	615 1 34	711 3 0	296 17 6	316 0 0
Totals, ...	236	4,228 0 16	1,898 11 8	2,198 17 7	1,897 3 11
MUNSTER—					
Clare, ...	20	691 3 5	295 19 0	389 19 1	271 18 0
Cork, ...	66	2,163 1 21	577 0 0	1,170 12 3½	1,008 14 0
Limerick, ...	14	480 2 8	515 10 0	610 8 9	351 18 0
Tipperary, ...	1	177 1 19	318 0 0	500 0 0	250 0 0
Totals, ...	101	3,503 1 15	1,708 9 0	2,399 5 1½	1,881 10 0

IRELAND.

ULSTER, ...	406	8,095 2 12	4,852 10 8	4,848 6 10½	3,873 15 10½
LEINSTER, ...	130	4,297 1 13	2,920 5 0	3,477 9 11	2,760 9 0
CONNAUGHT, ...	236	4,228 0 16	1,898 11 8	2,198 17 7	1,897 3 11
MUNSTER, ...	101	3,503 1 15	1,708 9 0	2,399 5 1½	1,881 10 0
Totals, ...	873	19,924 1 16	10,875 15 4	12,419 19 6	9,857 18 9½

For Rents fixed upon Reports of Valuers, see page [illegible].

CIVIL BILL COURTS.

SUMMARY FOR APRIL, 1889.

Cases in which Judicial Rents have been fixed by Civil Bill Courts under the Land Law (Ireland) Act, 1881, and notified to the Irish Land Commission during the month of April, 1889.

Province and County.	Number of Cases in which Judicial Rents have been fixed.	Acreage.	Tenement Valuation.	Former Rent.	Judicial Rent.
		Statute Acres. A. R. P.	£ s. d.	£ s. d.	£ s. d.
ULSTER—					
Down, ...	2	18 3 13	21 0 0	29 0 0	20 3 0
Fermanagh, ...	2	25 0 10	25 10 0	27 0 0	22 10 0
Londonderry, ...	6	40 3 23	19 9 0	24 5 0	17 12 8
Monaghan, ...	1	13 2 36	9 15 0	10 9 6	7 10 0
Totals, ...	10	98 2 2	75 14 0	90 14 6	67 15 9
LEINSTER—					
[illegible], ...	68	5,097 2 25	3,060 6 8	3,876 5 9	3,316 1 5
CONNAUGHT—					
Mayo, ...	34	997 1 21	232 0 0	299 1 7	221 18 0
Roscommon, ...	1	31 3 3	15 0 0	13 0 0	7 16 0
Totals, ...	[illegible]	1,039 0 24	251 0 0	318 1 7	229 14 0
MUNSTER—					
Cork, ...	4	170 3 30	57 4 0	160 0 0	87 16 6
Kerry, ...	15	789 3 39	154 4 0	294 16 6	192 1 5
Tipperary, ...	16	965 1 5	183 16 0	197 3 10	153 14 6
Totals, ...	35	1,925 3 35	397 4 0	691 19 4	408 12 8

IRELAND.

[illegible]					
ULSTER, ...	10	98 2 2	75 14 0	90 14 6	67 15 9
LEINSTER, ...	68	5,097 2 25	3,536 6 8	3,876 5 9	3,316 1 5
CONNAUGHT, ...	35	1,039 0 24	251 0 0	612 1 7	229 14 0
MUNSTER, ...	35	1,925 3 35	397 4 0	691 19 4	408 12 8
TOTALS, ...	118	8,564 1 17	3,620 4 8	4,370 18 2	3,022 3 9

LEASEHOLDERS.

SUMMARY FOR APRIL, 1889.

Summary showing, according to Provinces and Counties, the Number of Cases in which Judicial Rents have been Fixed by Sub-Commissions under the Land Law (Ireland) Act, 1887, during the Month of April, 1889; and also the Acreages, Tenement Valuations, Former Rents, and Judicial Rents of the Holdings.

Province and County.	Number of Cases in which Judicial Rents have been fixed.	Acreage.			Tenement Valuation.			Former Rent.			Judicial Rent.		
		Statute Acres.											
		A.	R.	P.	£	s.	d.	£	s.	d.	£	s.	d.
ULSTER—													
Antrim, ...	56	2,087	2	14	1,649	4	1	1,819	1	11	1,835	17	6
Armagh, ...	24	194	3	31	180	6	6	154	8	6	173	1	6
Donegal, ...	8	165	3	20	61	5	0	135	11	6	106	1	3
Down, ...	63	1,047	1	39	1,058	5	0	1,254	6	1	689	16	6
Fermanagh, ...	1	74	0	0	45	0	0	15	0	0	31	0	0
Londonderry, ...	3	141	3	1	134	0	0	101	16	0	85	0	0
Tyrone, ...	16	1,535	0	25	966	10	0	2,036	18	11	778	11	0
Totals, ...	169	6,094	1	8	4,094	6	7	4,657	18	0	3,434	6	4
LEINSTER—													
Carlow, ...	17	1,633	0	18	1,194	6	0	1,432	18	9	1,216	19	0
Dublin, ...	2	196	0	35	267	0	0	300	0	0	296	0	0
Kildare, ...	5	606	3	0	603	0	0	373	6	6	418	0	0
Kilkenny, ...	25	1,349	1	37	842	10	6	965	4	11½	713	6	0
Longford, ...	23	1,144	2	17	528	9	6	851	17	6	582	6	6
Louth, ...	11	689	0	7	606	15	0	723	19	9	541	13	0
Meath, ...	60	1,731	3	13	1,718	0	0	2,373	3	11	1,766	0	10
Westmeath, ...	20	3,419	0	13	2,780	10	0	3,446	0	0	2,663	6	0
Wexford, ...	6	319	2	4	161	0	0	196	1	8	173	10	0
Wicklow, ...	4	443	1	15	297	10	0	294	16	0	259	10	0
Totals, ...	161	11,381	1	9	8,720	19	0	11,537	1	8½	9,004	7	10
CONNAUGHT—													
Galway, ...	19	448	1	18	276	17	6	284	9	6	250	17	6
Mayo, ...	33	605	1	19	328	11	6	471	7	9	308	3	8
Roscommon, ...	48	1,556	0	27	995	16	0	1,168	13	8½	901	19	6
Sligo, ...	1	21	2	8	9	0	0	13	0	0	7	10	0
Totals, ...	61	2,631	0	36	1,611	5	6	1,967	9	11½	1,468	5	8
MUNSTER—													
Clare, ...	46	2,149	1	21	687	16	0	1,298	19	10	920	18	0
Cork, ...	33	1,717	1	30	739	7	10	1,101	6	8	764	19	8
Limerick, ...	84	4,557	3	14	1,766	7	10	2,943	11	8	2,100	16	3
Tipperary, ...	1	15	0	18	—			11	17	3	9	0	9
Waterford, ...	1	60	0	17	50	13	6	66	6	0	43	18	6
Totals, ...	166	8,469	3	19	3,463	6	8	5,441	14	8	3,770	13	6

IRELAND.

ULSTER, ...	169	6,094	1	8	4,094	6	7	4,657	18	0	3,434	6	4
LEINSTER, ...	161	11,381	1	9	8,720	19	0	11,537	1	8½	9,004	7	10
CONNAUGHT, ...	61	2,631	0	36	1,611	5	8	1,967	9	11½	1,469	5	8
MUNSTER, ...	166	8,469	3	19	3,463	6	8	5,441	14	6	3,770	16	8
TOTALS, ...	577	27,487	1	29	17,889	17	0	23,604	9	10	17,677	15	6

CIVIL BILL COURTS.

LEASEHOLDERS.

SUMMARY FOR APRIL, 1888.

Cases in which Judicial Rents have been fixed by Civil Bill Courts, under the Land Law (Ireland) Act, 1887, and notified to the Irish Land Commission during the Month of April, 1889.

Province and County.	[illegible]	Acreage.	Tenement Valuation.	Former Rent.	Judicial Rent.
		Statute Acres. A. R. P.	£ s. d.	£ s. d.	£ s. d.
ULSTER—					
Fermanagh, ...	2	104 2 28	97 0 0	103 4 2	80 9 0
Londonderry, ...	6	72 1 18	41 0 0	48 16 10	35 19 0
Totals, ...	8	176 3 37	134 0 0	152 1 0	116 8 0
LEINSTER—					
Meath, ...	14	911 2 28	678 0 0	986 9 5	719 15 0
CONNAUGHT—					
Galway, ...	1	87 0 27	43 16 0	83 10 6	63 10 6
Mayo, ...	2	148 0 4	80 8 0	103 6 0	79 18 0
Totals, ...	3	235 0 31	124 4 0	186 16 6	143 8 6
MUNSTER—					
Cork, ...	1	69 3 8	61 10 0	70 0 0	37 0 0
Kerry, ...	13	756 0 19	222 10 0	370 19 0	245 18 0
Totals, ...	14	825 3 27	284 0 0	440 19 0	282 18 0

IRELAND.

ULSTER, ...	8	176 3 37	138 0 0	152 1 0	116 8 0
LEINSTER, ...	14	911 2 28	678 0 0	986 9 5	719 14 0
CONNAUGHT, ...	3	235 0 31	124 4 0	186 16 6	143 3 6
MUNSTER, ...	14	825 3 27	284 0 0	440 19 0	282 18 0
TOTALS, ...	39	2,149 3 33	1,204 4 0	1,696 7 11	1,256 8 6

PROVINCE OF

COUNTY OF

Names of Assistant Commissioners by whom Cases were decided.	No.	Name of Tenant.	Name of Landlord.	Townland.
Head Commissioner.	3681	Robert Young,	Earl of Antrim,	Ballymarlagh,
Assistant Commissioners—	3682	Hugh Smith,	Sir Richard Wallace, Bart.,	Ballynadolly,
E. Greer (Legal)	3683	George Fleming,	do.	Crew,
R. [illegible]				
J. M. Weir.	3684	John McGarrity,	do.	Ballymacward,
	3685	Do.,	do.	do.
	3686	Richard McKinney,	do.	W[illegible] (part of.)
	3687	John Bennett,	do.	M[illegible],
	3688	Thomas Hull,	do.	Ballymaloy,
	3689	Mary Palmer,	do.	do.
	3690	Do.,	do.	Magalurry,
	3691	William Megowan,	do.	[illegible],
	3692	Richard Robinson,	do.	[illegible],
	3693	Arthur Peel,	do.	Aghadalgan,
	3694	Philip Magee,	do.	Tullyrusk,
	3695	William J. Park,	do.	Lower Ballinderry,
	3696	Thomas McCarroll,	do.	Pomeroy,
	3697	Patrick McGeogh,	do.	Aghalee,
	3698	Christian G. Brown,	do.	Ballyellough,
	3699	Nathaniel Law,	do.	Moyrusk,
	3700	George Dawson,	do.	Ballycarrickmaddy,
	3701	Dalway Bell,	do.	Magheragall,
	3702	Patrick Phillips,	do.	Ballyclough,
	3703	William Topping,	Marquis of Hertford,	Broughmore,
	3704	John McConnell,	John Quiery and another, Trustees of Joseph Quiery.	Ballykeown,

ULSTER.

ANTRIM.

Extent of Holding. Statute.	Poor Law Valuation.	Former Rent.	Judicial Rent.	Observations.	Value of Tenancy.
A. R. P.	£ s. d.	£ s. d.	£ s. d.	£ s. d.	£ s. d.
1 3 8	1 15 0	3 0 0	1 2 0		
24 0 5	16 15 0	17 5 8	12 0 0		
16 2 11	unascertained,	8 0 5	7 5 0		
12 0 7	10 0 0	5 1 0	6 10 0		
5 3 25	5 15 0	1 15 5	4 16 8		
17 1 10	9 10 0	9 9 3	7 0 0		
7 2 21	9 0 0	7 18 0	5 10 0		
27 0 15	23 10 0	28 10 0	20 15 0		
11 0 0	14 10 0	10 0 0	8 15 0		
9 3 0	11 15 0	11 8 8	5 5 0		
20 1 6	20 10 0	22 13 4	17 10 0		
31 1 30	25 0 0	22 11 3	16 10 0		
18 1 20	24 0 0	21 11 8	17 0 0		
25 2 8	21 10 0	20 8 8	18 11 0	Rent changed in 1862 from . . . 18 6 4 ; 1880 19 3 5	
11 3 0	19 10 0	15 1 6	18 0 0		
17 2 0	unascertained,	17 6 5	10 10 0		
1 5 33	4 15 0	5 15 0	2 10 0		
17 2 29	19 15 0	20 10 6	14 10 0		
23 1 9	23 5 0	23 14 5	24 10 0		
15 0 0	14 10 0	15 8 2	9 10 0		
13 2 12	21 10 0	16 18 10	11 15 0		
24 0 0	19 10 0	17 0 0	31 0 0		
24 2 0	40 0 0	28 0 0	20 0 0	1848 28 7 0	
11 3 20	16 0 0	15 0 0	10 16 0	1855 15 0 0	

COUNTY OF

Names of Assistant Commissioners by whom Cases were decided.	No.	Name of Tenant.	Name of Landlord.	Townland.
Assistant Commissioners—				
E. Greer (Legal). R. Sproule. J. M. Weir.	3705	Joseph Savage, ...	Arthur J. Johnston, ...	Ballymena, ...
	3706	William Lee, ...	Mrs. I. M. Duncan and others,	Drumadraugh,
	3707	Samuel McCormick, ...	Jane Simpson and others, Reps. of Mrs. Jane Munroe.	Carrowmoney, ...
	3708	Joseph McCullough, ...	Viscount Templetown, ...	Altanalbey, ...
	3709	Alexander McCaughan,	Colonel J. McDonald, ...	Broalrussy, ...
	3710	Hugh McCaughan, ...	do.	do. ...
	3711	John McDougall, ...	James S. Moore, ...	Drumcullion, ...
	3712	Randal McDonnell, ...	Dr. John B. Dunlop, ...	Tavnaghboy, ...
	3713	Do., ...	do.	Kilroberts, ...
	3714	John McCaughan, ...	do.	do. ...
	3715	Robert Macartney, ...	Alexander George Fullerton,	Magheramenagh, ...
	3716	Francis McCormick, ...	John Turnley, ...	Brokagh, ...
	3717	John McGrew, ...	George William Cuppage and another, Trustees of the Entailed Alexander Cuppage.	Unshinagh, ...
	3718	Francis McGoughan, ...	do.	Agolah, ...
	3719	Patrick McKay, ...	do.	Drumnagessan, ...
	3720	Sarah Christy, ...	Sir Frederick Boyd, Bart., ...	Ballydurnan, ...
	3721	William J. Mulmoran,	Kenneth MacK. Wray, ...	Prolusk, ...
	3722	William Chambers, ...	do.	do. ...
	3723	John McGregor, ...	do.	do. ...
	3724	Daniel McAuley, ...	do.	do. ...
	3725	Jane Clarke, ...	do.	do. ...
	3726	John McGill, ...	do.	do. ...
	3727	Alexander McIntyre, ...	do.	do. ...
	3728	John Chambers, ...	do.	do. ...
	3729	John McLean, ...	do.	Craigalappin, ...
	3730	William Taggart, ...	do.	do. ...
	3731	Daniel McCurdy, ...	do.	do. ...
	3732	Patrick McCurdy, ...	do.	do. ...
				Total, ...

ANTRIM—*continued.*

Extent of Holding. Statute.	Poor Law Valuation.	Former Rent.	Judicial Rent.	Observations.		Value of Tenancy.
A. R. P.	£ s. d.	£ s. d.	£ s. d.		£ s. d.	£ s. d.
13 3 0	15 10 0	20 11 11	14 0 0			
48 3 0	56 10 0	78 9 8	68 0 0			
13 0 31	unascertained.	83 0 0	21 0 0			
155 2 0	108 0 0	84 0 0	80 0 0	Rent changed in 1876 from	78 0 0	
23 3 16	18 15 0	17 0 0	13 0 0			
34 0 4	17 10 0	17 0 0	12 10 0			
16 1 13	7 10 0	10 19 0	9 0 0			
43 3 22	9 15 0	19 0 0	7 10 0	And two acres grazing.		
20 1 24	11 0 0	9 17 3	7 0 0			
46 1 20	15 0 0	15 3 0	12 17 0	By consent.		
55 1 20	33 15 0	36 0 8	37 0 0			
25 1 0	9 19 0	9 5 8	9 8 9	And 4½ acres grazing.		
256 0 5	20 16 0	23 0 0	24 0 0			
25 3 5	23 10 0	24 16 6	15 15 0			
33 0 0	10 3 0	20 0 0	10 0 0			
22 1 10	13 6 0	11 11 8	7 10 0			
17 1 16	16 0 0	14 0 0	8 10 0			
15 2 25	6 0 0	5 0 0	5 0 0			
13 1 20	8 10 0	10 0 0	7 0 0			
26 1 29	7 5 0	7 0 0	5 10 0			
23 0 23	11 10 0	11 0 0	9 0 0			
46 2 37	14 15 0	25 0 0	13 0 0			
14 1 20	8 15 0	6 0 0	6 0 0			
9 1 25	7 5 0	6 0 0	5 0 0			
16 3 9	7 0 0	7 5 0	5 10 0			
19 0 0	9 15 0	9 15 0	7 15 0			
20 1 10	15 15 0	16 10 0	11 15 0			
18 0 24	6 10 0	7 5 0	5 10 0			
1,403 1 14	513 7 0	512 14 8	408 7 9			

COUNTY OF

Names of Assistant Commissioners by whom Cases were decided.	No.	Name of Tenant.	Name of Landlord.	Townland.
Assistant Commissioners:— D. Tierney (Legal). M. K. Sentwell. H. Johnston.	5745	Margaret McGlay, Ltd. Admix. of Jas. McGlay.	Reps. of John Henry, ...	Sheriff Rathbane,
	5746	Rachel Carroll, Ltd. Admix. of Robert Carroll.	do. — —	do. —
	5747	Mathew Kane, ...	do.	do. —
	5748	John Eastwood, —	do.	Ballymore, —
	5749	John McConville, —	James Hanratty, ...	Loughross, —
	5750	Dominick Burke, ...	do. — ...	Clonduane, —
	5751	John Ley, — —	do. — —	Rathbane, ...
	5752	Patrick Haley, ...	Jasper and Mrs. Erskine, —	Greenhill, —
	5753	Owen Carragher & anor.,	do.	do. —
	5754	Alice Carr, — —	do.	do. —
	5755	Patrick Kelly, —	do. — ...	do. —
	5756	Patrick McKeown, —	Mary J. Allen, ...	Drumbally, —
	5757	Francis Henry, ...	do.	do. —
	5758	Michael Hearty, ...	do. — ...	do. —
	5759	Patrick Lambe, ...	do. — ...	do. —
	5760	Edward McGeeney, —	do. — ...	do. —
	5761	Owen Keenan, ...	do. ... —	Lisnigan, —
	5762	John McGeeney, —	do. — —	do. —
	5763	William P. Sullivan, ...	R. T. Wakefield, ... —	Clonagh and anor.,
	5764	Francis Gallaghy, —	Robert J. McGeough, —	Aughnaleck, —
	5765	John Carroll, —	Captain R. McG. R. Shelton,	Altnamackin, —
	5766	Mary Harvey, Limited Admix. of Pat Harvey.	Michael Kelly and another, Execs. of Denis Kelly.	Drumboy, —
	5767	James Watson, ...	do.	do. —
	5768	Patrick Hughes, Ltd. Admr. of Mary Hughes.	do. — ...	do. —
	5769	John O'Neill, —	do.	do. —
	5770	Peter Callan, ...	do. — —	Aughnagun, —
	5771	John Malia, Limited Admr. of Pat Malia.	Helen F. Reid and another,	Cassly McCabbagh.
	5772	Owen Daly, — —	do. — —	Carnabane, —
	5773	Bernard McKenna, —	do. — —	Carnabane and another.
	5774	Patrick Callaghan, —	do.	do. —
	5775	Bryan Callaghan, —	do.	do. —
	5776	Pat McKenna, ...	do.	do. —
	5777	Edward Fleming, ...	do. — ...	do. —
	5778	James Boyle, ...	do. — ...	[illegible], —
	5779	Do., ... —	do. — —	do. —

ARMAGH.

Extent of Holding. Statute.	Poor Law Valuation.	Former Rent.	Judicial Rent.	Observations.	Value of Tenancy.
A. R. P.	£ s. d.	£ s. d.	£ s. d.		£ s. d.
9 2 33	7 0 0	5 15 0	5 0 0		
11 3 20	5 15 0	6 0 0	8 0 0		
3 1 2	3 3 0	3 0 7	2 0 7		
66 1 30	53 15 0	81 1 7	25 5 0	By consent.	
4 1 0	2 15 0	2 10 6	1 13 0		
8 1 0	5 16 0	8 0 0	4 10 0		
6 3 10	4 0 0	6 5 0	4 5 0		
11 0 35	6 10 0	6 0 0	3 15 0		
40 3 0	24 15 0	23 0 0	15 10 0		
6 0 30	3 17 6	4 7 6	2 15 0		
15 2 5	11 0 0	10 5 0	6 0 0		
9 1 15	4 15 0	6 15 5	3 3 0		
10 0 10	5 15 0	5 19 10	4 0 0		
14 0 15	7 5 0	7 3 0	5 16 0		
9 3 30	6 5 0	4 12 0	4 5 0		
6 3 10	4 10 0	3 10 0	5 0 0		
5 0 37	5 10 0	8 14 9	7 2 0		
8 1 32	5 15 0	7 10 0	9 0 0		
27 2 35	18 5 0	23 6 11	17 10 0	do.	
10 3 23	5 15 0	6 6 3	5 0 0		
13 3 30	11 5 0	10 11 9	8 5 0		
19 0 15	12 0 0	6 1 5	5 10 0		
10 0 30	5 15 0	4 0 0	4 0 0		
7 1 31	6 5 0	3 14 9	3 0 0	And undivided half of 1a. 1r. 33p.	
20 3 25	11 0 0	7 0 6	4 0 0	And undivided half of 3a. 2r.	
5 0 20	2 5 0	1 18 4	1 5 0		
6 1 5	5 5 0	8 15 0	4 0 0		
9 3 5	7 5 0	6 4 8	4 15 0		
23 0 35	15 5 0	13 6 2	12 0 0		
8 0 25	unascertained.	6 17 0	6 5 0		
7 1 5	do.	5 19 0	4 0 0		
16 3 0	13 0 0	10 0 0	8 10 0		
6 3 7	5 0 0	4 18 5	3 10 0		
9 3 25	7 14 0	5 18 6	5 0 0		
6 1 35	6 10 0	3 9 10	2 5 0		

COUNTY OF

Names of Assistant Commissioners by whom Cases were decided.	No.	Name of Tenant.	Name of Landlord.	Townland.
Assistant Commissioners—				
G. Toomey (Legal). H. K. Barrows. H. Jameson.	5780	Michael McGuinness,	John P. Reid and another,	Managullia,
	5781	John Wilson,	do.	Glasdrummanagrey,
	5782	Bernard McNulty,	Horace Thorp and another, Reprs. of Thomas P. Ball.	Kearvin,
	5783	Bridget Hughes,	do.	do.
	5784	Peter McGough,	do.	do.
	5785	Peter Morgan,	do.	do.
	5786	Charles Smith,	do.	do.
	5787	Peter McNulty,	do.	Ballyhearn, Big,
	5788	Arthur McMahon,	do.	do.
	5789	John Carragher,	do.	do.
	5790	Patrick Donnelly,	do.	do.
	5791	Francis Carragher,	do.	do.
	5792	Terence Carragher,	do.	do.
	5793	Peter Hanratty,	do.	Carlan,
	5794	John McElroy, Ltd. Admx. of Phoebe McElroy,	do.	do.
	5795	Peter McGough,	do.	Shanderim
	5796	Peter Quinn,	do.	do.
	5797	Patrick McNulty,	do.	do.
	5798	Bridget Quinn, Limited Admix. of Pat Quinn,	do.	do.
	5799	Alice McGuinness,	do.	Aunsaure,
	5800	Henry McCabe,	do.	do.
	5801	Bernard McCabe,	do.	Tom,
	5802	Hugh McConville,	do.	do.
	5803	John McCreesh, Rep. of Pat McCreesh,	do.	do.
	5804	Henry McCabe,	do.	do.
	5805	Patrick Sheils,	do.	Ureker,
	5806	Denis Nugent,	do.	do
	5807	John McCreesh, Rep. of Pat McCreesh,	do.	Drumlagher,
	5808	John McCarney,	do.	do.
	5809	Charles McShane,	do.	do.
	5810	Arthur Brooks, Rep. of Pat McShane,	do.	do.
	5811	Rose Ward,	do.	do.
	5812	Alice Lennon,	do.	Crossmaglen,
	5813	Owen Treanor,	do.	Crossoharent,
				Total,

ARMAGH—*continued.*

Extent of Holding. Statute.	Poor Law Valuation.	Former Rent.	Judicial Rent.	Observations.	Value of Tenancy.
A. R. P.	£ s. d.	£ s. d.	£ s. d.		£ s. d.
27 0 6	13 15 0	10 6 8	8 0 0		
10 1 28	8 0 0	7 1 9	5 5 0		
6 2 20	4 15 0	4 11 0	4 5 0		
14 2 25	10 15 0	9 10 0	8 10 0		
24 0 5	11 8 0	15 1 0	10 18 0		
5 0 30	2 10 0	3 5 0	2 15 0		
5 0 25	5 12 0	3 6 6	3 6 6		
14 2 17	8 0 0	6 14 0	6 14 0		
4 3 3	2 10 0	2 10 0	1 18 0		
24 2 25	16 0 0	12 10 0	13 0 0		
5 1 25	4 5 0	3 10 0	2 10 0		
4 1 33	4 0 0	2 17 0	2 10 0		
19 1 35	12 0 0	10 0 0	9 0 0		
4 0 24	3 18 0	2 10 0	1 18 0		
27 0 5	unascertained.	16 5 0	16 5 0		
12 3 12	8 0 0	7 0 0	7 0 0		
6 0 0	2 10 0	3 0 0	3 0 0		
9 1 30	5 15 0	4 1 8	3 16 0		
11 3 0	5 15 0	7 13 6	7 0 0		
42 2 30	17 10 0	18 7 4	13 7 6		
4 3 20	3 10 0	5 10 0	2 10 0		
8 3 10	6 5 0	4 15 0	3 15 0		
15 0 11	10 5 0	9 6 8	8 0 0		
4 3 0	6 10 0	3 4 0	2 10 0		
19 1 28	16 5 0	10 16 10	10 0 0		
19 0 5	15 10 0	15 7 0	10 10 0		
15 1 31	9 16 0	8 10 0	6 10 0		
9 0 8	5 5 0	5 10 0	4 4 0		
10 3 6	8 0 0	7 8 3	5 15 0		
6 1 34	1 0 0	3 17 10	2 17 10		
31 0 20	27 15 0	19 9 0	18 9 0		
5 2 20	6 5 0	6 14 0	2 15 0		
7 2 0	7 10 0	6 7 0	6 0 0		
10 0 20	... 6 0 0	5 10 0	4 10 0		
584 2 11	350 1 5	301 16 11	231 17 1		

Name of Assistant Commissioners by whom Cases were decided.	No.	Name of Tenant.	Name of
Head Commissioners.	2794	David Faulkner, ...	Henry & Sm

Assistant Commissioners—	6400	Bryan Mongey, ...	Reps. of Sir now Charles
D. Tuohy (Legal). G. N. Caldwell. J. H. McConnell.	6401	John Mooney, ...	Joseph Stew
	6402	Bernard McGuinness, ...	Hon. Ernest others.
	6403	Bryan McLoughlin, Ltd., Admor. of Cornelius McLoughlin.	do.
	6404	Mary Duffy, Limited Ad-mix. of Brian Duffy.	Charles B. H.
	6405	Margaret McLoughlin, ...	do.
	6406	John Falconer, ...	John McCre
	6407	Patrick Breslend, ...	do.
	6408	Charles Doherty, ...	do.
	6409	Denis McLoughlin, ...	John Doherty
	6410	Captain James Kavanagh,	do.
	6411	Patrick Doherty, ...	William Hart
	6412	James Walker, ...	John Doherty
	6413	James Lindsay, ...	Alexander A
	6414	Charles Cavanagh, ...	Robert Stew
	6415	Neal Doherty, Admor. of	do.

4	19	0	4	5	0	
6	7	4	3	18	0	
10	0	0	6	0	0	
8	10	0	4	10	0	And [illegible] right of grazing over 80 acres of mountain.
5	18	0	2	17	6	And [illegible] right of grazing over 80 acres of mountain.
2	10	0	3	0	0	
8	12	0	8	5	0	
8	15	10	5	9	6	
8	0	0	3	15	0	
5	0	0	4	15	0	
6	10	0	4	0	0	And right of grazing over [illegible] acres of mountain with 19 others.
4	0	0	3	0	0	do.
6	1	6	6	0	0	And right of grazing over [illegible] of 85 acres mountain.
8	5	0	8	5	0	do.
7	13	0	7	10	0	do.
4	0	0	3	0	0	And right of grazing over [illegible] of [illegible] acres mountain.
6	17	0	6	0	0	do.
5	15	0	5	0	0	do.
6	12	0	4	10	0	do.
1	18	1½	1	18	1½	
5	0	0	4	10	0	Right of grazing with 4 others over

COUNTY OF

Names of Assistant Commissioners by whom cases were decided.	No.	Name of Tenant.	Name of Landlord.	Townland.
Assistant Commissioners—				
D. Tuohy (Legal). G. H. Caldwell. J. H. McConnell.	6426	James Galbraith, ...	Isabella Harvey and another, Reps. of A. B. Cary.	Cashel, ...
	6427	Ashman Smith, ...	do.	do. ...
	6428	Patrick Ferren, ...	Georgina A. E. Dunbar, ...	do. ...
	6429	Owen Doherty, ...	do.	do. ...
	6430	John Devir, senior, ...	do.	do. ...
	6431	Thomas McLoughlin, Limited Admor. of Daniel McLoughlin.	do.	do. ...
	6432	Mary Doherty, ...	do.	do. ...
	6433	William Devir and anor.,	do.	do. ...
	6434	Catherine Doherty, ...	do.	do. ...
	6435	Michael Ferren, ...	do.	do. ...
	6436	Michael Devir, ...	do.	do. ...
	6437	John McLoughlin, ...	do.	Cashel Glenealy,
	6438	Isabella Boggs, ...	do.	Bree, ...
	6439	Patrick Moloy, ...	do.	do. ...
	6440	Mary Boggs, ...	do.	do. ...
	6441	James Heuston, ...	do.	do. ...
	6442	John Devir, Ltd. Admor. of Michael Devir, decd.	do.	Cashell, ...
	6443	James Harkin, ...	do.	do. ...
	6444	Michael Ferran, ...	do.	do. ...
	6445	Michael Doherty, ...	do.	do. ...
	6446	Mary McCauley, ...	do.	Buckill, ...
	6447	Patrick Gill, ...	Charles R. Harvey, ...	Minnawary, ...
	6448	Daniel Kelly, ...	do.	Dunaweenie, ...
	6449	Patrick McGee, ...	do.	Slackrin, ...
	6450	Charles Duffy, ...	do.	Lephin, ...
	6451	James Roddy, ...	do.	Urbalreagh, ...
	6452	John Friel, ...	do.	Letter, ...
	6453	Patrick Duffy, ...	do.	Kinnea, ...
	6454	Neal O'Gibbon, ...	do.	Dunaff, ...
	6455	Ellen Doherty, ...	do.	Tullagh, ...
	6456	Mary McDermott, Ltd. Admx. of Jas. McDermott,	do.	Urbalreagh, ...
	6457	Joseph Doherty, ...	do.	Letter, ...
	6458	William Devlin, ...	do.	do. ...
	6459	John Gubbins, Ltd. Admor. of Grace Gubbins.	do.	Kheel, ...

TABLE OF JUDICIAL RENTS.

DONEGAL—*continued.*

Extent of Holding. Statute.	Poor Law Valuation.	Former Rent.	Judicial Rent.	Observations.
A. R. P.	£ s. d.	£ s. d.	£ s. d.	
18 0 0	3 8 0	5 0 0	3 10 0	Right of grazing over 1/17 of 197 acres mountain.
27 3 18	16 0 0	14 2 0	10 10 0	do.
37 3 30	10 5 0	10 6 6	8 5 0	
39 3 28	9 15 0	9 7 0	7 10 0	
18 3 5	5 5 0	6 18 6	3 15 0	
14 3 20	6 15 0	6 19 0	5 10 0	
26 3 16	18 10 6	9 12 0	6 0 0	
61 0 12	14 10 0	14 16 0	12 0 0	
41 3 10	13 10 0	14 2 6	11 10 0	
13 0 36	5 15 0	5 12 0	4 15 0	
23 3 28	7 5 0	7 0 0	8 17 6	
14 3 21	6 0 0	5 11 0	8 11 0	
76 3 0	51 18 0	63 13 0	24 15 0	And 1/17 right of grazing over 640 acres mountain.
4 3 18	3 3 6	3 3 0	3 0 0	And 1/17 right of grazing over 640 acres mountain.
64 3 20	40 10 0	40 11 6	37 10 0	And 1/8 right of grazing over 640 acres mountain.
16 0 6	11 5 0	11 3 6	7 3 0	And 1/17 right of grazing over 640 acres mountain.
68 0 16	17 0 0	17 6 0	13 10 0	
14 3 26	10 0 0	8 4 0	5 15 0	
13 0 38	7 6 0	6 6 0	5 7 6	
63 0 0	44 6 0	36 8 0	30 0 0	
15 1 18	4 5 6	4 14 3	3 3 6	And 1/17 right of grazing over 167a. 2r. 13p. mountain.
18 1 16	3 10 0	5 18 0	2 0 0	
23 0 26	6 10 0	2 14 0	1 17 6	
21 3 0	3 15 0	3 7 6	3 7 6	
21 3 34	6 10 0	7 0 6	5 16 0	
11 2 30	3 6 0	3 0 6	3 5 0	
5 3 26	4 10 0	4 10 0	2 16 0	
11 2 5	2 0 0	4 0 0	1 18 0	
8 2 10	5 6 0	4 6 0	3 3 0	
6 3 36	1 5 0	7 10 0	1 5 0	
8 1 0	6 15 0	8 0 0	6 5 0	
6 1 0	4 0 0	4 10 0	2 15 0	
6 1 25	3 0 0	2 10 0	1 15 0	
16 3 0	6 10 0	5 10 0	4 3 6	

Names of Assistant Commissioners by whom Cases were decided.	No.	Name of Tenant.	Name of Landlord.	Townland.
Assistant Commissioners—	6460	Mary Tolan,	Charles R. Harvey,	Urbalreagh,
D. Tuohy (Legal).	6461	Bridget Carey, Limited Admix. of Pat Carey.	do.	do.
G. N. Gallwey.	6462	James Cary,	John Cary and another, Trustees of J. L. Cary, deceased.	[illegible]
J. H. McConnell.	6463	Thos. McLaughlin (John),	do.	do.
	6464	John Harold,	do.	do.
	6465	Joseph Atcheson,	do.	do.
	6466	John Smith (Isaac),	do.	do.
	6467	John Smith (John),	do.	do.
	6468	John Smith (Rob),	do.	do.
	6469	Brady McLaughlin,	do.	do.
	6470	Joseph Atcheson and another.	do.	do.
	6471	Michael McElhenny,	do.	do.
	6472	George Atcheson,	do.	do.
	6473	Robert Smith,	do.	do.
	6474	Thomas Galbraith,	do.	do.
	6475	Edward McLaughlin,	do.	do.
	6476	Thomas Galbraith,	do.	do.
	6477	John McKinley,	do.	do.
	6478	Grace Quigley,	do.	do.
	6479	Owen McLaughlin,	do.	do.
	6480	John Campbell,	do.	do.
	6481	Patrick Reddy,	Hon. Ernest Cochrane,	Meenaduff,
	6482	Susan O'Donnell,	do.	[illegible]
	6483	James O'Donnell,	do.	do.
	6484	Philip Doherty and anr.,	do.	do.
	6485	Robert O'Donnell, junr.,	do.	Glenagannon,
	6486	Daniel McCay,	do.	do.
	6487	James O'Donnell, junior,	do.	do.
	6488	John Logue,	do.	Trillick,
	6489	Daniel Barr,	do.	do.
	6490	Michael Doherty,	do.	Templemoyle,
	6491	Do.,	do.	[illegible]
	6492	Rev. William O'Doherty,	do.	Clonagh,
	6493	Rose McLaughlin,	do.	Fegart,
	6494	Pat Doherty (Neal Harry),	do.	do.

DONEGAL—*continued.*

Extent of Holding. Statute.	Poor Law Valuation.	Former Rent.	Judicial Rent.	Observations.
A. R. P.	£ s. d.	£ s. d.	£ s. d.	
2 2 20	3 0 0	2 12 0	1 15 0	
3 2 20	2 10 0	3 5 0	2 7 6	
24 1 31	7 14 0	8 8 0	7 0 0	And right of grazing over 1/17 of 197 acres mountain.
19 1 7	5 15 0	7 0 0	5 5 0	And right of grazing over 1/17 of 971 acres mountain.
8 3 25	1 8 0	2 6 0	2 12 6	And right of grazing over 1/17 of 197 acres mountain.
19 2 0	4 15 0	6 0 0	4 10 0	And right of grazing over 1/17 of 126 acres mountain.
5 1 15	3 15 0	5 11 6	3 0 0	do.
24 3 0	7 0 0	5 17 0	5 18 0	do.
10 2 10	4 5 0	4 19 0	3 17 6	do.
8 1 6	3 5 0	3 10 0	3 0 0	do.
7 2 24	3 13 0	3 10 0	3 7 6	And right of grazing 197 acres of mountain with thirteen others.
18 2 9	4 19 0	4 17 6	3 10 0	do.
20 0 20	4 17 0	4 11 0	4 5 0	do.
23 1 31	8 5 0	9 0 0	7 0 0	do.
20 0 22	4 5 0	6 7 0	3 13 6	do.
40 2 0	17 14 0	14 13 [illegible]	11 18 0	And right of grazing over 1/17 of 914 acres mountain.
12 2 24	4 1 0	4 10 0	3 5 0	And right of grazing over 197 acres mountain with thirteen others.
15 0 0	4 15 0	6 6 10	4 15 0	And right of grazing over 1/17 of 756 acres mountain.
26 0 6	12 0 0	12 0 0	8 0 0	And right of grazing over 197 acres mountain.
9 3 20	4 15 0	3 14 0	3 0 0	And right of grazing over 197 acres mountain with thirteen others.
73 1 21	25 7 0	22 14 0	21 0 0	do.
60 3 21	6 15 0	7 15 5	6 10 0	And right of grazing with five others over 144a. 0r. mountain.
27 3 18	5 19 0	6 7 8	6 0 0	
23 0 0	9 18 0	10 2 7	6 0 0	And 1/17 right of grazing over 176a. 3r. 30p., and 1/17 right over 91a. 1r. 10p. mountain.
40 2 24½	8 15 0	5 17 6	7 10 0	do.
24 0 0	4 5 0	5 10 6	4 5 0	
15 2 2	5 10 0	7 4 11	5 10 0	And 1/[illegible] right of grazing over 77a. 1r. 22p. mountain.
46 0 0	10 5 0	9 8 4	7 10 0	
30 1 20	3 15 0	4 17 8	1 0 0	
29 2 24	16 0 0	17 12 0	15 0 0	
24 3 14½	5 0 0	4 8 2	3 10 0	
71 0 23	24 15 0	20 14 9	25 0 0	
15 2 2	12 0 0	8 0 0	8 0 0	
4 2 25	2 0 0	2 0 11	1 12 6	
13 3 1	5 11 0	9 8 7	7 0 0	

COUNTY OF

Names of Assistant Commissioners by whom Cases were decided.	No.	Name of Tenant.	Name of Landlord.	Townland.
Assistant Commissioners— D. Tuckey (Legal). G. N. Callwell. J. H. McCurtin.	6495	Charles Doherty,	Hon. Ernest Cochrane,	Ballyfillin and ...
	6496	John McDaid, now Cecily McDaid, Ltd. Admix. of Stewart McDaid.	do.	Ballintallon,
	6497	Hugh Mulhern, Ltd. Admor. of Anne Mulhern.	do.	Glenmakee,
	6498	Michael Barr,	do.	Moneydaff,
	6499	Daniel Conaty,	do.	Ardagh,
	6500	John Doherty (Denis),	do.	do.
	6501	Charles Doherty,	do.	do.
	6502	Owen Durnigan,	do.	Moneydaff,
	6503	Edward Doherty, Ltd. Admor. of Philip Doherty.	do.	Ballyliffin,
	6504	Pat Bradley,	do.	Glenmakee,
	6505	Pat McLaverty,	do.	do.
	6506	Sarah Butler,	do.	do.
	6507	Bridget Barr,	do.	Moneydaff,
	6508	Margaret Barr,	do.	do.
	6509	Hugh Farren,	do.	Ballinlough,
	6510	Rose Sheriry, Ltd. Admix. of Wm. Sheriry.	do.	Lackagh,
	6511	James Gill (Pat),	do.	Altahaol,
	6512	Denis Doherty, Ltd. Admor. of Michael Doherty.	do.	Ardagh,
	6513	Mary Hegarty,	do.	Ballyhoskey,
	6514	Daniel McGuigan,	do.	Ardagh,
	6515	Rose McGuigan,	do.	Ocrannive,
	6516	Patrick McGeoghegan, Ltd. Admor. of Michael McGeoghegan.	do.	do.
	6517	Charles Doherty,	do.	do.
	6518	John McKeague,	do.	Glengad,
	6519	Samuel Long,	do.	do.
	6520	George McLaren,	do.	do.
	6521	Rebecca McLaren,	do.	Carrowbeagh,
				Total,

DONEGAL—*continued.*

Extent of Holding. Statute	Poor Law Valuation.	Former Rent.	Judicial Rent.	Observations.	Value of Tenancy.
A. R. P.	£ s. d.	£ s. d.	£ s. d.		£ s. d.
27 0 0	5 10 0	9 0 3	7 15 0	And 1/16 right of grazing over 589 acres, and 1/16 right over 803A. 1R. 27P. mountain.	
50 2 3	4 0 0	5 1 1	3 15 0	And 1/16 right of grazing over 116A. 3R. 38P. mountain.	
20 1 30	3 10 0	4 5 8	5 6 0	And 1/16 right of grazing over 847 acres mountain.	
38 0 20	8 10 0	8 5 0	7 0 0	And 1/8 right of grazing over 116A. 2R. 3P. mountain.	
6 2 8	5 10 0	9 11 4	3 15 0	And 1/16 right of grazing over 107 acres mountain.	
8 3 12	5 5 0	5 2 8	3 10 0	And 1/16 right of grazing over 107 acres mountain.	
9 2 18½	4 6 0	3 19 1	3 8 3	do.	
55 0 7	5 10 0	8 8 9	6 10 0	And right of grazing with five others over 166A. 0R. mountain.	
8 0 31	1 15 0	2 9 8	1 17 8	With 1/16 right of grazing over 803A. 1R. 27P. mountain.	
5 0 10	unascertained,	1 8 4	0 15 0	And right of grazing with eleven others over 617A. 0R. 11P. mountain.	
29 1 4	5 0 0	3 17 8	2 15 8		
9 0 28	3 15 0	4 0 1	2 13 8	do.	
60 3 0	6 5 0	7 1 1	6 17 6	And right of grazing with five others over 166A. 3R. mountain.	
40 0 11	5 5 0	7 4 1	5 12 6	do.	
17 0 0	7 0 0	8 10 6	5 15 0	And 1/16 right of grazing over 450 acres mountain.	
64 3 27	12 0 0	35 8 10	25 3 10		
8 2 20	2 0 0	1 16 1	1 2 6		
9 3 19	2 15 0	2 8 10	1 15 0	And right of grazing over 1/16 of 107 acres mountain.	
3 3 28½	5 6 0	4 18 4	3 10 0	do.	
7 3 7½	3 0 0	2 7 3	1 10 0	do.	
1 3 35	1 15 0	1 6 8	1 2 6		
5 2 0	4 4 0	3 17 0	3 0 0	And right of grazing over ½ of 124 acres mountain.	
6 2 0	6 17 0	4 3 0	3 7 6	do.	
17 1 4	5 5 0	5 18 1	3 16 0		
18 1 0	6 0 0	4 19 5	5 15 0		
18 2 5	4 15 0	5 0 0	4 0 0		
24 2 20	13 5 0	11 15 0	6 15 0		
2,085 3 37	251 4 5	297 16 1½	205 2 11½		

COUNTY OF

Names of Assistant Commissioners by whom Cases were decided.	No.	Name of Tenant.	Name of Landlord.	Townland.
Assistant Commissioners— E. Greer (Legal). J. Cuninghame, T. Smith.	5100	Robert McCleghan, ...	Viscount Bridport and anor., Trustees of Marquis of Downshire.	Tullinisky, ...
	5101	John M. Harron, ...	do.	Ballygowan, ...
	5102	William Harron, ...	do.	do. ...
	5103	John Lamb, ...	James Whitela, ...	Ballydougan, ...
	5104	Elizabeth Joyce, ...	do.	do. ...
	5105	Robert Pinkerton, ...	A. P. Henderson, ...	Shanaghan, ...
	5106	Do., ...	do.	do. ...
	5107	Bernard O'Hare, ...	General H. C. Magennis, ...	Finnis, ...
	5108	John Mitchell, ...	Earl of Clanwilliam, ...	Lisnaward, ...
	5109	Peter Keenan, ...	James Cleland, ...	Gargory (part of),
	5110	William Cheevers, ...	William J. Greer, ...	Glaskermore, ...
	5111	William Bell, ...	do.	do. ...
	5112	James Lindsay, ...	St. John T. B. Douglas, ...	Ballymacaramery,
	5113	John Mitchell, ...	do.	Balleny, ...
	5114	Edward Murray, ...	Earl Annesley, ...	Burren (part of),
	5115	Hugh McEvoy, ...	do.	Ballymagreehan (part of),
	5116	James McEvoy (Pat) and another,	do.	do. ...
	5117	John Connolly, ...	do.	Burren (part of),
	5118	John Cinnamond, ...	do.	Leitrim (part of),
	5119	Do., ...	do.	do. ...
	5120	Do., ...	do.	do. ...
	5121	James Owens, junior, and anor., Exors. of E. Kelly,	do.	Legananny, ...
	5122	Robert Steele, ...	do.	do. ...
	5123	Do., ...	do.	do. ...
	5124	Henry Kelly, Lad. Admor. of P. Kelly, deceased,	do.	do. ...
	5125	James Mooney, ...	do.	do. ...
	5126	James Burns and anor.,	do.	Bankaderry, ...
	5127	Felix Cunningham, ...	Earl of Kilmorey, ...	Ballyteal, ...
	5128	James McBurney, ...	do.	Moneydarraghbeg,
	5129	Patrick Hughes, ...	do.	Ballinran, ...
	5130	James McVeigh, ...	do.	Glasdrumman,
	5131	Joseph Moore, ...	do.	Moneydarraghmore,
	5132	Thomas McBurney, ...	do.	do. ...
	5133	Do., ...	do.	do. ...
	5134	John McCartan, ...	do.	Moneydrumman, ...

TABLE OF JUDICIAL RENTS.

DOWN.

Extent of Holding. Statute.	Poor Law Valuation.	Former Rent.	Judicial Rent.	Observations.
A. R. P.	£ s. d.	£ s. d.	£ s. d.	
6 3 10	8 10 0	6 10 0	4 10 0	
44 1 12	46 10 0	44 6 0	33 0 0	
60 3 15	68 15 0	61 3 0	45 0 0	
1 1 31	8 10 0	8 13 0	2 10 0	By consent.
10 0 0	12 0 0	10 14 10	7 10 0	
15 1 20	14 15 0	12 13 8	11 10 0	
65 1 20	67 13 0	95 10 0	86 10 0	
19 1 10	18 5 8	22 12 0	15 15 0	
61 2 0	65 15 0	54 0 0	48 0 0	
16 2 29	18 5 0	21 5 8	15 13 0	
8 1 25	10 5 0	14 0 0	7 10 0	
8 0 30	10 0 0	11 9 8	6 10 0	
4 2 15	—	5 0 0	6 10 0	
11 1 14	9 0 0	11 11 0	8 0 0	
13 0 37	unascertained.	7 13 4	7 18 4	
20 2 17	8 15 0	6 0 0	6 0 0	Rent changed in 1882 from . . . £7 0s. 0d.
19 0 23	8 15 0	6 5 0	4 15 0	
16 0 9	9 15 0	9 16 0	7 0 0	
11 3 34	10 13 0	7 0 0	6 0 0	1878 5 18 0
15 3 0	9 8 0	7 8 0	5 10 0	
6 3 20	5 0 0	5 17 0	4 0 0	
17 1 0	8 0 0	6 5 0	5 13 0	
39 1 13	6 1 8	10 5 0	7 0 0	
8 1 26	6 10 0	5 0 0	4 0 0	
23 1 22	6 10 0	10 4 0	6 0 0	do. 8 8 0
7 0 4	6 0 0	4 0 0	3 0 0	
21 0 16	11 0 0	10 0 0	8 0 0	
1 3 32	2 18 0	3 8 9	2 5 0	
21 0 15	18 8 0	14 19 8	11 0 0	
11 1 15	13 10 0	9 9 8	7 10 0	
23 1 0	16 0 0	13 6 2	11 0 0	
14 1 38	11 10 0	11 8 6	8 10 0	
16 0 25	17 0 0	10 8 0	9 5 0	
4 1 36	1 0 0	3 8 0	3 16 0	
4 0 7	1 0 0	1 19 8	1 5 8	

COUNTY OF

Names of Assistant Commissioners by whom Cases were decided.	No.	Name of Tenant.	Name of Landlord.	Townland.
Assistant Commissioners—				
E. Greer (Legal). J. Cunningham. T. Bewes.	5135	Robert McCormick,	Earl of Kilmorey,	Moneydarragh, Upper,
	5136	George Hanna,	do.	Aughnahoory,
	5137	Hugh Bush,	do.	Leitrim,
	5138	Patrick McKay,	do.	Drumcrow,
	5139	Robert Quinn,	do.	Kilkeel,
	5140	Michael Owens,	do.	Magheragh,
	5141	Owen McVeigh,	do.	Kilkeel,
	5142	Hugh Cunningham,	do.	Magheragh,
	5143	John Quinn,	do.	do.
E. Greer (Legal). R. Garland. S. Chambers.	5144	James Morgan, Ltd. Admor. of John Morgan,	Earl Annesley,	Slievenaboley,
	5145	Edw. Loughlin, Ltd. Admor. of Patk. Loughlin,	do.	do.
	5146	Bernard Dornan & anor., Exors. of Danl. Dornan,	do.	do.
	5147	Michael O'Hare,	do.	Clarkhill, part of,
	5148	John McManus,	do.	do.
	5149	Francis Murray, Ltd. Admor. of Daniel Murray,	do.	Slievenaboley,
	5150	John McClean,	do.	Drumskee, part of,
	5151	Luke Savage,	do.	Clarkhill,
	5152	Patrick Conlon,	Sir Edward P. Cowan,	Lisnoid, part of,
	5153	William Vesey,	do.	Ballyvaston, part of,
	5154	Daniel Carr,	James Craig,	Ballyclander, Lr.,
	5155	George Cleland,	Colonel G. R. Hamilton,	Corporation,
	5156	William Kennedy,	Major Robert P. Maxwell,	Dunnevilly, part of,
	5157	Edward Curran,	General Magenis,	Shanaghanstown, part of,
	5158	G. Gilchrist and others,	do.	do.
	5159	John Ringland,	Archd. R. Hamilton, a minor, by Rev. A. Poole, his Trustee,	Clonagh,
	5160	John Baird,	Robert P. Maxwell,	Granshaw,
	5161	Peter McAlister,	Richard K. Boyd,	Ballyduggan, part of,
	5162	John McAlister,	do.	do.
	5163	Sarah McNamara,	Aubrey deV. Beauclerk,	Ballydonety, Upper, part of,
	5164	James McIlmail,	do.	Ballygilbert, part of,
	5165	Do.,	do.	Bright, part of,
	5166	John Starkey,	do.	Rossglass, part of,
	5167	Sarah McNamara,	do.	Ballydonety, Upper, part of.

DOWN—*continued.*

Extent of Holding. Statute.	Poor Law Valuation.	Former Rent.	Judicial Rent.	Observations.	Value of Tenancy.
a. r. p.	£ s. d.	£ s. d.	£ s. d.	£ s. d.	£ s. d.
54 2 20	3 10 0	4 15 6	3 5 0		
23 3 4	11 10 0	14 18 6	10 0 0		
6 2 14	unascertained.	8 18 4	2 10 0		
29 0 7	16 15 0	13 11 4	11 0 0		
8 0 23	11 5 0	18 18 10	9 0 0		
16 1 20	18 5 0	18 18 6	13 10 0		
14 3 29	15 0 0	13 18 3	11 0 0		
17 1 0	15 10 0	15 7 10	11 10 0		
20 0 25	20 0 0	17 12 6	14 10 0		
8 3 18	8 0 0	3 14 6	8 0 0		
19 1 16	10 5 0	9 14 0	7 7 0	Rent changed in 1879 from - - - 8 8 0	
18 3 3	12 15 0	11 10 0	10 0 0	do. 15 6 10	
14 1 20	9 10 0	7 18 0	5 0 0		
20 3 0	4 0 0	5 5 0	4 4 0		
22 3 38	14 0 0	13 0 0	11 0 0	1879 11 9 6	
6 0 15	8 0 0	7 10 0	5 0 0		
12 0 15	6 0 0	5 0 0	4 0 0	do. 5 4 0	
8 2 26	2 10 0	8 18 10	3 5 0		
7 3 12	13 0 0	9 10 6	6 0 0		
16 0 10	19 0 0	18 15 0	18 5 0		
34 1 32	34 0 0	44 15 4	37 10 0		
20 2 16	37 0 0	36 0 0	27 0 0		
14 3 10	15 10 0	15 18 0	12 0 0		
30 3 5	52 10 0	51 5 0	43 0 0	1869 20 15 6	
6 1 37	unascertained.	3 3 4	2 17 0		
53 1 16	44 5 0	40 0 0	30 0 0	1848 41 7 4	
8 3 0	10 0 0	11 17 9	6 18 0		
16 1 22	16 0 0	14 0 0	10 10 0		
46 0 8	62 0 0	64 0 0	40 0 0	1872 57 8 8	
15 3 20	20 10 0	18 0 0	13 10 0		
3 3 15	5 0 0	4 10 0	3 5 0		
18 0 30	20 15 0	13 19 3	9 10 0		
18 0 0	18 0 0	23 2 6	13 0 0		

COUNTY OF

Names of Assistant Commissioners by whom Cases were decided.	No.	Name of Tenant.	Name of Landlord.	Townland.
Assistant Commissioners—				
E. Greer (Legal). R. Garland. S. Crawford.	5168	Daniel Pollen, ...	Lord De Ros, ...	Castlescreen, part of.
	5169	John McAleer, ...	do.	Bonecastle, part of,
	5170	William Magee, ...	Ven. Archdeacon Gibbs, ...	Kilclief, ...
	5171	Michael McIlravey, ...	Rev. James T. Hall, ...	Tullumgrange, part of.
	5172	James Napier, ...	do.	Tullumgrange, Up.
	5173	John Doherty, ...	do.	Ballyhornan, part of,
	5174	Do., ...	do.	do. ...
	5175	Edward McCann, ...	John Mulholland, ...	Lisban, part of,
	5176	Mrs. Jane Gracey, ...	General A. Nugent, ...	Tullycarnan, ...
	5177	Jas. and Wm. McNamara,	do.	Tullycarnan, part of.
	5178	Margaret Galway, ...	Estate of Alexander F. St. J. Gordon and others.	Carrowreagh, ...
	5179	Catherine Fitzsimons, ...	William Johnston, Rep. of James Johnston.	Kirkmabbin, ...
	5180	James Dorrian, ...	Hugh McMullan & anor., Extors. of Alexander McMullan.	Ballyward, ...
	5181	Ellen Moore, ...	Sir Edward P. Gowan, ...	Lisnacid, part of, ...
	5182	Thomas McCann, ...	Viscount Bridport and anor., Trustees of Marquis of Downshire.	Dundrum, ...
	5183	Archibald Kirkpatrick,	do.	Ballybannan, part of.
	5184	William Craig, ...	do.	Moneylane, ...
	5185	Do., ...	do.	Waterash, ...
	5186	William Donaldson, ...	William B. McConnell, ...	Clontonaglare, ...
	5187	Hugh Smyth, ...	John Cleland, Trustee of Hugh Cleland and others.	Castlebury, ...
	5188	John Connolly, ...	H. B. Meredyth, ...	Tyrvended, ...
	5189	Mary Connolly, ...	Rev. H. W. Johnston, ...	Balloo, part of, ...
	5190	Elizabeth Moore, ...	R. W. B. Ker, ...	[illegible], ...
	5191	James Hamilton, ...	Marquis of Londonderry, ...	Barnamaghery, part of.
				Total, ...

COUNTY OF

Head Commission.	2933	Francis Murphy, ...	Earl of Dartrey, ...	Redrum, ...
Assistant Commissioners— W. F. Bailey (Legal). J. H. Bell. W. S. Rutledge.	2934	James Henderson, ...	James M. Ross, ...	Aughnamullen, ...
				Total, ...

DOWN—*continued.*

Extent of Holding. Statute.	Poor Law Valuation.	Former Rent.	Judicial Rent.	Observations.	Value of Tenancy.
A. R. P.	£ s. d.	£ s. d.	£ s. d.	£ s. d.	£ s. d.
10 1 25	11 0 0	10 6 0	7 0 0		
25 1 39	[illegible] 5 0	25 3 0	21 0 0		
22 2 15	29 5 0	27 0 0	18 10 0		
20 1 32	22 0 0	20 0 6	14 0 0		
19 3 25	21 5 0	21 0 0	15 10 0		
23 2 34	29 15 0	25 10 2	20 0 0		
3 3 15	5 15 0	5 4 2	3 10 0		
7 0 7	9 0 0	7 10 0	5 12 0		
25 2 20	22 10 0	23 5 6	18 10 0		
25 1 25	29 15 0	30 0 0	27 0 0		
53 2 37	45 10 0	58 15 11	49 0 0		
0 2 25	1 5 0	2 0 0	1 5 0		
6 0 20	2 10 0	3 14 5	3 2 0	Rent changed in 1853 from 6 4 0	
9 0 6	13 12 0	10 0 0	7 5 0		
2 0 20	3 0 0	3 0 0	3 0 0		
31 1 20	17 5 0	15 15 0	13 5 0		
10 3 27	8 4 0	6 11 0	4 15 0		
26 3 28	25 0 0	20 5 0	18 10 0		
20 2 10	15 5 0	14 17 0	13 0 0		
18 3 35	—	15 15 11	13 0 0		
6 2 0	5 10 0	5 6 10	3 15 0		
5 0 18	4 15 0	7 0 0	4 10 0		
47 1 19	54 10 0	41 0 0	33 0 0	Provision has been made in this case as regards a Labourer.	
9 1 20	9 0 0	9 18 6	6 10 0		
1,636 3 25	1,303 12 6	1,440 12 11	1,064 15 4		

MONAGHAN.

COUNTY OF

Names of Assistant Commissioners by whom Case was decided.	No.	Name of Tenant.	Name of Landlord.	Townland.
Assistant Commissioners—	7377	John Conly, ...	Robert F. Gardner and another,	Drumrowan and another.
D. Turner (Legal). A. S. Drake. A. Dennis.	7378	John Ellison, ...	Maria R. Fleming, ...	Boydstown, ...
	7379	Henry Anderson, ...	Amy H. Eccles, a minor, by Thomas Dunne, her Guardian.	Killyfin, ...
	7380	James McDonald, ...	Charles Moorhead,	Drumard, ...
	7381	James McCrory, ...	Colonel J. G. Lowry, ...	Coolkeeghan, ...
	7382	Ellen Russell, Limited Admix. of John Russell.	Charles G. R. Kennedy, ...	Aghaloey, ...
	7383	Ellen Russell, ...	do.	do. ...
	7384	John Nugent, ...	Colonel Thomas E. A. Hall and another, Trustees of Countess of Caledon.	Mureslin, ...
	7385	Henry Shepherd, ...	John S. Johnston and another, Trustees of Mountjoy Estate.	Upper Bank, ...
	7386	Do., ...	do.	Lower Bank, ...
	7387	Patrick O'Rourke, ...	Julius Casement and another, Reps. of Robert Casement.	Eagh, ...
	7388	James Lowry and anor.,	Robert W. Lowry, ...	Cavanakeeran, ...
	7389	Patrick Kane, ...	Earl of Charlemont, ...	Dunamore, ...
	7390	Henry McCork, ...	Captain Henry Irvine, ...	Killeenan, ...
	7391	James Quin, ...	do.	Terrywinny, ...
	7392	Andrew McGaughey, ...	do.	Tullyland, ...
	7393	Michael McElroy, ...	Arthur E. Daniel, ...	Lower Mallen, ...
	7394	Robert J. Carr, ...	John S. Alexander, ...	Feranagh, ...
	7395	Do., ...	do.	Kilmascally, ...
	7396	John W. Fleming, ...	Rev. H. W. Stewart, ...	Ballymenagh, ...
	7397	Do., ...	do.	do. ...
	7398	Robert Wilson, ...	John Lindsey, ...	Sherrygroom, ...
	7399	John Blackley, ...	Rev. B. H. Blacker, ...	Carrywaghey, ...
	7400	Ellen Blackley, Admix. of Robert Blackley.	do.	do. ...
	7401	John Mallon, ...	William Duff	Aghnamullagh, ...
	7402	Charles Mallon, ...	do.	do. ...
	7403	Michael O'Hara, ...	do.	do. ...
	7404	Patrick Devlin, ...	do.	do. ...
	7405	Patrick O'Hara, ...	do.	do. ...
	7406	Andrew Brown, ...	do.	do. ...
	7407	John Cosgrove, ...	do.	do. ...
	7408	Elizabeth Cosgrove, ...	do.	do. ...
	7409	Bernard O'Hara, ...	do.	do. ...
	7410	Peter Devlin, ...	do.	do. ...

TYRONE.

Extent of Holding, Statute.	Poor Law Valuation.	Former Rent.	Judicial Rent.	Observations.	Value of Tenancy.
A. R. P.	£ s. d.	£ s. d.	£ s. d.		£ s. d.
14 0 8	17 10 0	12 10 0	10 10 0		
1 2 10	8 10 0	6 18 6	8 17 8	By consent.	
17 2 10	13 10 0	15 3 4	13 0 0	do.	
10 8 5	6 5 0	6 0 0	3 8 0		
8 1 19	6 0 0	3 18 8	2 10 0		
8 8 16	10 10 0	9 17 1	7 0 0		
13 0 0	15 10 0	18 17 6	16 0 0		
10 3 15	1 10 0	2 0 0	8 0 0		
10 0 33	unascertained,	10 6 11	7 10 0		
44 2 11	do.	34 13 5	24 0 0		
4 0 20	5 10 0	6 7 0	4 15 0		
23 0 10	7 10 0	6 0 8	6 0 0		
16 0 0	9 10 0	6 0 0	4 16 0		
11 2 25	1 5 0	2 8 0	1 6 0		
18 3 0	4 10 0	8 15 0	6 10 0		
23 3 10	15 10 0	11 0 0	10 0 0		
15 1 5	3 10 0	12 13 9	8 10 0		
10 1 10	3 15 0	5 4 6	3 18 0		
19 1 30	6 10 0	7 15 9	6 13 0		
19 3 5	10 6 0	9 6 0	9 8 0		
7 3 30	10 0 0	11 7 0	8 10 0		
70 1 20	54 10 0	53 0 0	48 0 0		
56 8 10	29 0 0	25 8 0	20 10 0	do.	
8 1 20	3 5 0	3 16 3	3 0 0	do.	
14 1 15	13 16 0	11 11 0	8 17 0		
4 0 26	3 15 0	5 17 0	3 12 6		
8 3 25	8 0 0	7 1 2	5 10 0		
9 3 10	9 0 0	6 9 10	6 8 0		
3 1 25	5 0 0	4 12 6	5 8 0		
7 3 20	7 3 0	8 11 8	6 18 6		
5 3 20	6 6 0	5 8 0	4 10 0		
4 8 0	2 13 0	3 16 8	2 14 0		
8 3 22	3 10 0	3 5 8	2 8 0		
11 8 3	10 0 0	9 11 0	7 10 0		

COUNTY OF

Names of Assistant Commissioners by whom Cases were decided.	No.	Name of Tenant.	Name of Landlord.	Townland.
Assistant Commissioners—				
D. Tuckett (Legal). A. S. Drane. A. Dunlop.	7411	Rev. Robert Mount, —	Sir Nathaniel A. Staples, Bart.	Tamnylennan, —
	7412	Patrick Coffey, —	do. — —	Crossnagh, —
	7413	Paul Risty, — —	Col. Thos. Erskine & anr., Trustees of [illegible] of Castlestewart.	Brackaruse, —
	7414	Patrick Gilmore, —	do. — —	do. —
	7415	Do., — —	do. — —	do. —
	7416	Patrick Murphy, —	do. — —	Mulnagh, —
	7417	James McNally, —	do. — —	Killeenan, —
	7418	Thomas Devlin, —	do. — —	do. —
	7419	Thomas Devlin, Ltd. Admr. of John Devlin.	do. — —	do. —
	7420	John McDonald, —	do. — —	do. —
	7421	Francis Conway, Ltd. Admr. of Pat Conway.	do. — —	do. —
	7422	Patrick Hare, —	do. — —	do. —
	7423	Do., — —	do. — —	do. —
	7424	John Logan (Francis),	do. — —	do. —
	7425	Owen Grimes, Limited Admr. of Arthur Grimes.	do. — —	do. —
	7426	Owen Grimes, —	do. — —	do. —
	7427	Anne Logan, Limited Admr. of Pat Logan.	do. — —	do. —
	7428	John Tierney, —	do. — —	Murnells, —
	7429	Felix McIlwaine, —	do. — —	Mulnagh, —
	7430	Francis McGurk & anr.,	do. — —	Killeenan, —
	7431	Bernard Mullan, —	do. — —	do. —
	7432	William Patton, —	do. — —	do. —
	7433	Bridget Nugent, —	do. — —	Crossnamill, —
	7434	Patrick Quinn, —	do. — —	do. —
	7435	Patrick Quinn (John),	do. — —	do. —
	7436	Peter Mallin, —	do. — —	Tamnaskeeny, —
	7437	David Loughlin, —	do. — —	Tullyreavy, —
	7438	James Nugent, —	do. — —	Murnells, —
	7439	Alice Nugent, —	do. — —	do. —
	7440	Peter Cunningham, —	do. — —	Gorteskady, —
	7441	Maria McGovern, —	do. — —	do. —
	7442	Charles Grimes, —	do. — —	Cloghfin, —
	7443	John McDonald, —	do. — —	Brackaruse. —

TYRONE—*continued.*

Extent of Holding. Statute.	Poor Law Valuation.	Former Rent.	Judicial Rent.	Observations.	Value of Tenancy.
A. R. P.	£ s. d.	£ s. d.	£ s. d.		£ s. d.
17 0 22	21 15 0	24 10 4	20 0 0		
25 2 20	14 10 0	12 12 0	10 5 0		
56 3 18	5 5 0	5 0 0	3 10 0		
31 1 15	2 0 0	2 0 0	2 0 0		
15 1 25	2 5 0	3 10 0	3 10 0		
12 2 10	1 15 0	8 0 0	8 0 0		
23 2 9	5 10 0	4 10 0	4 0 0		
17 0 0	2 15 0	2 19 0	3 12 0		
7 1 10	1 6 0	1 10 6	1 10 6		
24 0 8	4 0 0	4 4 4	4 0 0		
61 1 10	Unascertained,	7 14 0	6 6 0		
16 2 4	3 0 0	5 0 0	3 15 0		
19 0 0	6 5 0	5 0 0	3 10 0		
23 1 30	5 5 0	5 2 10	4 10 0		
17 1 5	4 0 0	4 1 7	5 10 0		
17 1 4	5 5 0	4 1 7	3 10 0		
15 1 20	3 0 0	3 5 4	3 12 6		
25 1 0	6 15 0	3 0 0	3 0 0		
16 3 20	5 0 0	4 5 10	4 6 10		
60 1 18	10 1 0	12 4 10	9 4 0		
67 2 10	7 0 0	6 0 0	4 5 0		
29 2 15	4 5 0	3 0 0	3 0 0		
22 0 12	5 12 0	6 0 0	4 12 0		
20 1 18	7 10 0	6 0 5	5 5 0		
60 0 0	8 10 0	6 10 0	7 10 0		
6 3 0	6 0 0	5 15 0	4 0 0		
17 1 0	31 0 0	20 0 0	7 15 0		
10 0 12	2 10 0	2 0 0	1 18 0		
40 2 0	2 0 0	3 0 0	2 0 0		
61 2 35	15 10 0	15 0 0	9 0 0		
25 0 10	5 5 0	7 13 4	5 7 6		
15 0 30	8 15 0	6 17 8	4 8 0		
30 2 10	3 10 0	8 0 0	3 10 0		
15 2 10	2 5 0	2 10 0	2 5 0		
1,023 3 8	469 10 0	341 10 2	431 7 4		

PROVINCE OF

COUNTY OF

Names of Assistant Commissioners by whom Cases were decided.	No.	Name of Tenant.	Name of Landlord.	Townland.
Head Commissioners.	607	John Fagan and anor.,	Rev. A. W. Durdin, ...	Cranemore, ...
	608	Thomas Kavanagh, ...	do.	do. ...
Assistant Commissioners—	609	Michael Whelan, Rep. of P. Byrne,	E. P. Brennan and anor., Trustees of Mrs. Mary Gray,	Upper Scabie, ...
R. Reeves, Q.C. (Legal)	610	Patrick B. Kehoe, ...	Charles E. H. Dunbott, ...	Ballinaboley, ...
S. Mowbray.	611	Patrick Kelly, ...	Sir Charles Burrowes, Bart., ...	Pollerton, Big, ...
F. P. Jeffers.	612	John Brennan, ...	Rev. Frederick J. Durdin, ...	Rathmapick, ...
	613	John Whelan, ...	do.	do. ...
	614	John Corcoran, ...	R. A. & F. Brewster, ...	Rossmickery, ...
	615	Patrick Kelly, ...	Hardy Eustace, ...	Rathmapick, ...
	616	John Dowling, Rep. of E. S. Dowling	Mrs. E. T. Bunbury, ...	Cranavonane, ...
	617	Michael Kealey, ...	do.	do. ...
				Total, ...

COUNTY OF

Assistant Commissioners—	1548	Thomas Quinn, continued instead of Robert Quinn, his Legatee.	Hon. O. Ballew Bryan, ...	Pollagrove, ...
R. Reeves, Q.C. (Legal).	1549	Edmund Rochford, ...	William Owen, Trustee of Rev. G. Ayres, deceased.	Grangefort, ...
J. J. Guiry.	1550	Edmund Kelly, ...	do.	do. ...
H. C. Nash.	1551	William Doran, ...	do.	do. ...
	1552	Joseph Dooley, ...	Robert Stannard, ...	Rathbaugh, ...
	1553	James Delaney, ...	William Butler, ...	Tomanbeety, ...
	1554	Michael Hobbes, ...	do.	Mountbispalaniren,
	1555	Thomas Marshall, ...	do.	do. ...
	1556	Bridget Glendon, ...	Lord Mountgarrett, ...	Clomantagh Mountgarrett.
	1557	Michael Dwyer, ...	do.	do. ...
	1558	Michael Bowden, ...	do	do. ...
	1559	Mary Dwyer, ...	do.	do. ...
	1560	Patrick Tobin, ...	Mrs. Ellen M. Cahill, ...	Ballyeamorry Beaker.

LEINSTER.

CARLOW.

Extent of Holding. Statute.	Poor Law Valuation.	Former Rent.	Judicial Rent.	Observations.	Value of Tenancy.
A. R. P.	£ s. d.	£ s. d.	£ s. d.		£ s. d.
24 2 37	7 10 0	11 8 0	7 10 0	The rent in this case was fixed by consent of the parties at the sitting of the Court in Dublin.	
45 2 18	13 5 0	18 1 0	8 0 0	do.	
60 0 25	37 0 0	45 1 10	23 0 0		
62 6 34	41 0 0	55 16 11	42 0 0		
15 3 8	16 5 0	25 14 6	19 0 0		
8 1 20	4 10 0	10 0 0	6 10 0		
98 2 1	35 0 0	70 0 0	60 0 0		
13 0 27	16 0 0	18 0 0	15 0 0		
18 1 30	18 0 0	20 0 0	18 0 0		
16 1 00	9 10 0	15 0 0	12 0 0		
103 1 7	40 10 0	60 0 0	45 0 0		
480 0 33	222 10 0	323 2 2	242 0 0		

KILKENNY.

Extent of Holding. Statute.	Poor Law Valuation.	Former Rent.	Judicial Rent.	Observations.	Value of Tenancy.
74 8 9	51 0 0	54 4 0	45 0 0		
75 2 20	37 5 0	50 7 6	31 0 0		
120 0 30	79 5 0	103 10 0	76 10 0		
60 1 8	34 15 0	45 0 0	30 0 0		
8 8 18	8 0 0	11 5 8	7 10 0		
6 3 13	6 15 0	7 0 0	8 10 0		
16 1 18	8 0 0	5 10 0	4 0 0		
12 0 13	4 15 0	5 0 0	6 10 0		
16 0 16	10 0 0	7 18 4	8 10 0		
5 8 16	3 5 0	9 6 8	8 10 0		
13 2 38	18 10 0	23 8 4	17 0 0		
6 1 26	3 6 0	3 7 8	1 10 0		
40 3 5	25 15 0	28 0 0	20 0 0		

COUNTY OF

Names of Assistant Commissioners by whom Cases were decided.	No.	Name of Tenant.	Name of Landlord.	Townland.
Assistant Commissioners—				
R. Reeves, q.c. (Legal). T. A. Dillon. T. Davenport.	1561	Anastasia Hughes, ...	George Hely, ...	Farlismore, ...
	1562	Michael Bergin (Michl.),	do.	Donaghmore, Lr.,
	1563	Thomas Fitzsimons, ...	do.	Donaghmore, Upr.,
				Total, ...

COUNTY OF

Assistant Commissioners—	1616	Richard J. Galvin, ...	Antonio B. Edgeworth, ...	Aghafin, ...
R. E. Kane (Legal). F. Rowlette. W. S. Hunt.	1617	Rose Casey, ...	Michael Quinn, ...	Killeeny, ...
	1618	Patrick Newman, ...	Alexander K. McEntire and others, Assignees of Sir Walter Nugent, Bart.	Kanekavalley,
	1619	Honor Carr, ...	Patrick Dunnion, ...	Corglass, ...
	1620	Mary Brehon, Ltd. Admix. of Thomas Brehon.	R. C. Lyonton and another,	Killynaher, ...
	1621	Peter Dunican, junior, ...	Lord Annaly, continued in name of Hon. Henry White.	Lahary, ...
	1622	Michael Casey, ...	Earl of Longford, ...	Corboonry, ...
	1623	James McEntire, ...	do.	do. ...
	1624	John McBrien, ...	Patrick Dunnion, ...	Corglass, ...
	1625	William Armstrong, jun.,	Col. E. R. King-Harman, continued in name of W. H. King-Harman.	Ballyduran, ...
	1626	Terence McKeone, ...	William D. Phillips, Rep. of A. M. Crofton, continued in name of James Watson.	Clonmagasker, ...
	1627	James Gonlan, ...	do.	do. ...
	1628	Vincent Ferrall, ...	do.	Cloonbaurna, ...
	1629	Do., ...	do.	do. ...
	1630	Thomas Hughes, ...	John G. Ireland, ...	Esker, South, ...
	1631	Daniel Hughes, ...	do.	do. ...
	1632	John Brady, ...	do.	do. ...
	1633	Peter Corrigan, ...	do.	do. ...
	1634	Catherine Heslin, ...	George McCreedy, ...	Dernacross, ...
	1635	John McCarthy, ...	do.	Aughadowry, ...
	1636	Patrick Devine, ...	do.	Lettergonnell, ...
	1637	James Reilly, ...	do.	Clonelly, ...

KILKENNY—*continued.*

Extent of Holding (Statute).	Poor Law Valuation.	Former Rent.	Judicial Rent.	Observations.	Value of Tenancy.
A. R. P.	£ s. d.	£ s. d.	£ s. d.		£ s. d.
15 2 17	18 15 0	16 11 11	18 11 11		
5 0 0	5 0 0	6 0 0	5 7 6		
226 2 27	103 0 0	68 6 5	70 0 0		
730 5 15	418 5 0	451 14 8	338 9 8		

LONGFORD.

1 2 23	1 5 0	1 10 0	1 0 0	By consent.	
72 1 7	85 0 0	45 0 0	30 0 0		
6 1 35	Unascertained.	4 5 8	3 15 0		
50 2 10	9 0 0	9 0 11	8 0 11		
11 1 14	4 15 0	7 0 0	5 10 0		
23 3 9	9 15 0	0 14 0	7 10 0	Rent changed in 1874 from . . . £ s. d. 0 3 0	
64 1 20	33 10 0	67 0 0	63 0 0	1858 63 1 6	
84 1 25	30 10 0	33 10 0	30 0 0	do. 18 0 0	
13 2 20	6 5 0	5 11 4	3 15 0		
19 0 18	16 5 0	10 10 0	6 0 0		
17 2 0	9 0 0	8 5 10	4 15 0		
17 3 20	16 0 0	11 5 8	8 10 0	1853 4 0 0	
60 5 0	85 0 0	37 0 0	37 0 0		

COUNTY OF

Names of Assistant Commissioners by whom Cases were decided.	No.	Name of Tenant.	Name of Landlord.	Townland.
Assistant Commissioners—				
R. R. Kane (Legal). T. Robertson. W. S. Hunt.	1838	John Flynn, ...	Col. E. R. King-Harman, continued in name of Frances A. King-Harman.	Crossloughan, ...
	1839	Francis Gigley, ...	do.	Sheanwallagh, ...
	1840	Bernard Thompson, ...	do.	Crossloughan, ...
	1841	Francis Cassidy, ...	do.	Fardrumin, ...
	1842	Daniel Gordon, ...	do.	do. ...
	1843	John Masterson, ...	do.	Crossloughan, ...
	1844	Bernard O'Neill, ...	do.	do. ...
	1845	Mary Campbell, ...	do.	Fardrumin, ...
	1846	Mathew Molloy, ...	do.	Crossloughan, ...
	1847	William Cassidy, ...	do.	Fardrumin, ...
				Total, ...

COUNTY OF

Assistant Commissioners—				
R. R. Kane (Legal). T. S. Perrin. H. G. Gatenby.	1161	Patrick McPartland (Hugh).	Edward Purcell, Rep. of General Purcell.	Grassmore, ...
	1162	Owen McCann, ...	St. Clair E. M. Stobart, ...	Glenmore, ...
	1163	Michael Donnelly, ...	do.	do. ...
	1164	Martin Donnelly, ...	do.	do. ...
				Total, ...

COUNTY OF

Assistant Commissioners—				
R. R. Kane (Legal). T. S. Perrin. J. Beth.	1105	Mathew Reilly, ...	John A. Farrell, ...	Carrickspringan,
	1106	Patrick McGuinness, ...	Tankerville W. Chamberlain,	Chamberlainstown
	1107	Hugh Higgins, ...	do.	do. ...
	1108	Peter Smith, ...	do.	do. ...
	1109	Mary Sheridan, ...	do.	do. ...
	1110	Patrick Cassidy, ...	Miss H. Mayne, ...	Trinchorin, ...
	1111	Patrick Rogers, ...	George E. Radcliff, ...	Tobanstown, ...
	1112	Patrick Fay, ...	do.	do. ...

LONGFORD—*continued.*

Extent of Holding. Statute.	Poor Law Valuation.	Former Rent.	Judicial Rent.	Observations.	Value of Tenancy.
A. R. P.	£ s. d.	£ s. d.	£ s. d.		£ s. d.
26 0 7	9 15 0	16 17 8	8 0 0		
24 1 20	10 18 0	15 8 8	8 0 0		
30 0 0	9 11 0	14 4 0	8 10 0		
16 3 7	5 8 0	6 19 0	6 0 0		
48 0 0	15 15 0	20 0 4	16 0 0		
23 3 37	8 0 0	11 1 8	8 10 0		
13 3 4	4 16 0	8 0 0	3 8 0		
12 1 0	4 15 0	6 8 8	4 6 0		
11 1 0	4 10 0	4 11 8	3 10 0		
12 1 0	4 10 0	5 3 0	4 3 0		
685 1 5	220 0 0	371 15 9	279 19 11		

LOUTH.

17 3 37	9 5 0	13 0 0	8 10 0		
13 0 37	6 10 0	6 12 0	6 10 0	And right of grazing on 1,100 acres of Glenmore Mountain with 65 others.	
18 0 6	7 18 0	7 19 6	5 18 0	do.	
8 2 15	5 10 0	5 6 10	6 15 0	do.	
56 1 7	29 0 0	33 0 5	27 10 0		

MEATH.

7 0 3	1 10 0	2 1 8	3 1 8		
6 0 24	1 8 0	2 18 0	2 15 0		
4 3 35	1 5 0	3 0 0	2 10 0		
1 1 19	1 0 0	2 10 0	1 5 0		
2 1 20	1 15 0	6 0 0	1 18 0		
1 0 8	2 18 0	4 6 3	3 5 0		
4 2 6	2 5 0	3 4 8	2 1 6		
15 1 16	6 10 0	10 18 6	8 0 0		

COUNTY OF

Names of Assistant Commissioners by whom Cases were decided.	No.	Name of Tenant.	Name of Landlord.	Townland.
Assistant Commissioners— E. M. Kane (Legal). T. S. Porter. J. Byrne.	1113	Paul Mathews,	George E. Radcliff,	Trohanny,
	1114	Owen Carolan,	James Riordan,	Carrickleck,
	1115	Do.,	do.	do.
	1116	Rose Gallagher,	do.	do.
	1117	Owen Monaghan,	John G. Boram,	Newcastle,
	1118	James Monaghan,	do.	do.
	1119	James Lynch,	John Rathborne,	Skearke,
	1120	Bernard Smith,	do.	do.
	1121	Edward Martin,	James L. Naper,	Castlekeiran,
	1122	Patrick McBride,	do.	do.
	1123	Patrick Sheridan,	George S. Radcliff,	Trohanny,
	1124	Bridget Cruise,	John Jameson,	Marsh Hill,
	1125	Redmond McKenna and another, Admors. of Estates of Patrick McKenna and another.	do.	do.
	1126	Thomas McIvor, Admor. of Estate of Eliza McIvor, deceased.	do.	do.
	1127	Thomas Boyle,	do.	do.
	1128	John Tierney,	do.	do.
	1129	James O'Neill,	do.	do.
	1130	Philip Halton,	do.	do.
	1131	John McCormac,	do.	do.
	1132	Matthew McIvor, Admor. of Estate of Thomas McIvor, deceased.	do.	do.
	1133	John McKeever,	do.	do.
	1134	Mary Farrelly,	do.	do.
	1135	Michael McEnery, Admor. of Estate of Nicholas Bradley.	Chard Chaloner,	Loughan,
	1136	John Mulhendal,	do.	do.
	1137	Mary Bradley,	do.	do.
	1138	Mary A. Moylan,	do.	do.
	1139	Patrick Halton,	Richard White,	Barley Hill,
	1140	Michael Rogers,	Captain William Alexander,	Allenach,
	1141	John H. Kirk,	Charles E. Caldwell,	Part of New Grange.
	1142	William Kelly,	Francis C. Osborne,	Ballymad,
	1143	Patrick Wall,	F. A. Woods,	Bolies, Great,
				Total,

MEATH—*continued.*

Extent of Holding. Statute.	Poor Law Valuation.	Former Rent.	Judicial Rent.	Observations.	Value of Tenancy.
A. R. P.	£ s. d.	£ s. d.	£ s. d.		£ s. d.
7 2 10	3 10 0	4 9 6	4 0 0		
43 1 37	34 10 0	53 15 10	42 18 10		
8 3 0	9 16 0	3 6 4	2 15 0		
11 1 8	6 0 0	6 4 5	5 0 0		
17 2 1	10 10 0	15 1 4	9 15 0		
15 1 [illegible]	8 0 0	11 3 6	6 10 0		
40 1 17	27 0 0	37 12 10	27 10 0		
18 0 23	7 10 0	12 4 0	9 10 0		
[illegible] 0 0	23 10 0	26 10 0	23 15 0		
24 3 27	18 0 0	16 15 0	16 18 0		
2 1 13	8 0 0	1 16 10	1 10 0		
31 3 13	18 5 0	20 0 0	18 0 0		
11 1 27	9 10 0	13 9 2	10 0 0		
2 0 34	1 10 0	2 13 0	2 0 0		
33 3 [illegible]	20 5 0	25 10 3	21 0 0		
5 0 0	3 5 0	3 17 10	3 17 10		
8 1 20	6 0 0	8 11 6	6 10 0		
11 1 [illegible]	7 0 0	6 14 6	7 15 0		
7 1 13	4 15 0	4 16 0	3 15 0		
5 1 5	3 10 0	7 5 3	5 0 0		
6 3 [illegible]	6 10 0	5 15 4	5 0 0		
21 0 25	18 0 0	23 6 4	17 15 0		
25 2 19	13 10 0	18 7 6	14 10 0		
10 0 20	9 15 0	11 9 8	9 0 0		
13 3 9	13 10 0	20 7 4	12 10 0		
27 0 23	20 0 0	27 5 10	24 0 0		
11 1 14	8 10 0	10 0 10	7 0 0		
7 2 23	not separately valued.	6 0 0	5 0 0		
346 0 17	271 10 0	252 4 9	212 0 0	By consent.	
51 0 34	50 0 0	56 5 1	45 0 0	do.	
13 3 23	13 5 0	15 13 0	10 0 0	do.	
744 2 10	658 0 0	745 7 10	609 5 10		

QUEEN'S

Names of Assistant Commissioners by whom Cases were decided.	No.	Name of Tenant.	Name of Landlord.	Townland.
Assistant Commissioners—				
R. Reeves, Q.C. (Legal). T. A. Dillon. T. Davidson.	1209	Patrick Tobin, ...	Lord Castletown, ...	Graigue Drisly,
	1203	Michael Farrell, ...	John Dagan, ...	Shanahoe, ...
				Total, ...

COUNTY OF

Head Commission.	1259	John Allen and another, Exors. of Michael Allen, deceased.	Mrs. Elizabeth M. Greppan and another.	Bantelistown, ...
Assistant Commissioners—	1260	Maurice Dalton, ...	Sir Edward Greppan, Bart.,	Moyvore, ...
H. N. [illegible] (Legal). J. F. [illegible]. J. Gibson.	1261	Margaret Cormack, ...	do.	do. ...
	1262	Edward Ham, ...	do.	do. ...
	1263	Do., ...	do.	do. ...
	1264	Patrick Mahon, ...	do.	do. ...
	1265	Patrick Lynch, ...	do.	do. ...
	1266	Peter Bannon, ...	do.	do. ...
	1267	George Moore, ...	do.	do. ...
	1268	Do., ...	do.	do. ...
	1269	Dennis Kenny, ...	do.	do. ...
	1270	John Murray, ...	Thomas Manley, ...	Maryrath, ...
	1271	Owen Murray, ...	Captain P. J. Murphy, ...	Kilbeggan Abbey,
	1272	Catherine Martin, ...	do.	Bricken, ...
	1273	Denis Bannon, Rep. of Laurence Bannon.	Mary Mulvihill, Rep. of Owen Mulvihill.	Aughafin, ...
J. F. Dowling. W. S. Hunt.	1874	James Killen, ...	Mrs. Elizabeth J. Bent, ...	Jamestown, ...
	1875	James Newman, ...	E. Ashburnt Gradwell, ...	Balrath, ...
	1876	James Reilly, ...	Lord Harlech, ...	Togher, ...
	1877	Christopher Gilsenan, ...	Hon. F. R. Greville Nugent,	Liscloghar, Little,
	1878	Patrick Parlon, ...	Thomas Murray, ...	Carrydonnellan,

TABLE OF JUDICIAL RENTS.

COUNTY.

Extent of Holding. Statute.	Poor Law Valuation.	Former Rent.	Judicial Rent.	Observations.
A. R. P.	£ s. d.	£ s. d.	£ s. d.	
16 2 19	5 5 0	8 8 6	9 8 4	
4 1 25	6 0 8	7 0 0	5 0 0	By consent.
19 0 4	14 5 0	16 8 6	14 8 4	

WESTMEATH.

335 3 6	295 10 0	378 0 0	315 0 0	The rent in this case was fixed [illegible] consent of the parties at [illegible] sitting of the Court in Dublin
71 1 4	51 0 0	56 0 0	43 10 0	By consent.
44 1 16	19 15 0	20 0 0	18 10 0	do.
37 3 10	25 0 0	37 1 6	29 10 0	do.
131 0 23	100 10 0	131 11 10	96 0 0	do.
20 0 0	21 15 0	21 15 0	18 10 0	do.
41 1 0	36 0 0	40 15 0	33 0 0	do.
79 0 0	75 5 0	78 0 0	63 10 0	do.
131 3 28	79 0 0	90 0 0	70 0 0	do.
131 0 16	120 10 0	135 0 0	110 0 0	do.
6 2 0	3 5 0	4 5 0	3 7 6	do.
1 2 19	unascertained.	1 0 0	1 0 0	
11 3 0	6 15 0	7 0 0	6 0 0	Rent changed in 1852 from . . . £ 5 s. 7
15 2 10	11 10 0	9 15 0	8 5 0	1856 11 7
3 1 20	4 0 0	3 0 0	1 15 0	By consent.
17 0 0	16 0 0	16 15 0	13 15 0	
29 1 23	22 4 0	25 10 0	20 0 0	Rent changed in 1851 from . . . £ 23 s. 5
5 1 17	5 0 0	5 15 0	3 15 0	1862 4 10
25 1 26	25 10 0	20 4 8	18 0 0	
20 2 10	23 15 0	25 4 8	18 0 0	do. 20 14

COUNTY OF

Names of Assistant Commissioners by whom Cases were decided.	No.	Name of Tenant.	Name of Landlord.	Townland.
Assistant Commissioners—				
J. Bowden. W. S. Roney.	1279	John Flood, ...	Henry M. Smythe, ...	Callinstown and Gravelly.
	1280	John Mann, ...	Major Fetherston Whitney,	Rathowen, ...
	1281	Anne Killane and anor., Admxs. of John Murphy, deceased.	do.	do. ...
	1282	John Moran, ...	do.	do. ...
	1283	Do., ...	do.	Derrydooan, ...
				Total, ...

COUNTY OF

Names of Assistant Commissioners by whom Cases were decided.	No.	Name of Tenant.	Name of Landlord.	Townland.
Assistant Commissioners— R. Reeves, Q.C. (Legal). S. Mowbray. F. F. Jeffers.	627	Peter Reilly, ...	Catherine Hudson and others,	Ballygarragh, ...

PROVINCE OF

COUNTY OF

Names of Assistant Commissioners by whom Cases were decided.	No.	Name of Tenant.	Name of Landlord.	Townland.
Assistant Commissioners— M. T. Crean (Legal). F. O'Callaghan. John Wilson.	7463	Thomas Norton, ...	Bernard W. Bagot and anor., Trustees of C. H. Bagot, deceased.	Emmafield, ...
	7464	Peter J. Crehan and anor.,	John Blakeney, ...	Gallagh, ...
	7465	Mathew Crehan (Mark),	John Fallon, ...	Ruckenstown, ...
	7466	Pat Donnelly, ...	do.	do. ...
	7467	John Mulligan, ...	do.	do. ...
	7468	Pat Fallon, ...	do.	do. ...
	7469	Catherine Crehan, Ltd. Admix. of Martin Crehan, deceased.	do.	do. ...
	7470	John Cunningham, ...	do.	do. ...
	7471	James Conway, ...	do.	do. ...
	7472	John Crehan (Mark), ...	do.	do. ...
	7473	Patrick Tully, ...	do.	do. ...
	7474	Mary Crehan, Limited Admix. of John Crehan, deceased.	do.	do. ...
	7475	Jno. Cunningham (Larry),	do.	do. ...

WICKLOW.

43 3 9	16 5 0	25 10 0

CONNAUGHT.

GALWAY.

31 1 13	7 5 0	9 12 0
18 9 18	16 0 0	17 6 6
5 9 27	3 15 0	3 12 0
21 1 0	4 0 0	6 15 6
7 3 20	3 16 0	4 16 6
7 3 8	4 0 0	4 11 6
8 0 16	4 0 0	4 15 5
9 0 24	4 0 0	4 16 5
4 0 21	8 8 0	8 7 8
4 3 33	1 16 0	9 7 4

Names of Assistant Commissioners by whom Cases were decided.	No.	Name of Tenant.	Name of Landlord.
Assistant Commissioners—			
M. T. Crean (Legal). F. O'Callaghan. J. Wigham.	7476	William Cunningham, ...	John Fallon, ...
	7477	Thomas Devine, ...	do. ...
	7478	John Ward, ...	do. ...
	7479	Peter Ward, ...	do. ...
	7480	John Martin, ...	do. ...
	7481	Pat Ward, ...	do. ...
	7482	Honor Crehan, ...	do. ...
	7483	Mary Crehan, Limited Admix. of John Crehan, deceased.	do. ...
	7484	Pat Conway, ...	do. ...
	7485	John Crehan (Tom), ...	do. ...
	7486	Ellen Crehan, Rep. of Owen Crehan.	do. ...
	7487	Thomas Cunningham, ...	do. ...
	7488	Michael White, ...	do. ...
	7489	Michael Cunningham, ...	do. ...
	7490	Pat Crehan, ...	do. ...
	7491	Catherine Cunningham,	do. ...
	7492	John Casey, ...	Bernard W. Regan as Trustee of Will of Regan, deceased.
	7493	Michael Naughton, ...	do. ...
	7494	Roger Lennon, ...	do. ...
	7495	Mathew Hogan, ...	do. ...
	7496	Catherine Nolan, ...	do. ...
	7497	Thomas Smyth, ...	do. ...
	7498	Michael Geraghty, ...	do. ...
	7499	Patrick Connolly, ...	do. ...
	7500	John Nolan, ...	do. ...
	7501	Thomas Devany, ...	do. ...
	7502	John Nolan, ...	do. ...
	7503	Patrick Connolly, ...	do. ...
	7504	Michael Clarke, ...	do. ...
	7505	Martin Gurley, ...	do. ...
	7506	Thomas Clarke, ...	do. ...
	7507	Martin Finnerun, ...	do. ...

GALWAY—*continued.*

Extent of Holding. Statute.	Poor Law Valuation.	Former Rent.	Judicial Rent.	Observations.	Value of Tenancy.
A. R. P.	£ s. d.	£ s. d.	£ s. d.		£ s. d.
14 0 27	5 15 0	7 0 6	5 10 0		
16 2 20	5 10 0	6 12 4	5 0 0		
7 1 0	6 0 0	6 10 5	2 16 0		
6 2 10	5 0 0	3 12 5	2 18 0		
11 0 34	6 0 0	8 14 9	4 16 0		
6 3 21	4 10 0	6 5 7	3 12 6		
10 2 20	4 18 0	6 9 6	4 13 0		
7 3 9	4 0 0	4 15 5	3 4 0		
6 2 10	4 0 0	4 15 5	5 10 0		
7 2 34	4 0 0	4 15 5	3 5 0		
2 1 31	4 0 0	4 15 5	3 14 0		
9 1 38	4 0 0	4 15 5	3 10 0		
8 1 10	4 0 0	5 16 5	3 10 0		
8 2 28	4 0 0	5 16 5	3 15 0		
9 0 13	4 0 0	5 16 7	3 4 0		
7 2 21	4 0 0	4 7 3	3 0 0		
2 3 31	1 5 0	3 0 4	2 0 0		
9 3 38	3 5 0	8 15 0	3 12 0		
9 3 34	5 10 0	5 5 0	4 5 0		
7 1 38	3 0 0	2 7 8	2 7 6		
21 2 23	12 15 0	16 12 0	11 10 0		
23 2 20	11 0 0	14 15 8	12 0 0		
16 3 23	5 10 0	6 3 8	3 5 0		
11 1 16	6 15 0	5 7 6	6 5 0		
67 0 20	9 10 0	7 13 8	7 12 6		
18 0 27	7 5 0	6 5 11	6 5 0		
36 2 7	12 15 0	14 0 0	10 0 0		
12 1 27	3 18 0	2 2 0	1 5 0		
40 0 0	18 10 0	23 4 2	17 10 0		
35 3 23	15 5 0	20 17 6	17 0 0		
18 0 6	7 5 0	7 6 0	5 0 0		
10 0 37	3 5 0	4 0 0	3 0 0		
10 0 19	5 10 0	5 16 0	3 10 0		
23 2 20	6 5 0	7 12 0	5 18 0		

COUNTY OF

Names of Assistant Commissioners by whom Cases were decided.	No.	Name of Tenant.	Name of Landlord.	Townland.
Assistant Commissioners—	7510	Patrick Dungan & anor.,	Robert B. Smyth,	Lisnabogan,
M. T. Cronan (Legal).	7511	Do.,	do.	do.
F. O'Callaghan.	7512	Martin Toole,	do.	do.
J. Wilson.	7513	Patrick Cunningham,	Thomas Cornwall,	Baggnaun,
	7514	Bridget Burke,	Howard Chevalier,	Clonebride,
	7515	Mary Flynn,	Michael J. Clemens,	Lisduff, West,
	7516	Peter Shaughnessy,	do.	do.
	7517	Michael Killeen,	do.	do.
	7518	Patrick Martin,	do.	do.
	7519	Martin Mitchell,	Captain John Blakeney,	Ashfield,
	7520	Ellen Manning,	Sir John Bradstreet, Bart.,	Carradell,
	7521	Michael Rohan,	Marquis of Clanricarde,	Oldling,
	7522	Catherine Connor, Ltd. Admix. of Thomas Connor,	do.	do.
	7523	Michael Egan,	do.	do.
	7524	Thomas Shiel,	Thomas Greene,	Gortnamona,
	7525	Michael Shiel,	do.	do.
	7526	Thomas Hanrahan,	do.	Ardevary,
	7527	Pat Gavin,	Barry Grehan and another,	Gallagh,
	7528	Peter Fallon,	Earl of Clancarty,	Killygrove,
	7529	Do.,	do.	Poolboy,
	7530	John Cogavin,	do.	Moher,
	7531	Joseph Dowling,	do.	Carrowreagh, Upr.,
	7532	Do.,	do.	do.
	7533	Michael Griffin,	W. A. H. Ussher and anor., Trustees of Will of Christopher Ussher, deceased,	Corraslin,
	7534	Patrick Biggins,	do.	do.
	7535	Mary Kennedy, Ltd. Admix. of Thomas Kennedy, deceased,	do.	Ballintaber,
	7536	Brian Connell,	do.	Ballintaber, East,
	7537	Mary Tarpy,	do.	do.
	7538	Bryan Monaghan,	do.	do.
	7539	Michael Sheridan,	do.	do.
	7540	John Ward,	The National Bank,	Baronsville,
	7541	Michael Ward,	do.	do.
	7542	Hugh Hehir,	do.	do.

GALWAY—*continued.*

Extent of Holding. Statute.	Poor Law Valuation.	Former Rent.	Judicial Rent.	Observations.	Value of Tenancy.
A. R. P.	£ s. d.	£ s. d.	£ s. d.		£ s. d.
19 2 0	unascertained.	7 0 0	4 10 0		
24 0 5	18 0 0	20 5 5	14 10 0		
24 1 7	8 5 0	16 1 5	8 5 0		
10 0 0	1 12 0	3 10 0	2 10 0		
3 1 20	1 5 0	2 0 0	1 10 0		
7 3 33	6 10 0	8 10 0	3 17 0		
13 0 24	6 15 0	7 8 6	5 0 0		
7 1 21	4 15 0	5 4 5	3 14 0		
3 3 0	3 0 0	4 5 4	3 10 0		
5 3 20	4 15 0	5 6 8	3 15 0		
4 1 8	2 9 0	2 8 0	1 15 0		
21 1 16	11 5 0	11 0 0	8 0 0		
16 3 26	9 0 0	7 16 8	6 10 0		
11 1 34	6 0 0	8 10 0	4 15 0		
15 3 0	10 5 0	11 10 5	8 15 0		
31 1 25	15 15 0	21 0 5	17 0 0		
22 3 35	10 0 0	13 7 0	9 10 0		
24 3 0	14 0 0	15 10 0	13 0 0		
4 0 30	3 5 0	3 10 0	1 17 0		
13 0 35	13 0 0	13 13 6	11 10 0		
16 2 11	5 10 0	9 14 10	5 0 0		
24 0 0	10 15 0	14 15 0	13 0 0		
107 0 18	67 0 0	120 0 0	70 0 0		
16 2 0	5 0 0	6 0 0	3 15 0		
15 0 7	6 10 0	8 5 0	5 0 0		
9 3 12	4 15 0	5 8 6	4 4 0		
1 3 10	0 15 0	3 0 0	1 1 0		
11 3 3	4 0 0	5 5 0	4 0 0		
21 3 15	6 15 0	11 15 5	7 15 0		
6 3 15	5 0 0	5 3 0	3 15 0		
3 1 28	3 0 0	3 0 0	1 18 0	And the right of grazing two collops on mountain in common with five other persons.	
2 0 18	2 15 0	4 0 0	2 0 0	do.	
4 2 20	1 10 0	2 13 0	1 6 0	And the right of grazing one collop over [illegible] Mountain.	

COUNTY OF

Names of Assistant Commissioners by whom Cases were decided.	No.	Name of Tenant.	Name of Landlord.	Townland.
Assistant Commissioners—				
M. T. Crean (Legal). T. O'Callaghan. J. Wilson.	7543	Michael Manning, ...	Lord Clonbrock, ...	Knockawn, ...
	7544	John Connelly, ...	do.	do. ...
	7545	Bridget Hardiman, ...	do.	do. ...
	7546	Catherine Hardiman, ...	do.	Gortlough, ...
	7547	Thomas Calleran, ...	do.	Cappamaginan,
	7548	Pat Hobbins, ...	do.	do. ...
	7549	Michael Kennedy, ...	do.	do. ...
	7550	Pat Head, ...	do.	Gortkeeva, ...
	7551	Bridget Reilly, ...	do.	Lisnabrogue, ...
				Total, ...

COUNTY OF

Names of Assistant Commissioners by whom Cases were decided.	No.	Name of Tenant.	Name of Landlord.	Townland.
Assistant Commissioners—	7969	John Bourke, ...	John N. Farrell, ...	Annaghdaugh, ...
R. O. MacDermott (Legal). J. Martin. T. Hall.	7970	Thomas McHugh, ...	do.	Bentigue, ...
	7971	Myles Walsh, ...	Marquis of Sligo, ...	Carrowkeel, ...
	7972	Darby Duffy, ...	Lord Ardilaun, ...	Drumshiel, Lower,
	7973	Do., ...	do.	do. ...
	7974	Hubert Jennings, ...	Alexander C. Lambert, ...	Lynch's Acres,
	7975	Richard Jennings, ...	do.	do. ...
	7976	Michael Kyne, ...	Charles Lynch, ...	Gortbrack, ...
	7977	Michael Kyne (Burke),	do.	do. ...
	7978	Pat Whelan, ...	do.	do. ...
	7979	Thomas Joyce, ...	do.	do. ...
	7980	Mary Canavan, ...	do.	do. ...
	7981	Thomas Moore, ...	do.	do. ...
	7982	John Prendergast, ...	Lord Clanmorris, ...	Rathmoncarry, ...
	7983	Henry Lenkin, ...	do.	do. ...
	7984	Thomas Lenkin, ...	do.	do. ...
	7985	Anthony Joyce, ...	do.	Curry McMoane,
	7986	Michael Heveran, ...	do.	Curryhirna and another,
	7987	James Prendergast, ...	do.	Curry McMoane,
	7988	Michael McCoy, ...	do.	Cashel, ...

GALWAY—*continued.*

Content of Holdings. Statute.	Poor Law Valuation.	Former Rent.	Judicial Rent.	Observations.
A. R. P.	£ s. d.	£ s. d.	£ s. d.	
23 2 6	8 16 0	6 18 6	8 18 6	
16 0 10	9 6 0	8 15 8	7 0 0	
17 3 1	11 0 0	9 0 0	8 0 0	
29 1 30	18 5 0	16 0 0	10 0 0	
20 3 8	9 8 0	7 18 5	7 0 0	
27 0 33	14 0 0	18 0 0	11 0 0	
16 0 13	8 10 0	8 0 0	7 0 0	
26 0 10	11 10 0	13 6 0	11 0 0	
23 0 23	18 10 0	18 4 0	11 5 0	
1,254 2 16	698 2 0	751 18 5	670 16 8	

MAYO.

18 3 3	7 10 0	6 10 0	5 18 0	
14 1 30	7 5 0	6 0 0	8 0 0	
24 1 38	9 10 0	8 0 0	7 0 0	
14 0 14	4 5 0	5 15 0	5 0 0	
8 0 19	7 10 0	1 7 4	3 13 0	
3 1 17	8 0 0	6 7 5	3 8 0	
7 1 11	4 0 0	6 5 8	4 0 0	
8 2 26	4 0 0	4 0 0	3 0 0	
6 0 13	5 5 0	3 5 0	1 3 0	
17 0 37	7 10 0	7 8 6	1 0 0	
13 1 35	7 15 0	7 2 6	5 10 0	
3 0 6	4 0 0	4 0 0	2 3 0	
8 3 4	8 0 0	3 0 0	1 3 0	
13 1 6	10 0 0	9 0 0	7 3 0	
21 0 11	9 10 0	8 0 0	7 0 0	
17 1 34	9 10 0	8 0 0	6 15 0	
9 3 10	4 15 0	5 10 6	4 10 0	
10 3 33	8 0 0	7 5 0	6 0 0	
21 3 31	10 8 0	9 10 0	8 10 0	
27 1 30	19 6 0	18 0 0	14 10 0	

COUNTY OF

Names of Assistant Commissioners by whom Cases were decided.	No.	Name of Tenant.	Name of Landlord.	Townland.
Assistant Commissioners—				
E. O. MacDevitt (Legal). J. Mahon. T. Hall.	7989	Pat Hynes,	Lord Clanmorris,	Carrowmenny,
	7990	James McHugh,	do.	Lisheenagh,
	7991	John Dun,	do.	Rathmurren,
	7992	Martin Hughes,	do.	do.
	7993	John O'Gara, Ltd. Admor. of Michael O'Dight,	do.	do.
	7994	John Burke,	do.	do.
	7995	Pat Noone,	Joseph M. Mahon,	Moorin,
	7996	Thomas Dyron,	do.	do.
	7997	Martin Barrett,	do.	do.
	7998	James Naughton,	do.	do.
	7999	Pat McTigue,	Colonel C. H. Knox,	Glynard,
	8000	Laurence Tierney,	do.	do.
	8001	James Thornton,	do.	do.
	8002	Thomas Walsh,	do.	Cloonlibber,
	8003	Patrick Killeen,	do.	do.
	8004	Pat Molloy, Ltd. Admor. of Thomas Molloy,	Lord Dillon,	Corraun,
	8005	Michael Finn,	do.	do.
	8006	Catherine Fureey,	do.	Gortaugarragh,
	8007	Bridget Eagan, Ltd. Admix. of James Eagan,	do.	Churchfield,
	8008	Bryan Byrne,	do.	Ballyroe undivided,
	8009	Bridget Byrne,	do.	do.
	8010	William Waldron,	do.	do.
	8011	Thomas Eagan,	do.	Callowbrack,
	8012	John Kearns,	do.	do.
	8013	Pat Lyons,	do.	Ballyroe,
	8014	Bridget Givern,	do.	Gortaugarragh & meadow,
	8015	Pat Waldron,	do.	do.
	8016	Thomas Cribbin,	do.	do.
	8017	John Finn,	do.	Gortmalcorn,
	8018	Michael Lydon,	do.	Forthill,
	8019	John Clyne, senior,	do.	Bargarriff,
	8020	Patrick Hunt,	do.	Kinaghard,
	8021	John Kilroy,	do.	Tavraghmore,
	8022	James Waldron,	do.	Drumkissane, South,
	8023	Martin Comber,	do.	Killsaler,

MAYO—*continued.*

Extent of Holding. Statute.	Poor Law Valuation.	Former Rent.	Judicial Rent.	Observations.	Value of Tenancy.
A. R. P.	£ s. d.	£ s. d.	£ s. d.		£ s. d.
8 3 20	8 7 0	8 14 0	8 0 0		
18 2 20	8 13 0	10 19 0	8 0 0		
16 8 6	8 10 0	8 0 0	8 10 0		
18 3 17	7 6 0	6 18 8	5 10 0		
21 1 19	10 15 6	16 10 0	15 10 0		
24 1 7	8 10 0	8 0 0	6 10 0		
24 1 7	6 8 0	9 9 0	5 10 0		
24 1 7	5 3 0	8 9 0	6 10 0		
32 0 10	16 5 0	16 16 6	9 10 0		
37 3 20	17 10 0	18 17 6	8 15 0		
7 3 30	8 0 0	8 5 0	8 18 0		
15 3 27	7 5 0	8 0 0	5 0 0		
15 0 9	7 5 0	8 0 0	4 10 0		
18 0 18	8 15 0	10 10 0	6 0 0		
7 0 16	5 0 0	8 10 0	8 8 0		
12 0 25	6 13 0	7 15 8	6 0 0		
19 0 37	5 8 0	8 12 0	4 0 0		
20 1 0	7 12 0	7 10 6	6 10 0		
17 2 14	6 10 0	6 8 0	5 0 0		
13 8 0	8 6 0	7 6 6	8 16 0		
18 2 18	7 15 0	8 11 5	7 10 0		
20 0 17	9 16 0	18 1 8	8 5 0		
18 0 11	6 5 0	8 5 0	5 10 6		
15 2 26	6 10 0	7 8 6	5 0 0		
18 3 0	6 8 0	7 2 6	5 14 0		
13 8 27	4 8 0	6 10 0	8 10 0		
19 2 17	6 8 0	6 9 10	9 10 0		
10 3 12	8 17 0	3 6 6	9 10 0		
27 1 20	7 5 0	7 13 0	6 7 0		
8 2 30	8 8 0	8 1 8	2 5 0		
26 8 15	4 9 0	6 17 10	6 0 0		
18 0 0	3 16 0	3 15 0	8 8 0		
15 8 8	8 11 0	3 1 5	2 5 0		
40 5 0	5 6 0	7 0 6	4 13 0		
23 3 6	4 2 0	4 6 0	3 16 0		

COUNTY OF

Names of Assistant Commissioners by whom Cases were decided.	No.	Name of Tenant.	Name of Landlord.	Townland.
Assistant Commissioners—				
E. O. MacDevitt (Legal). J. Marris. T. Hall.	8024	James Murphy,	Lord Dillon,	[illegible],
	8025	Patrick Dowry,	do.	do.
	8026	Mary Higgins, senr., Ltd. Admix. of John Higgins.	do.	[illegible],
	8027	Thomas Brehany, Ltd. Admx. of Murragh Brehany.	do.	[illegible],
E. O. MacDevitt (Legal). A. R. Montgomery. W. G. De La Poer.	8028	Martin Mulroy,	Barber E. [illegible],	[illegible],
	8029	John Donnelly,	do.	do.
	8030	Bridget Kelly, Ltd. Admix. of John Kelly.	Lord Clanmorris,	Limehurst,
	8031	John Walsh,	J. Fitzgerald Mahon,	Polliken,
	8032	Patrick Kirby,	do.	do.
	8033	Patrick Kelly,	do.	do.
	8034	Bridget Kelly, Ltd. Admix. of Peter Kelly.	do.	do.
	8035	Michael Bourk,	do.	do.
	8036	Pat Gibbins,	Charles L. Fitzgerald,	[illegible],
	8037	James Mullohen,	Miss Harriet Gardiner,	Kilmeane,
	8038	Patrick Devaney,	do.	Kilmeane & ann.,
	8039	Thomas Irwin,	do.	[illegible],
	8040	Mary Duffy and ann.,	do.	do.
	8041	Luke Lennon and ann.,	do.	[illegible],
	8042	Martin Conway,	do.	do.
	8043	James Walsh (Redmond),	do.	Lower Deerpark,
	8044	Martin Walsh,	do.	Higher and Lower Deerpark.
	8045	Martin Walsh (James),	do.	do.
	8046	Martin Henaghan,	do.	do.
	8047	Thomas Conway and ann.,	do.	do.
	8048	Thomas Tuohy,	Earl of Norbury,	Lack, East,
	8049	Mary Jordan, Ltd. Admix. of Patrick Jordan.	do.	do.
	8050	Patrick Doyle,	do.	Ballygarriff,
	8051	John Barrett,	do.	do.
	8052	Pat Flynn, Ltd. Admor. of John Flynn.	G. B. Miller and another,	Carrowkeel,
	8053	James Simmons, Rep. of Austin Simmons.	do.	do.
	8054	Bridget Stenson, Ltd. Admix. of Pat Stenson.	do.	do.
	8055	Pat Gannon,	do.	do.
	8056	Pat Mitchell,	do.	do.

MAYO—*continued.*

Extent of Holding. Statute.	Poor Law Valuation.	Former Rent.	Judicial Rent.	Observations.	Value of Tenancy.
A. R. P.	£ s. d.	£ s. d.	£ s. d.		£ s. d.
24 2 5	0 11 0	1 1 0	1 1 0		
19 0 9	1 12 0	2 4 0	1 17 0		
18 1 20	5 16 0	6 2 0	3 10 0		
12 3 16	3 17 0	6 8 7	4 0 0		
1 0 0	0 15 0	0 19 2	0 16 0		
4 0 0	2 7 0	2 0 0	1 10 0		
10 0 12	1 10 0	2 0 0	1 16 0		
19 0 30	6 16 0	6 0 0	5 0 0		
0 3 3	0 10 0	1 0 0	0 18 0		
15 2 0	6 0 0	5 0 0	4 0 0		
16 3 17	7 0 0	8 10 0	7 7 0		
9 3 26	5 15 0	4 5 0	3 0 0		
7 0 0	3 10 0	4 0 0	3 10 0		
6 0 16	3 16 0	5 0 2	3 16 0		
16 3 30	8 0 0	18 10 0	8 16 0		
16 3 17	7 4 0	8 1 6	6 15 0		
16 3 28	7 10 0	8 1 6	7 0 0		
11 2 20	6 10 0	6 10 0	4 12 0		
11 3 16	6 10 0	6 10 0	4 15 0		
9 0 22	3 16 0	3 13 4	3 10 0		
5 2 3	3 18 6	2 15 0	2 0 0		
4 0 33	2 0 0	2 6 0	1 17 0		
3 1 20	4 0 0	0 16 0	3 0 0		
21 0 27	6 15 0	6 17 6	5 15 0		
11 0 3	6 0 0	4 0 0	4 3 3		
18 2 30	8 13 0	5 0 3	5 0 2		
21 0 24	9 0 0	5 2 2	6 2 3		
19 0 26	7 10 0	7 10 2	7 10 7		
10 3 32	5 12 0	5 16 0	5 5 0		
10 3 6	6 7 6	6 0 10	5 10 0		
27 2 14	16 10 0	12 1 4	11 15 0		
9 3 11	5 0 0	6 5 10	5 5 0		
17 0 10	6 0 0	10 4 8	8 0 0		

COUNTY OF

Names of Assistant Commissioners by whom Cases were decided.	No.	Name of Tenant.	Name of Landlord.	Townland.
Assistant Commissioners—				
R. O. MacDevitt (Legal). A. R. Montgomery. W. O. De La Poer.	8057	Thomas McMaguire, ...	Sir R. H. Palmer, Bart., ...	Baltra, ...
	8058	Martin McTigue, ...	do.	do. ...
	8059	Mathew Fahey, ...	do.	do. ...
	8060	Catherine Flannery, ...	do.	do. ...
	8061	Thomas Flannery, Limited Admor. of M. Flannery.	do.	do. ...
	8062	Mary Flynn, ...	do.	do. ...
	8063	Owen Flannery, ...	do.	do. ...
	8064	John McLoughlin, ...	do.	do. ...
	8065	Pat Lally, ...	do.	do. ...
	8066	Bridget Doherty, ...	do.	do. ...
	8067	Richard Flannery, ...	do.	do. ...
				Total, ...

COUNTY OF

Assistant Commissioners— M. T. Gerety (Legal). H. G. Gardner. W. N. Martin.	4138	Pat Murray and another,	Colonel E. R. King-Harman, continued in name of Frances A. King-Harman,	Kingsland, ...
	4139	John Burns, ...	Luke Fallon, ...	Ballyconboirne,
	4140	Stephen Barrett, ...	Robert Caddell, ...	Scrabbagh, ...
	4141	James Collins, ...	do.	Cranin, ...
	4142	John Collins, ...	do.	do. ...
	4143	Mary Reynolds, ...	do.	Carrowcorr, ...
	4144	John Madden, ...	do.	do. ...
	4145	Michael Callary, ...	Lord Crofton, ...	Boherroe, ...
	4146	Do.	do.	Cartron, ...
	4147	Henry McDermott, Limited Admor. of Honoria McDermott, deceased,	do.	Cregganbeg, ...
	4148	Mark P. McDermott, ...	Mrs. Petronella Whyte, ...	Mountfield and another.
	4149	Bernard Dowd, ...	Henry William G. Crofton,	Culleenatreen, ...
	4150	Martin Dowd, ...	do.	do. ...
	4151	Patrick O'Dowd, ...	do.	do. ...
	4152	Thomas B. Cahill, ...	do.	do. ...
	4153	Maria Kerans (Widow),	do.	do. ...
	4154	Catherine Bryan, ...	do.	do. ...

MAYO—*continued.*

Extent of Holding, Statute.	Poor Law Valuation.	Former Rent.	Judicial Rent.	Observations.	Value of Tenancy.
A. R. P.	£ s. d.	£ s. d.	£ s. d.		£ s. d.
[illegible] 0 [illegible]	8 10 0	8 0 0	3 0 0	With commons of grazing over 267 acres with twenty others.	
[illegible] 0 15	4 0 0	5 0 0	4 5 0	do.	
[illegible] 3 27	4 0 0	6 5 0	4 10 0	do.	
[illegible] 3 [illegible]	6 0 0	7 15 0	6 15 0	do.	
46 1 14	8 15 0	7 10 0	5 12 0	do.	
[illegible] 0 34	2 15 0	3 10 0	2 15 0	do.	
[illegible] 2 10	4 10 0	5 15 0	4 16 0	do.	
43 2 1	6 5 0	7 0 0	6 0 0	do.	
30 1 20	3 10 0	8 5 0	4 12 0	do.	
67 1 8	5 10 0	4 10 0	3 10 0	do.	
80 5 [illegible]	3 15 0	5 0 0	4 0 0	do.	
1,7[illegible] 3 21	3[illegible] 2 3	645 12 8	4[illegible] 16 6		

ROSCOMMON.

8 2 20	5 0 0	5 10 0	4 4 0		
9 3 20	4 0 0	6 0 0	3 10 0		
9 2 0	3 5 0	4 4 0	3 10 0		
91 1 7	10 15 0	20 10 6	9 0 0		
57 1 18	14 20 0	17 1 6	14 10 0		
[illegible] 0 6	11 12 0	18 0 0	16 10 0		
15 1 30	18 8 0	14 6 0	10 10 0		
9 0 5	6 5 0	7 12 0	6 10 0		
9 3 35	7 0 0	8 8 5	6 15 0		
72 1 7	66 0 0	[illegible] 9 1	[illegible] 9 1		
33 3 15	15 10 0	34 11 8	43 0 0		
13 1 20	10 15 0	10 5 8	6 10 0		
16 0 20	9 0 0	10 0 0	7 10 0		
60 5 0	21 5 0	22 16 0	18 0 0		
18 3 8	11 15 0	13 0 0	8 0 0		
37 2 [illegible]	14 15 0	10 13 0	10 10 0		
42 3 64	20 0 0	[illegible] 10 6	18 0 6		

COUNTY OF

Names of Assistant Commissioners by whom Cases were decided.	No.	Name of Tenant.	Name of Landlord.	Townland.
Assistant Commissioners—				
M. T. Crean (Legal). H. G. Gregory. W. N. Magill.	4155	Margaret Donoher, ...	Henry William G. Grafton,	Cashelmuirane, ...
	4156	Michael Keally, ...	do.	do. ...
	4157	Owen Monaghan, ...	Countess of Kingston, ...	Foxhill, ...
	4158	Thomas Monaghan, ...	do.	do. ...
	4159	Pat Sweeney, ...	do.	Moyrane, ...
	4160	Margaret McGreevy, ...	do.	Tonroe, ...
	4161	Patk. Hegarty, Assignee of Catherine Hegarty.	do.	do. ...
	4162	Edward McGreevy, ...	do.	do. ...
	4163	Sarah Boland, Ltd. Admix. of Jas. Boland, decd.	do.	do. ...
	4164	Patrick Shannon, ...	Colonel E. R. King-Harman, continued in name of Frances A. King-Harman.	Lisnadera, ...
	4165	Nicholas Crummin, ...	do.	do. ...
	4166	Owen McGreevy, ...	Mrs. G. G. B. Whyte, ...	Tonmore, ...
	4167	Bernard Meenahan, ...	Mrs. Petronella Whyte, ...	Cloonamane, ...
	4168	Frances Cox, ...	Hon. George Greville, ...	Corbeg, ...
	4169	James Cox, ...	do.	do. ...
	4170	James Lloyd, ...	do.	Lemagh, ...
	4171	Michael Doyle, ...	do.	do. ...
	4172	Edward Cannon, ...	do.	do. ...
	4173	Thomas McLoughlin, ...	do.	Corry, ...
				Total, ...

COUNTY OF

Assistant Commissioners—	3618	James Kennedy, ...	J. P. McFadden, ...	Moyvore, East,
R. O. MacDermott (Legal). A. R. Montgomery. W. G. De La Poer.	3619	John O'B. Brabazon, ...	do.	do. ...
	3620	Hugh McLoughlin, ...	do.	do. ...
	3621	Michael Conlon, ...	do	Coolagarry, ...
	3622	Bernard Mullaney, ...	do.	Moyvore, East,
	3623	John Devine, ...	do.	do. ...

ROSCOMMON—*continued.*

Extent of Holding. Statute.	Poor Law Valuation.	Former Rent.	Judicial Rent.	Observations.	Value of Tenancy.
A. R. P.	£ s. d.	£ s. d.	£ s. d.		£ s. d.
17 1 20	17 15 0	19 11 10	10 10 0		
25 1 27	25 5 0	25 6 8	19 0 0		
47 3 27	20 10 0	25 0 0	16 10 0		
21 1 26	9 10 0	10 0 0	8 0 0		
28 3 25	10 5 0	9 14 0	8 0 0		
4 0 20	*—	8 14 0	1 12 6	* An undivided moiety of £3 15s.	
16 0 27	12 0 0	10 10 0	9 0 0		
8 3 13	3 0 0	3 0 8	2 5 0		
23 0 9	6 15 0	8 16 4	6 13 0		
16 3 7	9 5 0	10 3 8	9 0 0		
10 3 8	6 15 0	8 4 0	6 0 0		
11 0 5	7 15 0	11 9 1	7 10 0		
14 2 15	11 5 0	14 11 5	10 10 0		
9 3 20	6 5 0	6 17 0	5 15 0		
16 2 0	5 0 0	8 14 6	5 15 0		
15 3 25	10 0 0	11 6 0	9 10 0		
12 3 30	10 0 0	11 13 0	10 0 0		
9 2 10	4 5 0	5 5 0	4 0 0		
10 3 20	5 0 0	5 17 8	7 5 0		
727 0 25	480 5 0	502 15 4	415 8 7		

SLIGO.

COUNTY OF

Names of Assistant Commissioners by whom Cases were heard.	No.	Name of Tenant.	Name of Landlord.	Townland.
Assistant Commissioners—				
E. O. MacDevitt (Legal). A. R. Montgomery. W. G. De La Poer.	3624	John Conlan, ...	J. P. McFadden, ...	Drumbeg, West,
	3625	Michael Flynn and anor., Reps. of Patrick Flynn and another,	do.	Drumbeg, South,
	3626	John Harte, Rep. of Thady Harte,	do.	do. ...
	3627	John Burns, ...	do.	Cashelearly, ...
	3628	John Conlan, ...	J. F. H. Betts and others, Exors. of J. McDonagh	Cashmore, ...
	3629	Fitzmaurice Devine, ...	do.	Ballyfarnon, ...
				Total, ...

PROVINCE OF

COUNTY OF

Assistant Commissioners—	4591	Elizabeth Quinlivan, ...	Patrick M. Collins, ...	Lavalla, ...
J. S. Green (Legal). J. Armstrong. J. Carr.	4592	William O'Dea, ...	do.	do. ...
	4593	Thomas Hehir, ...	Lord Leconfield, ...	Lemna, ...
	4594	Thomas O'Gorman, ...	do.	Inishdadrid, ...
	4595	James Griffin, ...	do.	Lemna, ...
	4596	William Edwards, ...	John C. Scott, ...	Ballymacrinny, ...
	4597	John Malone, ...	do.	Shanakeamore, ...
	4598	Thomas O'Dea, ...	do.	do. ...
	4599	James Chambers, ...	Burdett Barclay and another,	Ballygeery, East,
	4600	Patrick Collins, ...	John Considine, ...	Furroor, ...
	4601	Patrick King, ...	Thomas R. Hone, ...	Shervinsley, ...
	4602	Martin Coughlan, ...	do.	Spa, ...
	4603	James O'Connor and anor.,	do.	Ballyvorig, ...
	4604	John Loughnane, ...	do.	Ballingaddy, ...
	4605	John Keane, ...	John C. Scott, ...	Shanakeamore, ...
	4606	Patrick Carey, ...	do.	do. ...
	4607	Patrick O'Connor, ...	Colonel White, ...	Collins, ...

SLIGO—*continued*.

Extent of Holding, Statute.	Poor Law Valuation.	Former Rent.	Judicial Rent.	Observations.	Value of Tenancy.
A. R. P.	£ s. d.	£ s. d.	£ s. d.		£ s. d.
[illegible] 2 0	[illegible] 5 0	63 7 10	[illegible] 0 0		
84 1 [illegible]	19 0 0	81 6 6	16 5 0		
[illegible] 0 [illegible]	18 0 0	[illegible] 1 5	18 0 0		
13 1 19	8 16 6	9 1 10	7 5 6		
14 0 [illegible]	31 7 0	18 0 0	15 0 0		
[illegible] 3 18	[illegible] 16 0	46 16 0	80 6 0		
416 1 24	311 2 0	[illegible] 17 6	316 0 0		

MUNSTER.

CLARE.

49 0 0	[illegible] 0 0	[illegible] 10 6	44 0 0		
6 1 20	6 5 0	5 10 0	3 3 0		
43 1 [illegible]	[illegible] 0 0	[illegible] 10 0	18 0 0		
[illegible] 0 16	[illegible] 4 0	180 17 2	[illegible] 10 0		
[illegible] 1 18	10 0 0	11 5 6	8 0 0		
24 1 0	19 18 0	[illegible] 0 0	16 18 0		
24 1 10	20 10 0	12 16 3	7 13 0		
5 1 33	1 10 0	8 10 6	1 15 0		
20 0 16	10 13 0	13 11 0	9 0 0		
7 2 [illegible]	(unvalued),	3 0 0	2 0 0		
64 1 [illegible]	25 5 0	25 0 0	20 18 0		
8 0 15	1 0 0	8 5 0	1 5 0		
16 3 0	7 15 0	21 0 0	6 0 0		
8 0 0	4 0 0	5 0 3	3 13 6		
18 1 0	6 10 0	9 0 0	7 4 0		
63 1 [illegible]	[illegible] 0 0	24 0 0	20 10 0		
0 3 30	1 5 0	4 0 0	1 5 0		

COUNTY OF

Names of Assistant Commissioners by whom Cases were decided.	No.	Name of Tenant.	Name of Landlord.	Townland.
Assistant Commissioners—				
J. E. Greer (Legal). J. Armstrong. J. Carr.	4608	Bridget Casey, ...	Colonel White, ...	Cailkee, ...
	4609	John Murphy, ...	do.	Caherum, ...
J. E. Greer (Legal). R. R. Kennedy. J. Rice.	4610	Patrick Naughton, ...	Sophia M. Massy and others,	Rylane, ...
				Tool, ...

COUNTY OF

Assistant Commissioners—	4758	Patrick McCarthy, ...	Earl of Bandon, ...	Ballyvorane, ...
L. Doyle (Legal). W. J. Gernon. W. Walpole.	4759	Michael Murphy, ...	Earl of Bantry, ...	Urhan, ...
	4760	Daniel Driscoll, ...	Richard M. Beamish, ...	Lahanaght, ...
	4761	Jerry McCarthy, ...	Richard Beamish, ...	Cappanabohy, ...
	4762	Charles McCarthy, ...	do.	do. ...
	4763	William Driscoll, ...	James O. Beamish, ...	Anglesville, ...
	4764	Denis Grissane, ...	Sir Henry W. Becher, Bart.,	Clashinimud, ...
	4765	Andrew Harrigan, senr.,	do.	do. ...
	4766	Jeremiah Regan, ...	do.	do. ...
	4767	John Hennessy, ...	do.	Balteen, ...
	4768	William Donovan, ...	do.	Kilbrenan and comm.
	4769	Ellen Nolan, ...	do.	Harbour's Mouth,
	4770	Catherine Driscoll, ...	do.	Kilbrown (North),
	4771	William Reilly, ...	do.	do. ...
	4772	Michael Connell, ...	do.	do. ...
	4773	Denis Nolan, ...	do.	do. ...
	4774	George Norris, ...	do.	Farranamanagh, ...
	4775	Bartholomew Desmond,	do.	Clodagh, South,
	4776	Florence Neill, ...	do.	do. ...
	4777	Ellen Regan, ...	do.	do. ...
	4778	Thomas Sullivan, ...	do.	Shreelane, ...
	4779	Michael Desmond, ...	do.	do. ...
	4780	Jeremiah McCarthy, ...	do.	Farranamanagh, ...
	4781	William Tope, ...	do.	do. ...
	4782	Mary Hourihane, Rep. of John Hourihan.	do.	Garranes, ...

CLARE—*continued.*

Extent of Holding. Statute.	Poor Law Valuation.	Former Rent.	Judicial Rent.	Observations.	Value of Tenancy.
a. r. p.	£ s. d.	£ s. d.	£ s. d.		£ s. d.
0 3 25	0 18 0	6 0 0	1 4 0		
4 2 0	unascertained,	3 10 0	2 3 0		
18 1 0	11 8 0	14 2 0	10 0 0		
491 3 1	381 19 0	588 12 1	371 16 0		

CORK.

40 0 0	21 18 0	27 18 6	21 0 0		
30 3 30	5 15 0	11 0 0	8 10 0	By consent.	
47 0 20	8 2 0	20 0 0	15 10 0		
8 2 2	4 15 0	8 10 0	5 0 0		
11 0 8	4 16 0	8 10 0	6 0 0		
37 0 9	23 15 0	31 5 0	31 5 0		
144 1 25	19 10 0	25 1 0	21 0 0		
41 3 4	8 5 0	13 0 0	10 0 0		
5 0 18	1 13 0	3 10 0	2 10 0		
53 1 20	20 0 0	25 0 0	17 0 0		
42 1 0	6 18 0	11 5 0	8 0 0		
31 3 2	8 5 0	0 17 0	8 5 0		
14 2 5	5 5 0	7 10 0	6 0 0		
12 0 0	5 13 0	0 0 0	7 7 6		
60 1 3	6 15 0	7 0 0	6 2 6		
16 0 0	6 5 0	7 0 0	6 0 6		
18 3 25	8 10 0	11 0 0	9 10 0		
20 1 30	5 15 0	9 10 0	7 10 0		
41 1 7	17 5 0	17 5 0	16 0 0		
25 0 31	6 0 0	8 3 6	5 10 0		
50 3 0	12 0 0	14 0 0	11 15 0		
71 3 31	8 10 0	10 0 0	8 10 0		
18 1 30	13 10 0	17 0 0	15 5 0		
31 1 16	11 10 0	14 12 6	12 17 6		
52 3 0	16 18 0	24 0 0	20 10 0		

COUNTY OF

Names of Assistant Commissioners by whom Cases were decided.	No.	Name of Tenant.	Name of Landlord.	Townland.
Assistant Commissioners—				
L. Doyle (Legal). W. J. Gorman. W. Walpole.	4783	Paul Kingston, ...	Sir Henry W. Becher, Bart.	Derrygurran, ...
	4784	William Goggin, ...	do.	Gortnaclogky, ...
	4785	Andrew Harrigan, junior,	do.	Clonakenna, ...
	4786	Patrick Regan, ...	do.	do. ...
	4787	Denis Cadogan, ...	John R. H. Becher, ...	Lissane, ...
	4788	Jeremiah McCarthy, Ltd. Admor. of Johanna McCarthy.	do.	do. ...
	4789	Michael Regan, ...	Mrs. E. M. Clarke, ...	Curraun, ...
	4790	John Brien, ...	Kate Deasy and others, ...	Drumkiddy, ...
	4791	Denis Mahony, ...	do.	Drumkiddy, Nth.
	4792	Cornelius McCarthy, ...	do.	do. ...
	4793	James Burke, ...	Charles Ellis.	Carrughbiney, ...
	4794	Michael Brien, ...	Martha E. Lewis, ...	Minane, ...
	4795	Daniel Donovan, ...	do.	do. ...
	4796	John Brien, ...	do.	do. ...
	4797	William Young, ...	do.	do. ...
	4798	Thomas French and another,	John Morris, ...	Ballyroe & [illegible],
	4799	John Cadogan and another,	Rev. Richard W. Morrison,	Ardagh, ...
	4800	Cornelius Donovan, ...	Mary Mahony and others, Reps. of George Mahony.	Lackey, Lower,
	4801	William Donovan, senior, and another.	William J. Hodges, ...	Carrigtowen, ...
	4802	Pat Brien, and another,	Catherine L. Power, ...	Knockmore, ...
	4803	Mary Wholey, ...	George Robinson, ...	Gurrane, South,
	4804	Timothy Sheehan, ...	Lieut.-Colonel George Roche,	Colom Marsh, ...
	4805	Timothy Walsh, ...	do.	do. ...
	4806	Mary Brien, ...	do.	Hawgers, ...
	4807	Stephen Brien, ...	do.	Drummanaclough,
	4808	Mary Barry, Limited Admix. of Pat Barry.	do.	do. ...
	4809	Patrick Harrigan, ...	do.	do. ...
	4810	Daniel Leary, ...	Robert H. Swanton, ...	Ballyjordan, ...
	4811	William Casey, Rep. of Dominick Casey.	St. Lawrence R. M. Tighe, ...	Big Marsh, ...
	4812	Daniel Driscoll, ...	do.	do. ...
	4813	Bartholomew Leary, ...	Rep. S. D. Wright, ...	Gorrancloghy, ...
	4814	Thomas Driscoll, ...	Joseph Whitehouse, ...	Lahertanavally,
	4815	Jeremiah Sullivan, ...	do.	do. ...
	4816	Daniel Hurley, ...	James Walsh, ...	Gnamelikeile, ...
	4817	James Hayes, ...	do.	do. ...

CORK—*continued.*

Extent of Holding. Statute.	Poor Law Valuation.	Former Rent.	Judicial Rent.	Observations.	Value of Tenancy
A. R. P.	£ s. d.	£ s. d.	£ s. d.		£ s. d.
11 0 0	14 0 0	20 0 0	14 0 0		
8 2 0	1 18 0	4 0 0	3 0 0		
41 8 4	4 5 0	13 0 0	10 0 0		
81 0 23	18 0 0	24 0 0	22 7 0		
25 0 0	9 0 0	12 0 0	10 0 0		
19 1 13	8 15 0	12 0 0	9 5 0		
34 0 22	6 0 0	20 0 0	4 15 0	With right of grazing one beast on mountain.	
84 1 0	9 19 0	22 0 0	17 10 0		
23 0 0	9 15 0	18 0 0	13 10 0		
49 8 30	18 0 0	41 0 0	31 0 0		
7 0 30	—	13 0 0	7 0 0		
11 2 0	4 0 0	6 16 0	3 12 0		
84 0 0	11 0 0	15 17 0	12 15 0		
20 0 0	6 0 0	8 5 0	8 0 0		
70 0 0	33 0 0	27 18 0	22 2 6		
82 0 0	34 0 0	60 0 0	45 0 0		
40 0 0	19 16 0	20 0 0	14 15 0		
7 0 0	0 18 0	4 0 0	2 10 0		
61 0 0	14 15 0	35 0 0	31 0 0		
41 0 0	4 15 0	12 0 0	9 17 6		
80 0 0	18 5 0	18 10 0	16 5 0		
10 0 1	11 10 0	18 0 0	11 0 0		
18 0 0	8 0 0	10 0 0	9 0 0		
35 3 4	17 0 0	21 14 0	16 0 0		
67 3 15	16 15 0	22 0 0	18 15 0		
11 0 25	12 0 0	14 15 0	12 0 0		
23 2 17	12 0 0	16 0 0	11 13 0		
88 0 3	79 10 0	87 0 0	77 10 0		
15 0 0	7 0 0	10 7 0	6 5 0		
14 0 0	9 18 0	10 15 0	0 0 0		
1 0 28	1 0 0	2 0 0	1 12 6		
13 2 24	10 0 0	11 0 0	9 16 0		
21 0 23	11 0 0	12 0 0	10 10 0		
35 0 24	7 5 0	12 0 0	9 0 0		
61 0 09	12 15 0	20 0 0	15 18 6		

COUNTY OF

Names of Assistant Commissioners by whom Cases were decided.	No.	Name of Tenant.	Name of Landlord.	Townland.
Assistant Commissioners—				
L. Doyle (Legal). W. J. Goodman. W. Walpole.	4818	Daniel Leyhane, ...	W. S. Bird and another, ...	Farranaw, ...
	4819	Timothy Sullivan, ...	Kate O'Donovan, ...	Gortnaskilla, ...
	4820	Timothy Riordan, ...	Mrs. Margaret M. McDonald,	Lahevan, ...
L. Doyle (Legal). E. O'Kelly. J. Gubbins.	4821	Maurice Bermingham, ...	Robert C. Bowen, ...	Farraly, ...
	4822	Jeremiah Howard & anor.,	Richard Hutchins, a minor, by S. N. Hutchins, his Guardian, and others.	Pranine, ...
L. Doyle (Legal). E. B. Bayly. O. R. Butler.	4823	Ellen Shinnick, ...	Earl of Listowel, ...	Killacloy, ...
				Total, ...

COUNTY OF

Names of Assistant Commissioners by whom Cases were decided.	No.	Name of Tenant.	Name of Landlord.	Townland.
Assistant Commissioners—	1938	James Hanlon, ...	Lord Monteagle, ...	Ballynorwood, ...
J. H. Rock (Legal). C. O'Keeffe. A. N. Currie.	1939	Michael Fitzgerald, ...	Sir Samuel B. Falls, ...	Ballyglassane, ...
	1940	Michael Buggane, ...	The Knight of Glin, ...	Ballinamaddagh,
	1941	Denis Cregan, junior, ...	do.	Kinnard, ...
	1942	Mary Costelloe, Admix. of Daniel Costelloe.	do.	Ballyglassane, ...
	1943	James Condon, ...	La Marchesa della Rocella, ...	Dromnyhane, ...
	1944	Edmund Sweeny, ...	Godfrey O. C. Massy, ...	Ballinakilbane, ...
	1945	Bridget Riordan, ...	do.	do. ...
	1946	Michael Dalton, ...	Rev. Edward O'Grady, ...	Kilmurrily, ...
	1947	Patrick Sullivan, ...	Godfrey O. Massy, ...	Ballydonnelly, ...
	1948	Daniel Griffin, ...	General Richard Bateson, ...	Loughill, ...
	1949	James Cleary, ...	do.	do. ...
	1950	Mary O'Shaughnessy, ...	do.	do. ...
	1951	James Hanrahan, ...	do.	do. ...
				Total, ...

COUNTY OF

Names of Assistant Commissioners by whom Cases were decided.	No.	Name of Tenant.	Name of Landlord.	Townland.
Assistant Commissioners—				
J. H. Rock (Legal). C. O'Keeffe. A. N. Currie.	2530	William Moriarty, ...	Earl of Donoughmore, ...	Newtown Mahon

CORK—*continued.*

Extent of Holding. Statute.	Poor Law Valuation.	Former Rent.	Judicial Rent.	Observations.	Value of Tenancy.
A. R. P.	£ s. d.	£ s. d.	£ s. d.		£ s. d.
33 0 10	17 18 0	23 0 0	20 0 0	With right of grazing on mountain.	
23 3 39	18 6 0	19 18 0	16 10 0	do.	
13 1 31	7 10 0	9 10 0	9 0 0		
45 2 0	31 16 0	43 10 1½	35 0 0	By consent.	
74 1 34	15 0 0	147 17 10	110 0 0	do.	
71 0 0	48 16 0	68 0 6	33 0 0		
2,165 1 25	877 0 0	1,870 12 3½	1,001 16 0		

LIMERICK.

63 2 25	7 0 0	10 13 6	9 5 0		
30 0 0	8 10 0	8 10 0	4 0 0		
39 0 12	7 15 0	15 0 0	10 0 0		
6 0 0	0 16 0	1 10 0	1 6 0		
31 2 17	21 15 0	30 7 6	25 0 0		
41 3 32	23 16 0	27 14 0	74 0 0		
83 3 24	41 0 0	52 1 7	70 0 0		
21 0 8	18 10 0	23 9 3	18 0 0		
4 0 11	9 10 0	5 0 0	8 3 0		
12 3 55	6 5 0	13 10 0	7 0 0		
35 2 0	23 16 0	31 15 0	23 10 0		
68 3 39	57 0 0	81 0 0	65 0 0		
23 0 1	16 18 0	25 0 0	18 10 0		
58 3 10	38 16 0	43 0 0	35 0 0		
480 3 6	316 10 0	440 0 9	331 16 0		

TIPPERARY.

377 3 18	318 0 0	300 0 0	216 0 0	By consent.	

CIVIL BILL

PROVINCE OF

COUNTY OF

County Court Judge.	No.	Name of Tenant.	Name of Landlord.	Townland.
T. [illegible], Q.C.	1	John Bradley, ...	Daniel Spence, ...	[illegible],
	2	Thomas McConville, ...	James Johnston, ...	Lisnaboy, ...
				Total, ...

COUNTY OF

County Court Judge.	No.	Name of Tenant.	Name of Landlord.	Townland.
J. C. Neligan, Q.C.	90	Robert Dixon, ...	Earl of Enniskillen, ...	Drumsaw, ...
	91	Thomas J. Watson, ...	Constantine Maguire, a lunatic,	Ednamore, ...
				Total, ...

COUNTY OF

County Court Judge.	No.	Name of Tenant.	Name of Landlord.	Townland.
J. C. Neligan, Q.C.	[illegible]	Mary Anne Fulton, ...	Margaret J. McGowan, ...	Grange, ...
	267	Edward Wilson, ...	Trustees of Elizabeth McIntyre,	Ballymaglagan,
	268	Hugh Magreary, ...	do.	do. ...
	269	Daniel Duggan, ...	The Drapers' Company, ...	[illegible], ...
	270	Edward Duggan, ...	do.	[illegible], ...
				Total, ...

COUNTY OF

COURTS.

ULSTER.

DOWN.

Extent of Holding. Statute.	Poor Law Valuation.	Former Rent.	Judicial Rent.	Observations.	Value of Tenancy.
A. R. P.	£ s. d.	£ s. d.	£ s. d.		£ s. d.
3 0 7	5 0 0	5 0 0	3 15 0		
15 [illegible] 6	16 0 0	25 0 0	16 10 0		
18 3 13	21 0 0	30 0 0	20 5 0		

FERMANAGH.

21 2 15	21 0 0	22 0 0	[illegible]		
3 1 35	6 10 0	5 0 0	4 0 0		
25 0 10	25 10 0	27 0 0	21 10 0		

LONDONDERRY.

6 0 3	1 0 0	3 0 0	1 12 0		
4 3 13	3 0 0	5 7 3	4 0 0		
8 1 20	3 5 0	6 13 4	3 0 0		
10 2 31	3 5 0	3 1 8	3 0 0		
11 3 34	7 0 0	5 8 0	4 11 8		
40 3 21	19 0 0	24 3 0	17 12 8		

MONAGHAN.

PROVINCE OF

COUNTY OF

County Court Judge.	No.	Name of Tenant.	Name of Landlord.	Townland.
Gerald Fitzgerald.	137	Robert Henery, ...	Thomas Boylan, ...	Ballyvenaun, ...
	138	Peter Waters, ...	James L. Hogan, ...	Pottlebane, ...
	139	Mary Gargan, ...	F. C. High and another, ...	Agnagh, ...
	140	Mary Geary, ...	J. C. Moore and another, ...	Kilsarry, ...
	141	Mary Geary, Rep. of Hugh Geary,	do.	do. ...
	142	Peter Wilkinson, ...	do.	do. ...
	143	Do., ...	do.	do. ...
	144	Do., ...	do.	do. ...
	145	Francis Reilly, ...	Edward McEvoy, ...	Grange, ...
	146	William Tormey, ...	do.	Flaughtown, Little,
	147	Edward Garvel, ...	do.	Grange, ...
	148	John Martin, ...	do.	Grange, ...
	149	John Carr, ...	do.	Grangeboyne, ...
	150	James Cusack, ...	M. Swetenham, ...	Carlanstown, ...
	151	Austin Hewitt, ...	W. B. Ryan, ...	Kilmody, ...
	152	Mathew Lynch, ...	Edmund O'Connor, a minor, by M. R. O'Connell, his Guardian.	Ross, ...
	153	Katie McDonnell, ...	Kathleen E. Rowley and ors.,	Seymourstown, Kush.
	154	Laurence Byrne, ...	do.	Balnagee, ...
	155	Margaret McGuinness,	Captain W. Alexander, ...	Altmush, ...
	156	Julia Reilly, ...	Trim Town Commissioners,	Part of Corporation Lands, 1st Division.
	157	John Smart, ...	do. ...	Corporation 7th Division.
	158	John McGrath, ...	Earl of Darnley, ...	Rathmore, ...
	159	John F. Bamford, ...	George F. Bamford, ...	Drumlargan, ...
	160	Hugh Geary, ...	John Tisdall, ...	Anghilaker, ...
	161	Peter Smith, ...	Trustees of Thomas Bligh, ...	Gerrardstown, ...
	162	Peter Alwell, ...	do.	Faugh, ...
	163	Bernard Garry, ...	Henry Hodgens, ...	Rackinagh, ...
	164	Ellen Martin and anor.,	James W. Drury and others,	Knightstown, ...
	165	Thomas O'Keeffe, ...	Edmund Swetenam, ...	Bramandstown,
	166	Thomas Connor, ...	Lord Fingall, ...	Gallowstown, ...

LEINSTER.

MEATH.

Extent of Holding. Statute.			Poor Law Valuation.			Former Rent.			Judicial Rent.			Observations.
A.	R.	P.	£	s.	d.	£	s.	d.	£	s.	d.	
31	2	27	30	0	0	40	0	0	32	10	0	
20	0	0	17	5	0	16	2	4	13	0	0	
21	2	16	13	5	0	16	5	8	14	0	0	
177	3	33	136	0	0	148	0	0	120	0	0	
258	1	14	196	0	0	220	0	0	180	0	0	
50	1	1	38	5	0	44	10	8	37	0	0	
26	2	20	18	15	0	20	0	0	17	0	0	
117	2	30	88	10	0	116	4	0	87	10	0	
140	0	20	103	10	0	180	4	0	92	0	0	
45	1	0	33	5	0	33	14	0	28	0	0	
63	0	13	40	5	0	71	2	0	54	0	0	
106	1	25	78	0	0	78	2	6	60	0	0	
38	2	23	23	0	0	26	0	0	18	0	0	
11	3	35	8	0	0	9	18	11	8	0	0	
96	0	0	71	0	0	143	0	0	95	0	0	
53	0	35	38	0	0	47	0	0	30	0	0	
78	3	30	51	10	0	55	5	1	42	0	0	
5	0	5	1	5	0	6	7	8	2	10	0	
4	0	0	7	18	0	6	0	0	5	16	0	
9	1	0	unascertained.			5	0	0	5	0	0	
7	0	5	5	5	0	7	7	2	5	17	0	
150	1	5	150	0	0	180	0	0	200	0	0	
336	0	12	324	18	5	400	4	0	330	0	0	
68	0	28	61	15	0	65	0	0	52	0	0	
18	2	10	15	0	0	10	10	0	9	10	0	
6	0	0	6	0	0	3	18	0	5	10	0	
30	0	0	20	0	0	20	0	5	15	10	0	
305	1	23	231	5	0	285	3	8	190	0	0	
51	0	34	28	5	0	30	0	0	22	10	0	
17	3	20	10	10	0	11	0	0	9	0	0	

COUNTY OF

County Court Judge.	No.	Name of Tenant.	Name of Landlord.	Townland.
Gerald Fitzgerald.	167	Thomas Gleeson, ...	Lord Fingall, ...	Gallaystown, ...
	168	Nicholas McNally, ...	Edward A. Patterson, ...	Alexander Reid, part of
	169	Mary Geraty, Admix. of Hugh Geraty,	Richard B. E. Chambers, ...	Ardbracken, .
	170	Thomas Lynch, ...	Lord Lansdowne, ...	Killaskillen,
	171	Thomas Dowd, ...	Walter Burrowes, Exor. of H. R. Burrowes, deceased.	Leamore, ...
	172	James Hughes, ...	do.	Dangan, ...
	173	William Dunne, ...	do.	Unlemstown, Laide,
	174	Michael Reilly, ...	R. E. K. Chambers, ...	Marshalstown, ...
	175	Bryan Gorman,	do.	do. ...
				Total, ...

PROVINCE OF

COUNTY OF

J. H. Richards.	3053	Margaret Gallagher, ...	George T. S. Carter, ...	Kilmilagh, ...
	3054	John Murphy, ...	Patrick D. Tyrell, ...	Aranagh, ...
	3055	Catherine Thompson, ...	Reps. of Henry Bruen, ...	Pribbaun, ...
	3056	Pat Thompson and anor.,	do.	Crumgummy, ...
	657	William Thompson, ...	do.	Pribbaun, ...
	3058	Michael Gibbons, ...	Sir Roger W. H. Palmer, Bart.,	Cashel, ...
	3059	Thomas McAndrew, ...	John E. Ferde, ...	Forerile, ...
	3060	John Murphy, ...	Sir Compton M. Domvile, Bart.	Drumadaforya, ...
	3061	Joseph Kelly, ...	Charles J. O'Donel, ...	Cloonawillen, ...
	3062	Martin Connor and ors.,	Frederick T. Lavin, ...	Derry, .
	3063	James Conway and anor.,	Colonel W. Clive, ...	do. ...
	3064	John McNamara and another,	John McDermott, ...	Claremorris, ...
	3065	James Prendergast and another,	James Tuite, ...	Gortnagry, ...
	3066	Patt Birrane, ...	Robert W. Orme, ...	Firrew, ...
	3067	Do., ...	do.	Lakeanwaddagh,
	3068	Thomas Boynton, ...	Lord Clanmorris, ...	Woodstock, ...
	3069	John Murray, junior, ...	Lord Dillon, ...	Cloonlyon, ...
	3070	Patrick Convey, ...	do.	do. ...

MEATH—*continued.*

Extent of Holding, Statute.			Poor Law Valuation.			Former Rent.			Judicial Rent.			Observations.
A.	R.	P.	£	s.	d.	£	s.	d.	£	s.	d.	
131	0	25	108	10	0	186	15	10	100	0	0	By consent.
66	1	8	50	0	0	64	13	0	45	17	5	do.
254	3	16	100	0	0	126	5	0	150	0	0	do.
19	3	30	11	16	0	9	10	0	6	0	0	do.
18	0	21	11	0	0	11	14	0	6	5	0	
11	0	35	13	15	0	11	15	0	8	15	0	
15	0	27	10	0	0	18	0	0	9	5	0	
226	3	1	277	10	0	255	7	0	190	0	0	
16	2	38	9	10	0	11	0	10	7	10	0	
3,097	0	35	2,800	0	6	3,276	8	9	2,816	1	5	

CONNAUGHT.

MAYO.

250	2	0	10	15	0	7	0	0	5	0	0	
0	1	16	1	5	0	0	1	0	1	5	0	
9	2	35	3	10	0	4	0	0	3	5	0	
unascertained.			4	5	0	4	10	0	3	0	0	
5	3	37	3	7	0	4	0	0	3	5	0	
16	3	33	6	5	0	7	0	0	5	0	0	
1	2	0	1	0	0	1	10	0	1	5	0	With right of grazing two cows free.
45	2	23	15	9	0	20	0	0	16	0	0	
113	2	7	37	15	0	65	0	0	62	0	0	
25	0	24	17	5	0	21	0	10	17	0	0	
unascertained.			14	15	0	25	0	0	17	0	0	
23	2	0	6	0	0	5	0	0	5	10	0	
31	0	11	6	5	0	8	15	0	5	0	0	
141	0	0	18	0	0	10	0	0	10	0	0	
18	0	0	4	5	0	5	0	0	4	17	0	
13	0	30	26	15	0	30	0	0	23	10	0	
77	1	10	4	15	0	5	1	0	3	15	0	

COUNTY OF

County Court Judge.	No.	Name of Tenant.	Name of Landlord.	Townland.
J. H. Richards.	3071	John Callinan, ...	Lord Dillon, ...	Glenlyon, ...
	3072	Thomas Curley, ...	do.	do. ...
	3073	Mary Costelloe, ...	Lady E. O'Grady, ...	Aughaterawy,
	3074	Edward Lyons, ...	do.	do.
	3075	Bridget Mulrennin, ...	do.	do.
	3076	John E. O'Reilly, ...	do.	Aughamore,
	3077	Martin Muldowney, ...	do.	Aughaterawy, ...
	3078	Pat Muldowney, ...	do.	do. ...
	3079	Thomas Hession, ...	do. ...	do. ...
	3080	Michael Roberts, ...	do.	do. ...
	3081	William Boland, ...	do.	do. ...
	3082	Pat Congrave, ...	Colonel John P. Brabazon,	Tullinahoo, ...
	3083	Pat Foley, ...	do.	do. ...
	3084	Pat Devine, ...	do.	do. ...
	3085	Michael Geary and anor.,	do.	do. ...
	3086	James Flynn, ...	David Ruttledge, ...	Rockfort, ...
				Total, ...

COUNTY OF

William O'Connor Morris.	459	Michael Turley, ...	John A. Mather, ...	Cornalara, ...

PROVINCE OF

COUNTY OF

Robert Ferguson, Q.C.	132	William Donegan, ...	Timothy Cotter, ...	Clashbredane, ...
	150	John Hurley, ...	Earl of Bandon, ...	Dromaleigh, ...
	314	Thomas Spriggs, ...	William J. Blandy, ...	Downeen, ...
	336	Thomas Hill, ...	Patrick McCarthy, ...	Cnockfilish, ...
				Total, ...

MAYO—*continued*.

Extent of Holding, Statute.	Poor Law Valuation.	Former Rent.	Judicial Rent.	Observations.	Value of Tenancy.
a. r. p.	£ s. d.	£ s. d.	£ s. d.		£ s. d.
11 1 0	8 0 0	2 5 0	1 15 0		
10 8 0	6 6 0	4 1 0	3 18 0		
12 1 30	1 5 0	1 10 0	1 10 0		
9 3 6	2 0 0	3 0 0	2 10 0		
21 1 30	1 10 0	4 10 0	2 10 0		
11 2 37	2 0 0	3 18 0	2 10 0		
10 0 13	3 8 0	3 10 0	2 10 0		
10 0 35	3 10 0	4 0 0	2 15 0		
11 3 37	3 0 0	6 15 0	3 10 0		
10 0 0	1 5 0	2 0 0	1 10 0		
unascertained.	1 13 0	3 13 0	2 0 0		
5 1 0	8 10 0	8 10 0	2 15 0		
unascertained.	2 14 0	5 13 9	4 13 0		
do.	3 3 0	6 1 0	3 5 0		
do.	2 19 0	5 0 0	2 16 0		
11 1 14	7 0 0	10 0 0	7 10 0		
997 1 31	738 0 0	299 1 7	221 19 0		

ROSCOMMON.

84 3 3	13 0 0	18 0 0	7 15 0		

MUNSTER.

COUNTY OF

County Court Judge.	No.	Name of Tenant.	Name of Landlord.	Townland.
I. A. Curran, q.c.	149	Michael Keeffe, ...	Stephen E. Collis, ...	Moyeens, ...
	150	Jeremiah Foley and anor.,	Denis G. MacGillycuddy, ...	Kenmare, ...
	151	John Foley, ...	do.	do. ...
	152	Michael Mulvihill, ...	John R. Kleman, ...	Kilcurry, Upper, ...
	153	John McCarthy and anor., Executors of Charles McCarthy, deceased.	F. C. Bendon, ...	Leith, ...
	154	Owen Moriarty, ...	John Foley, ...	Cloonbarragh, ...
	155	Florence Sullivan, ...	Francis B. Chute, ...	Carraghglass, &c.
	156	Michael Kennelly, ...	Jeremiah Behane, ...	Ballyoguane, ...
	157	James Murphy, ...	Mende C. Denis, ...	do. ...
	158	Denis Goulding, ...	Marion Fitzgerald and others,	Coolineare, ...
	159	Denis Conway, ...	Earl of Kenmare, ...	Coolick, ...
	160	Mary Clifford, ...	Mary A. McD. Mahony, ...	Castlequin, ...
	161	Jeremiah Cronin, ...	Marquis of Lansdowne, ...	Gurtcageennad, ...
	162	John Sullivan, ...	Wilson Gun, ...	Tullamore, ...
	163	Do., ...	do.	do. ...
				Total, ...

KERRY.

Extent of Holding, Statute	Poor Law Valuation.	Former Rent.	Judicial Rent.	Observations.	Value of Tenancy.
A. R. P.	£ s. d.	£ s. d.	£ s. d.		£ s. d.
10 0 27	24 0 0	50 0 0	35 0 0		
36 0 8	16 7 0	16 15 10	13 10 0		
38 1 34	16 17 0	18 14 8	12 0 0		
1 0 0	unascertained,	3 0 0	1 5 0		
138 3 33	33 0 0	56 0 0	47 0 0		
1 0 0	0 5 0	1 0 0	0 10 0		
311 1 31	5 5 0	13 0 0	10 0 0		
8 1 38	.	5 18 0	3 0 0		
71 0 35	20 0 0	37 0 0	27 0 0		
13 3 5	7 10 0	8 18 6	7 6 8		
56 1 23	17 0 0	21 0 0	18 15 0		
8 0 16	3 10 0	10 10 0	6 0 0		
41 1 38	7 10 0	9 12 0	7 10 0	With right to graze ½ of adjoining mountain, containing forty acres.	
5 0 0	—	1 10 0	1 10 0		
1 3 33	—	1 0 0	0 16 0		
789 3 33	164 6 0	294 16 0	193 1 8		

TIPPERARY.

164 0 0	62 5 0	60 0 0	50 0 0		
35 3 37	39 0 0	36 0 0	30 0 0		
35 0 33	34 0 0	33 6 0	30 0 0		
3 3 26	1 15 0	5 13 0	3 0 0		
10 3 0	5 10 0	11 9 10	10 0 0		
23 1 7	9 15 0	12 18 9	8 0 0		
11 1 14	4 0 0	5 0 0	4 0 0		
11 1 14	4 0 0	5 0 0	4 0 0		
36 0 0	5 10 0	7 0 0	5 0 0		
24 0 0	5 0 0	7 0 0	6 0 0		

COUNTY OF

County Court Judge	No.	Name of Tenant	Name of Landlord	Townland.
James E. Wall, q.c.	290	Michael Houlihan, ...	David Clarke, ...	[illegible], ...
	291	Joseph Slattery, ...	do.	[illegible], ...
	[illegible]	Ellen J. Guynan, ...	do.	[illegible], ...
	293	Do., ...	do.	do., ...
	294	Do., ...	do.	do., ...
	295	Do., ...	do.	do., ...
				Total, ...

Rents fixed upon the Reports of Valuers Appointed by the Irish Land

PROVINCE OF

COUNTY OF

Number.	Name of Tenant.	Name of Landlord.	Townland.
21	William J. Watson, ...	D. S. M. Baird, ...	Deer Park, ...

PROVINCE OF

COUNTY OF

43	Austin Gilbert, ...	Mary C. Bentley, a minor, by S. Perry, her Guardian,	[illegible], ...

TIPPERARY—*continued.*

Extent of Holding. Statute.	Poor Law Valuation.	Former Rent.	Judicial Rent.	Observations.	Value of Tenancy.
A. R. P.	£ s. d.	£ s. d.	£ s. d.		£ s. d.
8 1 13	3 10 0	5 0 0	8 8 0		
1 2 25	1 10 0	2 0 0	1 0 0		
6 3 32	6 5 0	8 17 10	7 10 0		
9 0 8	1 10 0	2 11 0	1 10 0		
1 2 11	5 10 0	8 10 0	1 11 8		
8 2 4	3 15 0	4 0 0	2 17 0		
318 1 8	153 18 0	197 2 10	156 11 6		

Commission on the Joint Applications of Landlords and Tenants.

ULSTER.

TYRONE.

Extent of Holding. Statute.	Poor Law Valuation.	Former Rent.	Judicial Rent.	Observations.
A. R. P.	£ s. d.	£ s. d.	£ s. d.	
18 3 10	10 5 0	12 11 10	10 0 0	

LEINSTER.

WEXFORD.

PROVINCE OF MUNSTER.

COUNTY OF CLARE.

[illegible]	[illegible]	[illegible]	[illegible]	[illegible]	[illegible]	[illegible]	[illegible]	[illegible]
				a. r. p.	£ s. d.	£ s. d.	£ s. d.	
[illegible]	[illegible]	[illegible]	[illegible]	[illegible]	[illegible]	[illegible]	[illegible]	
[illegible]	[illegible]	do.	do.	[illegible]	[illegible]	[illegible]	[illegible]	
[illegible]	[illegible]	[illegible]	[illegible]	[illegible]	[illegible]	[illegible]	[illegible]	
[illegible]	[illegible]	do.	do.	[illegible]	[illegible]	[illegible]	[illegible]	
[illegible]	[illegible]	do.	do.	[illegible]	[illegible]	[illegible]	[illegible]	
[illegible]	[illegible]	[illegible]	[illegible]	[illegible]	[illegible]	[illegible]	[illegible]	
			Total,	[illegible]	[illegible]	[illegible]	[illegible]	

[illegible]

LAND LAW (IRELAND) ACT, 1887.

LEASEHOLDERS.

PROVINCE OF

COUNTY OF

Names of Assistant Commissioners by whom Cases were decided.	No.	Name of Tenant.	Name of Landlord.	Townland.
Head Commission.	501	Thomas Gardner, —	Eliza Wilson, — —	[illegible], —
	502	John McCurdy, —	Sir Charles Lanyon, —	Tannybrake, —
	503	James Wilson, —	Anne B. Hay, ... —	[illegible], —
	504	William Martin, —	Andrew Pollock, — —	[illegible], —
	505	William J. Johnston, ...	Major J. J. Rowan, —	[illegible], —
	506	James Todd, —	Mrs. Anne McCormick, ...	Carnkenny, —
	507	John McAuley, senior, continued in name of Denis McAuley.	Major H. W. Coppage, —	[illegible], —
	508	Michael McAuley, —	do. — —	do. —
	509	Randall McDonnell, ...	do. — —	do. —
	510	James Carton, —	William Moore, ... —	Livery, Upper,
	511	Hamilton Patton, —	do. — ...	[illegible], —
Assistant Commissioners— E. Greer (Legal). R. Spencer. J. M. Weir.	512	John Templeton, —	William G. Forbes —	Jordanstown, —
	513	Roger Crossland, ...	Captain Alexander McNeill,	Broughshane, —
	514	James Sharpe, —	do. ... —	[illegible], —
	515	John McNeill, Admr. of Hugh Kyle, deceased, and another.	Whitewell Print Works Co.,	Glengormley, —
	516	Jane Barklimore & ors.	John Chisholm and another.	Collinward, —
	517	James Williamson and another.	Rev. J. Gordon-Smyth & ors.	Ballyhought, —
	518	Francis McAuley, —	Emily Macauley, Admix. of Alex. Macauley, deceased.	[illegible], —
	519	Catherine Murray, —	Alexander Macauley, a minor, by Mrs. Geo. A. Rotheram and another, his Guardians.	Ballytrask, —
	520	Denis McAlinney, ...	John Cameron, ... —	Ballyvordagh, Sth.
	521	James Woodside, ...	Mrs. Jane Dunlop, —	Gortconney —
	522	John McBride, —	Earl of Antrim, — —	Greenann, —

ULSTER.

ANTRIM.

Extent of Holding. Statute.	Poor Law Valuation.	Present Rent.	Judicial Rent.	Observations.	Value of Tenancy.
A. R. P.	£ s. d.	£ s. d.	£ s. d.		£ s. d.
10 1 8	13 0 0	17 0 0	13 0 0	The rent in this case was fixed by consent of the parties at the sitting of the Court in Dublin.	
*77 0 37	14 0 0	18 0 0	13 18 0	do.	* And 5 acres [illegible] Lyle [illegible]
48 3 37	30 0 0	64 0 0	46 0 0	do.	
75 1 28	4 15 0	7 8 4	5 14 8	do.	† And an undivided fourth of Craigduff, containing [illegible] acres.
7 1 15	9 0 0	9 0 6	6 0 0	do.	
24 3 30	22 0 0	34 0 0	27 0 0	do.	
18 0 0	13 10 0	16 10 0	10 10 0	do.	
19 0 0	15 0 0	16 10 0	10 10 0	do.	
17 0 0	11 15 0	13 18 0	8 18 0	do.	
40 3 10	41 0 0	41 15 8	34 10 0	do.	
48 2 24	45 0 0	60 0 0	40 0 0	do.	
85 0 30	58 0 0	72 10 0	60 0 0		
64 0 34	74 5 0	75 0 0	48 0 0		
45 1 15	50 0 0	60 0 0	44 0 0		
59 1 39	58 8 0	80 17 4	52 10 0		
98 1 25	45 0 0	80 0 0	61 0 0		
28 3 20	29 0 0	45 5 0	30 0 0		
32 1 30	16 0 0	15 17 4	31 0 0		
39 0 14	18 15 0	37 7 10	18 0 0		
174 1 31	68 5 0	84 0 0	65 0 0		
17 3 30	23 0 0	21 0 0	15 10 0		
34 3 37	17 10 0	20 17 3	14 10 0		
23 3 4	11 10 0	14 0 0	9 0 0		

Names of Assistant Commissioners by whom Cases were decided.	No.	Name of Tenant.	Name of Landlord.	Townland.
Assistant Commissioners—				
R. Gamble (Legal). [illegible] J. M. Weir.	524	John McKilloy, —	George William Cuppage and another, Trustees of Alexander Cuppage.	Gortnaroggan, —
	525	Alexander O'Neill, —	do. — —	do. —
	526	Daniel McDonnell, —	do. — —	do. —
	527	Neal McGarry, —	do. — —	Breid, —
	528	James Hamilton, —	do. — —	Ramaragh, —
	529	John McAlernon, —	do. — —	Glynleghan, —
	530	Daniel McNeill, —	do. — —	Broughanlease,
	531	Neal McGarry, —	do. — —	Clogher, —
	532	Joseph Lamont, —	Sir Richard Wallace, Bart.,	Ballynarrickmaddy
	533	William J. Lamont, —	do. — —	Derrykillelagh,
	534	Thomas Fleming, —	do. — —	Glenstorrif and another,
	535	Francis Morrow, —	do. — —	Tullyrusheen, —
	536	William J. Phillips, —	do. — —	do. —
	537	Francis Morrow, —	do. — —	do. —
	538	David Calwell, —	do. — —	Ballynally, part of,
	539	James Johnston, —	do. — —	Glenary, —
	540	Michael F. Armstrong,	do. — —	do. —
	541	Anne J. Brown, —	do. — —	Ballyclough, —
	542	John H. Campbell, —	do. — —	do. —
	543	John Kane, — —	do. — —	Ballycullen, —
	544	John Dickey	do. — —	Cairnloughan, —
	545	Ann Leverty, —	Sir Frederick Boyd, Bart., continued in name of Lady Alice E. S. Boyd.	Broughshane, —
	546	John McComb, —	do. — —	Tortmile, —
	547	James McClements, —	do. — —	Caryfad, —
	548	William McKinley, —	do. — —	Ballyreagh, Lr.,
	549	Robert Butler, —	do. — —	Caryfad, —
	550	James McClements, —	do. — —	do. —
	551	William McKinley, —	do. — —	Carnsaley, —
	552	Archibald Kelly, —	do. — —	Ballydurnian, —
	553	William Taylor, —	do. — —	Broomore, —
	554	Francis Black —	do. — —	Ballylammon, —
	555	Jane McCaughey, —	do. — —	Mullaren, —
	556	Samuel Simpson, —	do. — —	Drumnavaley, —
	557	Jane McCaughey, —	do. — —	do. —

ANTRIM—*continued.*

Extent of Holding, Statute.			Poor Law Valuation.			Former Rent.			Judicial Rent.			Observations.
A.	R.	P.	£	s.	d.	£	s.	d.	£	s.	d.	
20	3	37	13	18	0	16	15	5	10	0	0	
4	2	10	5	0	0	6	4	0	4	10	0	
13	2	25	6	15	0	8	12	0	6	15	0	
17	1	24	10	10	0	8	7	0	7	0	0	
73	1	37	18	10	0	25	12	2	9	10	0	
26	3	0	16	19	1	15	0	0	8	10	0	And [illegible] grazing
67	2	4	7	10	0	9	10	0	5	10	0	do.
41	3	3	10	14	0	10	10	0	7	10	0	
33	1	16	33	10	0	31	14	5	24	10	0	
67	3	31	44	5	0	38	18	4	34	10	0	
65	2	20	114	10	0	103	16	0	80	0	0	
5	3	38	5	10	0	4	6	6	3	10	0	
85	0	7	41	15	0	50	1	2	35	0	0	
15	2	27	11	15	0	9	10	8	8	15	0	
97	1	0	45	16	0	36	10	0	35	0		
33	0	19	35	0	0	31	17	4	27	10	0	
7	1	1	[illegible]			5	0	0	6	18	0	
33	0	30	61	10	0	35	19	0	36	0	0	
53	3	21	51	0	0	57	11	0	38	0	0	
19	1	23	64	0	0	53	15	0	44	0	0	
10	3	33	10	0	0	9	13	0	8	0	0	
8	3	0	5	5	6	10	0	0	6	10	0	
63	3	7	21	15	0	37	0	0	28	0	0	
15	0	0	5	10	0	6	0	0	5	15	0	
115	0	0	36	15	0	80	0	0	57	0	0	
48	1	20	30	5	2	21	0	0	14	0	0	
10	0	0	7	0	0	4	10	0	5	0	0	
103	2	37	43	10	0	64	0	0	45	0	0	
19	0	0	10	5	0	11	4	3	6	10	0	
37	2	0	19	15	0	23	0	6	18	10	0	
56	0	0	73	10	0	23	18	6	18	0	0	
18	0	0	11	0	0	12	0	0	5	5	0	
31	3	19	10	10	0	15	0	0	10	0	0	
35	0	0	19	0	0	17	0	0	11	0	0	

COUNTY OF

Names of Assistant Commissioners by whom Cases were decided.	No.	Name of Tenant.	Name of Landlord.	Townland.
Assistant Commissioners— E. Greer (Legal). R. Stronge. J. M. Weir.	558	John Robinson, ...	Sir Frederick Boyd, Bart., continued in name of Lady Alice E. R. Boyd.	Carnduff, ...
	559	Do., ...	do.	do. ...
	560	James Woodside, ...	do.	Clare, ...
	561	John White, ...	do.	Drummaville, ...
	562	John Christy, ...	do.	Drumagarvley, ...
	563	John McArthur, ...	do.	Ballyreagh's and another,
	564	Hugh Boyd, ...	do.	Ballymacaldrack, ...
	565	Denis McLaughlin, ...	do.	do. ...
	566	Michael P. Armstrong,	Sir Richard Wallace, Bart.,	Glenstry, ...
	567	Crawford Sefton, ...	do.	Ballyclamper, ...
	568	Joseph Kell, ...	Rev. A. H. Pakenham, ...	Malbeck, ...
				Total, ...

COUNTY OF

Head Commission.	202	Francis J. Ross, ...	Edward S. Ord, ...	Ballinacary, ...
	203	Joseph Weir, ...	Baroness Von Stieglitz, ...	Brough, ...
	204	John Watson, ...	do.	Lavaghery, ...
	205	Do., ...	do.	do. ...
	206	Edward Devlin, ...	do.	Muntiny, ...
	207	Henry Devlin, ...	James C. Rand, ...	do. ...
	208	Do., ...	do.	do. ...
	209	John Connolly, ...	do.	do. ...
	210	Henry Devlin, ...	do.	do. ...
	211	Do., ...	do.	do. ...
Assistant Commissioners— D. Tierney (Legal). H. K. Fairbairn. H. Johnston.	212	John Grimes, ...	Mary J. Allen, ...	Drumbally, ...
	213	Bryan Loy, ...	do.	Lisnalgan, ...
	214	John Murphy, ...	Robert J. McGeough, ...	Tullygallaghan,
	215	James McMahon, ...	Hibernian Joint Stock Company, Limited.	Tullyvallen, ...

ANTRIM—*continued.*

Extent of Holding. Statute.			Poor Law Valuation.			Former Rent.			Judicial Rent.			Observations.
a.	r.	p.	£	s.	d.	£	s.	d.	£	s.	d.	
15	0	0	18	10	0	20	0	0	15	0	0	
19	0	0	15	10	0	17	0	0	14	0	0	
23	0	0	25	10	0	28	0	0	23	0	0	
38	3	6	39	18	0	45	0	0	30	0	0	
21	0	0	14	0	0	20	0	0	15	0	0	
6	1	30	4	0	0	5	0	0	3	14	0	
19	1	0	27	0	0	34	10	0	27	0	0	
15	0	0	16	15	0	18	11	6	14	10	0	
10	0	38	unascertained.			10	13	0	7	15	0	
8	0	7	do.			3	2	0	2	18	0	
12	3	16	9	10	0	12	18	4	11	0	0	
2,077	3	36	1,649	6	1	1,619	1	11	1,338	17	6	

ARMAGH.

7	0	17	8	10	0	10	2	5	7	10	0	The rent in this case consent of the pa sitting of the Court
4	2	16	7	15	0	5	4	1	4	14	0	do.
5	1	0	6	0	0	6	5	4	6	16	6	do.
17	0	0	24	0	0	24	8	1	21	5	0	do.
16	0	15	14	5	0	18	4	4	11	10	0	do.
5	2	10	4	5	0	4	14	0	3	15	0	do.
8	0	10	9	10	0	9	0	11	6	15	6	do.
6	1	1	6	10	0	7	13	1	5	18	0	do.
6	0	19	6	18	0	5	18	7	5	15	0	do.
3	2	34	5	17	6	4	3	8	3	14	0	do.

COUNTY OF

Names of Assistant Commissioners by whom Cases were decided.	No.	Name of Tenant.	Name of Landlord.	Townland.
Assistant Commissioners—				
D. Tenney (Legal). H. K. Stevens. H. Johnston.	316	James McCally and another,	John Paton, ...	Tullyrallon, ...
	317	Do., ...	do.	do. ...
	318	James Tiffney, ...	Lord Lurgan, ...	Tunnahart, ...
	319	Joseph Hendron, ...	E. T. Wakefield, ...	Derryhennan, ...
	320	Do., ...	do.	do. ...
	321	John Hendron, ...	do.	do. ...
	322	John Stevenson, ...	Mrs. Roche, ...	Mackbury, ...
				Total, ...

COUNTY OF

Head Commission	160	Mary Neely, ...	Alexander J. R. Stewart, ...	Dromore, ...
	161	James Alexander, ...	do.	Clonmaryry, ...
	162	Thomas Martin, ...	James A. Shaw, ...	Drumlerishan, ...
Assistant Commissioners—				
D. Tenney (Legal). G. N. Caldwell. J. H. McConnell.	163	James Lindsay, ...	Alexander A. Richardson, ...	Tullyvarren, ...
	164	William H. Caldwell, ...	Catherine Black, ...	Ballylawn, ...
	165	James Hamilton, ...	John Clarke, Rep. of Andrew Clarke.	Aught, ...
				Total, ...

COUNTY OF

Head Commission.	277	Charles Lennon, ...	Marquis of Dufferin and Ava,	Ballygilbert, ...
	278	Rev. John Quartz, ...	do.	do. ...
	279	John Flanagan, ...	Rowland Gray and another,	Annadoy, ...
	280	Hugh Watson, ...	Mrs. Edith Mercer, ...	Ballymacarrett, ...

ARMAGH—*continued.*

Extent of Holding. Statute.	Poor Law Valuation.	Former Rent.	Judicial Rent.	Observations.	Value of Tenancy.
A. R. P.	£ s. d.	£ s. d.	£ s. d.		£ s. d.
13 1 0	unascertained.	3 15 0	3 4 0		
20 0 0	do.	7 1 7	6 16 0		
3 3 20	10 15 0	16 0 0	9 0 0	By consent.	
8 1 35	Unascertained.	4 13 6	3 0 0	do.	
7 1 7	do.	13 0 0	8 5 0	do.	
7 3 0	do.	11 0 0	9 10 0	do.	
73 0 0	33 10 0	80 0 0	81 5 0	do.	
154 2 31	150 0 6	221 5 4	179 1 6		

DONEGAL.

13 0 20	4 5 0	6 0 0	4 10 0	The rent in this case was fixed by consent of the parties at the sitting of the Court in Dublin.	
33 1 27	4 13 0	6 10 0	6 0 0	do.	
17 1 25	8 10 0	8 7 0	7 3 3	do.	
23 3 0	unascertained.	30 0 0	30 0 0		
40 1 4	34 0 0	70 0 0	50 0 0		
13 0 5	7 15 0	13 14 6	6 10 0	By consent.	
135 3 35	81 5 0	133 11 6	103 3 3		

DOWN.

31 0 20	33 0 0	36 0 0	31 0 0	The rent in this case was fixed by consent of the parties at the sitting of the Court in Dublin.	
43 1 14	40 10 0	55 2 0	44 5 0	do.	
37 1 33	33 15 0	40 6 8	30 0 0	do.	
46 3 35	79 5 0	110 0 0	70 0 0	do.	

COUNTY OF

Names of Assistant Commissioners by whom Cases were decided.	No.	Name of Tenant.	Name of Landlord.	Townland.
Assistant Commissioners—				
E. Greer (Legal). R. Garland. S. Chambers.	281	John Ringland, ...	Archibald Hamilton, a minor, by Rev. A. Boyd, his Trustee.	Clontagh, ...
	282	Do., ...	do.	do. ...
	283	Do., ...	do.	do. ...
	284	James Duff, ...	do.	do. ...
	285	Mrs. Jane Greeny, ...	General A. Nugent, ...	Tonaghy, ...
	286	Sarah Fitzpatrick, ...	S. R. Woods, ...	Ballyregan, part of.
	287	Samuel Rea, ...	Mary W. Birch, ...	Craigbeg, ...
	288	David Jamison, ...	Henry H. Stewart, ...	Ballyrussell, ...
	289	John Shaw and another,	John Mulholland, ...	Ballymaglaff, ...
	290	William Ennis, ...	Francis Hewson, ...	Ballybranagh, ...
	291	Alexander Rainey, ...	James G. Allen, ...	Ballygowan, ...
	292	Daniel Murray, ...	B. and H. McCartan, ...	Clanvaraghan, ...
	293	Hugh Watson, ...	Thomas Armstrong, junior, and another,	Ballymacashen, ...
	294	John Hanna, ...	Robert G. Dunville, ...	Carrickmannan, part of.
	295	Hugh McIlroy, ...	Earl Annesley, ...	Ballymagreehan, part of.
	296	Luke Savage, ...	do.	Shanknockery, ...
	297	Edward Murray, ...	do.	Bann, part of, ...
	298	James Crosby, ...	W. R. McConnell, ...	Lisnaw, ...
	299	William J. Forwood, ...	do.	Clontinaglare, ...
	300	Agnes Campbell, ...	do.	do. ...
	301	James Crosby, ...	do.	do. ...
	302	John Harper, junior, ...	James McCauley, ...	Ballygowan, ...
	303	James Coulter, ...	do.	do. ...
	304	John Lowther, ...	do.	do. ...

DOWN—*continued.*

Extent of Holding. Statute.	Poor Law Valuation.	Former Rent.	Judicial Rent.	Observations.
A. R. P.	£ s. d.	£ s. d.	£ s. d.	
11 1 [illegible]	unascertained,	17 0 0	9 5 0	
64 1 5	27 10 0	23 13 7	19 10 0	
[illegible] 0 [illegible]	[illegible] 10 0	[illegible] 6 3	[illegible] 0 0	
101 3 16	117 5 0	111 0 0	[illegible] 0 0	
[illegible] 1 24	—	40 17 8	39 10 0	
61 3 [illegible]	27 10 0	[illegible] 3 8	17 10 0	
11 1 18	13 10 0	12 6 0	13 5 0	By account.
[illegible] 0 17	43 10 0	44 10 0	43 0 0	
[illegible] 1 [illegible]	41 10 0	[illegible] 0 0	[illegible] 0 0	
48 3 6	71 15 0	[illegible] 16 9	60 [illegible] 0	
[illegible] 3 28	68 10 0	11 8 1	38 0 0	
16 [illegible] [illegible]	9 16 0	15 10 0	7 6 0	
72 [illegible] 14	101 0 0	166 0 0	110 0 0	
27 1 21	28 16 0	31 5 6	19 10 0	do.
[illegible] [illegible] 19	14 0 0	17 10 8	11 10 0	
[illegible] 3 [illegible]	12 14 0	10 0 0	8 0 0	Rent changed in 1879 from . . . .
[illegible] 3 30	unascertained,	[illegible] 15 6	[illegible] 0 0	
[illegible] [illegible] 6	42 0 0	[illegible] 4 10	[illegible] 0 0	
41 3 36	43 0 0	43 5 0	31 10 0	
16 [illegible] 24	9 5 0	11 [illegible] [illegible]	8 0 0	
12 [illegible] 29	13 0 0	18 10 8	10 10 0	
6 0 [illegible]	6 [illegible] 0	4 10 0	4 10 0	
31 0 [illegible]	65 0 0	63 8 0	38 10 0	
16 [illegible] 20	15 0 0	20 17 0	12 0 0	
13 [illegible] 29	13 0 0	16 6 0	10 10 0	

COUNTY OF

Names of Assistant Commissioners by whom Cases were decided.	No.	Name of Tenant.	Name of Landlord.	Townland.
Head Commission.	108	John Murphy, ...	Ethel E. Tennent, a minor, by Hon. Mrs. C. Butler and another, her Guardians.	Baugh, ...

COUNTY OF

Head Commission.	846	Sarah McIlwaine, ...	The Hon. The Irish Society,	Culmore, ...
	847	John Thompson, ...	do.	do. ...
	848	Joseph Cochrane, ...	Sir H. H. Bruce, Bart., ...	Quilly, ...
				Total, ...

COUNTY OF

Head Commission.	306	Andrew Hamilton, ...	Samuel Colquhoun, ...	[illegible] ...
	307	John McCormick, ...	Captain William Knox, ...	Kildoag, ...
	308	James Erskine, ...	do.	do. ...
	309	Jane Hamilton, ...	do.	do. ...
Assistant Commissioners— D. Twomey (Legal). A. S. Deane. A. Dudgeon.	310	Edward Bird, ...	George C. Leadrum, ...	Moorfield, ...
	311	Henry Anderson, ...	Amy A. Rea, a minor, by Thomas Duncan and others, her Guardians.	Killyclea, ...
	312	Eliza Hinckley, Admix. of Robert Hinckley.	Rev. Beaver H. Blacker, ...	Hackirmore, ...
	313	Thomas Musgrave, ...	do.	do. ...
	314	Euphemia Hinckley, ...	do.	Garvaghey, ...
	315	Michael Grilly, ...	Sir Nathaniel A. Staples, Bart.,	Crewragh, ...
	316	Robert Henry, ...	do.	Tamnyleenan, ...
	317	Michael Smart, ...	do.	Unagh, ...
	318	John Mullen, ...	William W. Harris, now Reginald T. Harris.	Ballymully, ...

FERMANAGH.

Extent of Holding. Statute Measure.	Poor Law Valuation.	Former Rent.	Judicial Rent.	Observations.	Value of Tenancy.
A. R. P.	£ s. d.	£ s. d.	£ s. d.		£ s. d.
74 0 0	48 0 0	45 0 0	37 0 0	The rent in this case was fixed by consent of the parties at the sitting of the Court in *Dublin*.	

LONDONDERRY.

18 2 10	17 0 0	18 0 0	15 0 0	The rent in this case was fixed by consent of the parties at the sitting of the Court in Dublin.	
86 1 6	86 10 0	0 0	60 0 0	do.	
76 3 25	30 10 0	69 15 0	51 0 0	do.	
181 2 1	134 0 0	101 15 0	66 0 0		

TYRONE.

87 0 15	43 0 0	87 10 0	48 10 0	The rent in this case was fixed by consent of the parties at the sitting of the Court in Dublin.	
78 2 15	40 10 0	65 0 0	38 5 0	do.	
71 0 8	30 0 0	35 0 0	17 5 0	do.	
64 1 38	36 5 0	40 0 0	32 10 0	do.	
259 1 30	160 10 0	197 8 10	150 0 0	By consent.	
22 1 35	18 5 0	16 10 0	14 0 0	do.	
58 3 19	37 0 0	59 0 0	35 0 0	do.	
40 3 20	29 0 0	29 13 4	24 0 0	do.	
46 3 11	35 0 0	30 18 10	25 0 0	do.	
38 0 10	16 0 0	16 4 7	12 0 0		
8 0 22	14 10 0	19 3 10	7 15 0		
9 1 35	6 18 0	8 13 11	6 10 0		
61 1 6	61 10 0	76 18 1	59 0 0		

COUNTY OF

Names of Assistant Commissioners by whom Cases were decided.	No.	Name of Tenant.	Name of Landlord.	Townland.
Assistant Commissioners—				
D. Tuohy (Legal). A. S. Drake. A. Dunlop.	219	James Dickson,	James Crossle,	Edendrett,
	220	Jane Kelly,	Joseph O'Neill,	Ballywhinny,
	221	Robert J. Stewart,	do.	do.
	222	John Joyce,	Samuel E. White,	do.
	223	Felix Lavery,	Julius Casement and anor., Reps. of Robert Casement,	Hagh,
	224	John Lavery,	do.	do.
	225	Peter Devlin,	Colonel Thomas E. A. Hall and another, Trustees of Countess of Castlestuart,	Cavanagh,
	226	Robert A. Ferguson,	Thomas H. H. Black & anor., Trustees of Thomas H. Black,	Tullygarn,
	227	James McCrory,	Colonel J. C. Lowry,	Castlemahon,
	228	Patrick McGlinn,	do.	Bracklagh,
	229	John McGlinn,	do.	do.
	230	Maria Stuart,	Colonel J. A. Caulfeild,	Drumaharn,
	231	Felix Taggart,	do.	Drumcare,
	232	Do.,	do.	do.
	233	Mary Orr,	Amy H. Bruce, a minor, by Thomas Dunne and others, her Guardians,	Drumnamoid,
	234	James Houston,	do.	Rathmore,
	235	Richard King and anor.,	do.	Cumber,
	236	William Johnston,	do.	Rathronnan,
	237	James Hosmer,	do.	Fomon,
	238	James Moffatt,	do.	Killyblo,
	239	Joseph Wilson,	do.	Ardbinny,
	240	Andrew Kidd,	do.	Sheron,

TYRONE—*continued.*

Extent of Holding. Statute.	Poor Law Valuation.	Present Rent.	Judicial Rent.	
a. r. p.	£ s. d.	£ s. d.	£ s. d.	
10 2 4	6 15 0	8 15 0	6 10 0	
41 1 34	46 10 0	41 8 0	30 0 0	
43 0 38	48 10 0	43 17 2	31 0 0	
[illegible] 3 10	24 10 0	21 15 8	20 0 0	
14 0 [illegible]	unascertained,	14 8 8	8 10 0	
9 1 15	8 10 0	8 18 0	5 0 0	
23 2 24	7 0 0	9 18 4	6 10 0	
10 2 0	10 15 0	20 0 0	10 0 0	
11 1 20	14 0 0	10 9 9	10 9 9	
13 8 0	7 0 0	10 18 3	7 10 0	By consent.
12 1 18	unascertained,	10 8 2	7 10 0	do.
5 3 5	do.	5 4 10	4 6 0	
6 1 20	6 0 0	5 17 10	3 18 0	
21 2 7	21 0 0	22 10 0	17 0 0	
49 0 30	36 10 0	34 15 8	29 0 0	do.
7 3 6	7 5 0	9 0 0	5 5 6	do.
23 0 10	23 10 0	25 0 0	18 15 0	do.
60 2 8	43 0 0	59 11 8	43 7 9	do.
19 1 30	15 5 0	14 18 9	12 10 0	do.
41 0 26	23 10 0	30 15 0	[illegible] 0 0	do.
30 2 8	22 0 0	20 14 4	17 10 0	do.
17 1 23	18 10 0	18 14 0	10 3 8	do.
19 1 6	16 5 0	12 1 4	10 5 0	do.
9 2 30	6 10 0	6 15 0	5 0 0	do.
17 2 18	8 10 0	11 1 8	9 8 4	do.

PROVINCE OF

COUNTY OF

Names of Assistant Commissioners by whom Cases were decided.	No.	Name of Tenant.	Name of Landlord.	Townland.
HEAD COMMISSIONER.	203	Bridget Cummerford, ...	Sir Thomas Esmonde, Bart., ...	Aughnamaddy, ...
	204	James McDonald, ...	Right Hon. Henry Bruen, ...	Coolrue, ...
	205	William Kidd, ...	Rev. A. W. Dardis, ...	Crossmore, ...
Assistant Commissioners— R. Reeves, Q.C. (Legal). S. McCarthy. F. F. Jeffers.	206	James Lawlor, ...	Gwynne Dyer, ...	Marshallstown, ...
	207	William Campbell, ...	Miss Eliza Byrne, ...	Rathdrum, ...
	208	Thomas McDonald, ...	Sir Thomas F. Bellew, Bart.,	Coolnakisha, ...
	209	Thomas Furnace, Exor. of Eliza Kehoe, decd.	do.	do. ...
	210	William Kane, ...	do.	Lacey, ...
	211	Mathew Butler, ...	do.	Cloughbawn, ...
	212	Do., ...	do.	Forestown & amp;c.
	213	John Cummins, ...	do.	Clonmahon, ...
	214	Jane Teehan, ...	do.	Forestown, ...
	215	Mary E. Lennon, ...	Robert C. Browne, ...	Carrigabrey, ...
	216	Richard Smith, ...	John Alexander, ...	Ballinakill, ...
	217	Timothy Hughes, ...	do.	do. ...
	218	Richard Thunderbury, ...	Hon. Thomas G. Smith, ...	Ardristan, ...
R. Reeves, Q.C. (Legal). M. F. Lynch. A. Dicken.	219	William Kidd, ...	Rev. A. W. Dardis, ...	Crossmore, ...
				Total, ...

COUNTY OF

LEINSTER.

CARLOW.

Extent of Holding. Statute.	Poor Law Valuation.	Former Rent.	Judicial Rent.	Observations.	Value of Tenancy.
A. R. P.	£ s. d.	£ s. d.	£ s. d.		£ s. d.
16 0 31	6 0 0	10 0 0	7 0 0	The rent in this case was fixed by consent of the parties at the sitting of the Court in Dublin.	
21 3 17	15 15 0	20 14 0	13 10 0	do.	
25 0 0	unascertained.	18 10 0	6 10 0	do.	
86 1 25	53 0 0	36 0 0	66 0 0		
44 1 27	31 5 0	42 12 6	35 15 0		
102 0 18	55 15 0	70 0 0	60 0 0		
150 3 34	104 0 0	174 12 0	144 0 0		
23 0 10	15 10 0	31 0 0	26 5 0		
160 0 27	171 0 0	167 4 0	167 4 0		
173 3 35	114 10 0	176 18 2	131 5 0		
189 0 [illegible]	163 10 0	203 4 6	203 4 6		
[illegible] 2 19	71 15 0	81 10 0	80 0 0		
20 0 35	11 10 0	23 15 8	16 0 0		
79 2 0	28 10 6	36 0 0	32 0 0		
143 1 5	145 0 0	127 15 0	130 0 0		
94 1 38	86 5 0	78 19 4	79 16 4		
43 2 17	31 0 0	26 7 6	14 10 0		
1,[illegible] 0 18	1,164 5 0	1,[illegible] 14 2	1,316 19 0		

DUBLIN.

Names of Assistant Commissioners by whom Cases were decided.	No.	Name of Tenant.	Name of Landlord.
Head Commission.			
	136	John Dunphy, ...	Captain H. F. Smyth ...
	137	Sarah Walsh, ...	Earl of Carysfort,
	138	John Byrne, ...	do. ...
	139	Patrick Tierney, ...	Archibald R. Butler,
	140	Miss Anne McEvoy, ...	Earl of Carysfort.

KILDARE.

Extent of Holding, Statute.	Poor Law Valuation.	Former Rent.	Judicial Rent.	Observations.	Value of Tenancy.
A. R. P.	£ s. d.	£ s. d.	£ s. d.		£ s. d.
35 0 31	26 10 0	30 0 0	28 0 0	The rent in this case was fixed by consent of the parties at the sitting of the Court in Dublin.	
213 3 34	168 15 0	190 0 0	165 0 0	do.	
61 0 26	50 15 0	38 15 4	39 0 0	do.	
115 1 27	77 15 0	125 10 0	80 0 0	do.	
118 1 34	111 5 0	155 0 0	130 0 0	do.	
576 3 0	409 0 0	573 0 6	443 0 0		

KILKENNY.

80 3 12	47 0 0	56 18 0	43 10 0		
60 1 34	39 0 0	48 0 0	40 0 0		
189 0 31	83 0 0	106 10 0	78 0 0		
197 2 19	129 15 0	163 0 0	130 0 0		
30 1 6	26 0 0	40 15 4	29 0 0		
63 1 30	23 0 0	33 0 0	29 0 0		
11 4 4	5 10 0	6 10 0	5 5 0		
34 1 5	9 0 0	13 7 0	9 10 0		
85 1 15	20 0 0	45 0 0	30 0 0		
87 0 35	30 0 0	39 9 0	31 0 0		
58 2 16	47 10 0	63 0 0	48 0 0		
101 3 1	51 0 0	57 10 0	48 5 0		
5 1 21	5 5 0	8 5 0	5 10 0		
6 2 5	4 0 0	5 0 0	5 10 0		
53 1 34	43 15 0	56 0 0	33 0 0		
49 3 7	30 5 0	35 5 0	30 0 0		
21 1 8	14 0 0	16 0 0	12 0 0		
55 3 14	23 0 0	26 0 0	19 0 0		
34 1 11	16 0 0	19 2 1½	15 0 0		
44 1 32	45 0 0	47 15 0	40 15 0		

COUNTY OF

Names of Assistant Commissioners by whom Cases were decided.	No.	Name of Tenant.	Name of Landlord.	Townland.
Assistant Commissioners— R. Reeves, Q.C. (Legal). T. A. Dillon. T. Davidson.	144	Jeremiah Brown, —	George Daly, — —	Dunaghmore, —
	145	Kyran Bergin, —	do. — —	Dunaghmore, Lr.,
	146	John Hearne, —	do. — —	do. —
	147	James Sweeney, —	do. — —	do. —
	148	Michael Brennan, —	do. — —	[illegible] and another,
				Total, —

COUNTY OF

Names of Assistant Commissioners by whom Cases were decided.	No.	Name of Tenant.	Name of Landlord.	Townland.
Head Commission.	94	Rev. Francis O'Farrell,	Shirley A. W. H. S. Ball and others, minors, by Mrs. Cecilia S. Ball.	Abbeyland, —
Assistant Commissioners— R. R. Kane (Legal). T. Roberts. W. T. Hewt.	95	John Kenny, —	George Greville, — —	Clonbrin, —
	96	Maria Kennedy, —	Earl of Granard, — —	Coolelder, —
	97	William Coyle, contd. in name of James Coyle.	Dr. John S. Ireland, —	Upper Ralen, —
	98	Willoby Reid, a minor, by Anne McCarthy, his Guardian.	Robert Chevenix, —	Aughaboy, —
	99	James Martin, —	Captain John Newton, —	Tirlagan and another.
	100	Patrick Gill, —	Maxwell Fox, — —	Cloonbrony, —
	101	Francis [illegible], —	[illegible] Moore, — —	Aughamore[illegible]
	102	Henry Shaw, —	Mrs. Francis E. Woodward,	Cloontark, —
	103	Patrick Reilly, —	Col. King-Harman, continued in name of Frances A. King-Harman.	Streamstown, —
	104	Eugene O'Beirne, —	Sergeant-Major James O'Reilly,	Queensland, —
	105	Denis Rivers, —	Mrs. Jane Guy, — —	Kilmacty, —

KILKENNY—*continued.*

Extent of Holding. Statute.	Poor Law Valuation.	Former Rent.	Judicial Rent.	Observations.	Value of Tenancy.
A. R. P.	£ s. d.	£ s. d.	£ s. d.		£ s. d.
40 3 23	23 15 0	37 0 0	31 7 6		
24 1 14	18 0 0	17 18 6	14 7 6		
9 0 14	5 5 0	6 5 0	5 0 0		
31 2 16	18 10 0	21 0 0	14 15 6		
33 3 18	20 0 0	31 0 0	16 10 0		
1,269 1 37	808 10 0	943 4 11½	719 5 0		

LONGFORD.

65 2 15	27 0 0	24 13 11	22 10 0		
28 0 13	18 0 0	25 5 0	20 0 0		
76 1 35	66 0 0	84 11 6	54 0 0		
14 1 37	7 10 0	8 2 9	6 10 0		
27 0 34	10 5 0	18 10 0	18 0 0		
79 3 0	48 0 0	73 7 0	62 10 0	Rent changed in 1874 from . . . £65 0s. 0d.	
53 3 26	35 0 0	35 0 8	28 0 0		
65 1 20	58 10 0	57 0 0	38 0 0		
210 1 13	123 0 0	148 0 0	110 0 0		
23 3 26	7 5 0	6 7 11	6 0 0		
93 2 5	48 10 0	81 0 6	76 0 0	By consent.	
20 0 35	11 5 0	14 0 0	8 18 0		
15 1 18	6 0 0	6 4 8	4 6 0	By consent. And grazing on Ls. Co. Hls.	
33 3 17	19 0 0	28 4 0	18 7 0		
18 2 4	16 0 0	14 0 0	10 10 0	Rent changed in 1877 from . . . £15 12s. 0d.	
63 1 22	unascertained,	45 0 0	35 0 0		
28 2 27	13 0 0	17 0 0	8 0 0	do. £10 5s. 0d.	
31 1 33	16 15 0	14 10 0	10 10 0	do. £16 17s. 6d.	

COUNTY OF

Names of Assistant Commissioners by whom Cases were decided.	No.	Name of Tenant.	Name of Landlord.	Townland.
Assistant Commissioners—				
R. R. Kane (Legal). T. Robinson. W. T. Huff.	115	James Newman, —	Alex. K. McEntire and anor., Assignees of Sir W. Nugent.	Knockavalley, —
	116	John Newman, —	do. — —	do. —
				Total, —

COUNTY OF

Head Commission.	91	Elizabeth Matthews, —	Arthur P. H. Lonsdale, —	Carntown, —
	92	Do., — —	do. — —	Carntown and another.
	93	Joseph Murphy, —	do. — —	do. —
	94	Bridget Reade, —	do. — —	do. —
	95	George Allen, —	do. — —	do. —
	96	Michael Murphy, —	do. — —	do. —
	97	Do., — —	do. — —	do. —
	98	John N. Dunne, —	Incorporated Society for promoting English Protestant Schools in Ireland.	Ardgatwick, —
	99	Do., — —	do. — —	Rathendy, —
	100	Nicholas Halligan, —	Richard J. Montgomery, —	Balltown, —
Assistant Commissioners— R. R. Kane (Legal). T. S. Porter. H. C. Greaney.	101	William Campbell, —	Vincent Mansergh and Forward,	Whiteriver & anor.
				Total, —

COUNTY OF

Head Commission.	182	William Hopkins, —	Francis W. Kackburne, —	Fosterstown, —
	183	Patrick Tobin, —	John G. Barnes, — —	Turkstown, —
	184	John Mathews, —	do. — —	do. —
	185	Mathew Lynch, —	do. ... —	[illegible], —
	186	John Dunning, —	Nugent T. Everard, —	Kilberry, —
	187	John Daly, — —	Chad Chalmers, — —	Loughan, —

LONGFORD—*continued.*

Extent of Holding. Statute.	Poor Law Valuation.	Former Rent.	Judicial Rent.	Observations.
A. R. P.	£ s. d.	£ s. d.	£ s. d.	
31 3 18	unascertained,	21 0 0	15 15 0	
31 3 13	do.	22 0 0	14 16 0	
1,144 3 17	635 9 0	601 17 4	485 5 0	

LOUTH.

46 0 30	70 0 0	75 16 0	55 0 0	The rent in this case w consent of the part sitting of the Court b
41 1 29	51 15 0	73 6 0	65 0 0	do.
55 1 15	39 0 0	83 16 0	57 0 0	do.
47 0 14	49 0 0	57 6 0	51 0 0	do.
6 0 7	7 0 0	6 13 0	4 18 0	do.
7 3 6	unascertained,	6 3 0	6 10 0	do.
9 3 10	do.	10 0 0	5 0 0	do.
105 3 26	140 0 0	168 17 0	130 5 0	do.
54 3 15	55 0 0	71 5 0	55 0 0	do.
141 1 14	165 10 0	173 0 0	136 0 0	do.

Name of Assistant Commissioners by whom Cases were decided.	No.	Name of Tenant.	Name of Landlord.
Assistant Commissioners— R. E. Kane (Legal). T. S. Fowler. J. Reeve.	188	Charles Reilly, ...	John A. Farrell, ...
	189	Joseph Reilly, ...	do. ...
	190	James Clarke, ...	do. ...
	191	Catherine Smith, ...	do. ...
	192	Thomas Kearney, ...	do. ...
	193	Mary A. Hoyle, ...	Chas. Chaloner, ...
	194	Bryan Farrelly, ...	Henry Crawford, tri... Mrs. Ann Armstro... Guardian.
	195	Thomas Monaghan, ...	John G. Bergen, ...
	196	Charles Reilly, ...	do. ...
	197	Michael Daly, ...	do. ...
	198	James Monaghan, ...	do. ...
	199	Gordon Jackson, ...	Georgiana A. Jenkins...
	200	Richard Booker, Guardian of Estate of John Booker, a lunatic,	Patrick Leavy, ...
	201	Patrick Gargan, ...	Henry W. Smith,
	202	Patrick McMahon, ...	do. ...
	203	Patrick Sheridan, ...	George E. Radcliff,
	204	Patrick Fay, ...	do. ...
	205	Do., ...	Patrick Fay, ...
	206	Richard Nixon, ...	Richard S. Murray,
	207	Hugh Brien, Admor. of the Estate of Ann Brien, deceased.	Rev. William Tren... minister, Reps. of Frederick F. Trench,
	208	Ann Kelly, ...	do. ...
	209	Do., ...	do. ...
	210	Do., ...	do. ...
	211	Christopher Farrell, ...	do. ...
	212	John Kiernan, ...	do. ...
	213	Rose Farrell, ...	do. ...
	214	James McDonagh, Admor. of the Estate of Mary McDonagh, deceased.	do. ...
	215	Margaret O'Brien, ...	John O'Reilly, comit... name of Farrell O'R...
	216	Mathew Reilly, ...	do. ...
	217	Gordon Jackson, ...	Ellen V. Fallon,

MEATH—*continued.*

Extent of Holding Statute.	Poor Law Valuation.	Former Rent.	Judicial Rent.	Observations.
A. R. P.	£ s. d.	£ s. d.	£ s. d.	£ s.
35 0 22	unascertained,	55 7 6	41 0 0	
21 1 5	27 10 0	32 15 6	29 0 0	
24 1 13	30 0 0	30 18 3	21 0 0	Rent changed in 1878 from . . . 30 16
35 0 31	35 10 0	43 10 0	36 0 0	
72 3 15	64 0 0	91 0 0	66 0 0	
6 0 0	10 0 0	10 4 8	6 0 0	
76 2 23	72 0 0	101 0 0	72 0 0	
31 0 36	16 0 0	25 13 2	17 10 0	
64 3 14	64 0 0	77 14 2	63 0 0	
15 0 22	8 0 0	11 5 6	8 0 0	
14 3 30	8 10 0	13 4 10	8 10 0	
*—	unascertained,	46 11 3	34 10 0	* Moiety of eighty acres.
190 3 26	120 15 0	160 11 5	122 0 0	
40 0 0	35 0 0	43 7 6	36 5 0	
28 2 1	15 0 0	20 19 5	15 10 0	
5 0 20	5 10 0	6 3 5	4 10 0	
13 3 6	6 10 0	6 10 10	6 0 0	
13 2 1	5 10 0	8 3 4	6 5 0	
25 3 14	27 0 0	14 0 0	27 18 5	By consent.
9 0 25	9 10 0	15 10 2	10 10 0	
4 3 29	5 0 0	4 8 0	5 0 0	
53 3 10	47 5 0	49 10 9	40 0 0	
9 3 35	10 15 0	13 2 6	10 17 0	
13 0 23	14 10 0	20 9 2	16 10 0	
73 3 14	39 10 0	37 6 6	36 0 0	
55 2 7	60 5 0	82 0 0	63 0 0	
16 0 27	13 5 0	22 14 6	17 10 0	
191 1 25	160 15 0	190 0 0	130 0 0	
70 3 30	75 10 0	92 8 0	75 0 0	
*—	unascertained,	46 15 3	34 10 0	* Moiety of eighty acres.
53 3 23	67 10 0	93 0 0	67 10 0	By consent.

COUNTY OF

Names of Assistant Commissioners by whom Cases were decided.	No.	Name of Tenant.	Name of Landlord.	Townland.
Assistant Commissioners—				
R. R. Kane (Legal). T. G. Fortune. J. Byrne.	219	James Sullivan, ...	Captain G. R. Caldwell, ...	Knowth, ...
	220	James Sampson, ...	Mrs. Elizabeth Brodan, ...	Drystown, ...
	221	Thomas Byrne. ...	George Kappes, assd. in estate of the Claremont Institution for the Deaf and Dumb,	Rathcoall.., ...
				Total, ...

COUNTY OF

Names of Assistant Commissioners by whom Cases were decided.	No.	Name of Tenant.	Name of Landlord.	Townland.
Head Commission.	85	Marcella Nugent and another,	S. R. Fetherston H., ...	Milltown, ...
Assistant Commissioners—	86	Joseph Brabazon and another, Admors. of J. H. Moore, deceased.	William Murray, ...	Cappagh, ...
R. R. Kane (Legal). J. F. Bourke. J. Gilmore.	87	Henry Smythe, ...	Lieut.-Col. F. E. B. Tighe, ...	Addinstown, ...
	88	Thomas Nugent, ...	William J. Delany, ...	Mabestown, ...
	89	T. and B. O'Beirne, ...	James Kiernan and another,	Clonmore, ...
J. F. Bourke. W. S. Hunt.	90	Bertie Whelehan and another.	Dame Letitia Nugent, ...	Ballinalig, ...
	91	Do., ...	do.	do. ...
	92	Mary Coolan, Admix. of William Coolan.	do.	Crookinstown, ...
	93	James Barney, ...	do.	do. ...
	94	James Murphy, ...	do.	Newtown, ...
	95	Patrick Hegarty, ...	Lady Nugent, ...	Killeagh, ...
	96	Christopher Dardis, ...	Elizabeth J. Reed, ...	Jamestown, ...
	97	Do., ...	do.	do. ...
	98	Anne Lynch, ...	Lord Rayleigh, ...	Annaspore, ...
	99	Patrick McCormick, ...	Robert F. Ellis, ...	Gillardstown, ...
	100	Patrick Murphy and another.	William Murray, ...	Cappagh, ...
	101	Richard Mulderry, ...	do.	do. ...
	102	Andrew Coffey, ...	Henry Smyth, ...	Collinstown, ...
	103	John Tallon, ...	do.	Berkeville and another.
	104	Margaret Martin, ...	William E. Smyth, ...	Grangestown, ...
				Total, ...

MEATH—*continued.*

Extent of Holding. Statute.	Poor Law Valuation.	Former Rent.	Judicial Rent.	Observations.	Value of Tenancy.
a. r. p.	£ s. d.	£ s. d.	£ s. d.		£ s. d.
126 0 24	1[illegible] 15 0	117 10 0	130 0 0	By consent.	
5 2 34	7 0 0	13 10 0	11 0 0	do.	
12 1 31	10 0 0	13 16 4	13 16 4	do.	
1,767 1 10	1,718 0 0	2,342 1 11	1,7[illegible] 0 10		

WESTMEATH.

Extent of Holding. Statute.	Poor Law Valuation.	Former Rent.	Judicial Rent.	Observations.	Value of Tenancy.
237 0 12	199 5 0	317 9 0	1[illegible] 0 0	The rent in this case was fixed by consent of the parties at the sitting of the Court in Dublin.	
240 1 [illegible]	12[illegible] 0 0	[illegible] 0 0	343 0 0	And right of grazing on 34a. 2r. 13p.	
643 0 10	4[illegible] 0 0	594 0 0	520 0 0		
216 3 31	164 0 0	3[illegible]4 7 6	187 0 0		
97 0 20	76 5 0	121 8 6	93 0 0		
77 0 24	unascertained,	23 10 0	[illegible] 0 0		
74 2 30	do.	72 8 0	58 0 0		
303 0 0	229 15 0	319 17 0	270 0 0		
341 2 15	212 10 0	276 5 4	233 0 0		
149 3 0	113 10 0	1[illegible] 0 0	105 0 0	Rent changed in 1859 from . . . £110 0 0	
281 1 [illegible]	230 0 0	308 16 4	225 0 0		
107 3 8	91 10 0	104 8 4	73 0 0		
31 1 0	38 10 0	38 11 7	22 15 0		
117 0 26	102 10 0	110 0 0	96 0 0		
196 3 0	131 8 0	170 0 0	133 0 0	18[illegible] 153 0 0	
181 0 19	102 8 0	142 0 4	107 0 0		
73 2 18	63 0 0	103 18 8	87 10 0		
31 1 3	18 10 0	37 0 0	31 0 0		
51 2 20	41 0 0	53 0 0	45 0 0		
163 1 0	150 0 0	213 4 9	155 0 0	1873 150 0 0	
3,419 3 19	2,129 10 0	3,648 0 8	3,035 5 0		

COUNTY OF

Names of Assistant Commissioners by whom Cases were decided.	No.	Name of Tenant.	Name of Landlord.	Townland.
Head Commission.	166	Charles Murphy, ...	Patrick J. Murphy, ...	Bohalog, ...
	167	Thomas Gilbert, ...	Miss Ellen Bousanne and ors.,	Crossleakil, ...
	168	Gabriel Congrave, ...	William Pillar, ...	Ballyinstogan, ...
	169	Peter Brown, ...	do.	do. ...
				Total, ...

COUNTY OF

Head Commission.	126	Laurence Cullen, ...	Henry F. Truell, ...	Ballinasre, ...
	127	Edward Nunan, ...	Earl of Carysfort, ...	Thomastown, ...
Assistant Commissioners—	128	James Lambe, ...	Sir Edward S. Hutchinson, Bart.	Rostyduff, ...
R. Reeves, Q.C. (Legal). B. Mulhall. F. F. Jeffers	129	John Kelly, ...	Mrs. Sam J. H. Cooper, ...	Sroughmanagh, ...
				Total, ...

PROVINCE OF

COUNTY OF

Assistant Commissioners— M. T. Crean (Legal). E. McCrea. W. Willans.	131	Joseph Morgan, ...	Mrs. Florence Hibbert, ...	Cappadaff, ...
M. T. Crean (Legal). F. O'Callaghan. J. Wilkes.	163	Michael Coigan, ...	John Ryan, ...	Ardrapatrick, ...
	133	John Hanrahan, ...	do.	do. ...
	134	Charles Campbell, ...	James Ryan, ...	Cheleen, ...
	135	Francis MacDermott, ...	James MacDermott, ...	Loughbeck, ...
	136	James Tierney, ...	Sir John M. Stewart, Bart.,	Ballydemagh, ...
	137	Do.	do.	do. ...
	138	Pat Dillon, ...	Andrew M. Conyn, ...	Ballyglass, ...
	139	Bridget Kelly, ...	do.	do. ...
	140	Pat Kenny, senior, ...	do.	do. ...
	141	John Ward, ...	John F. Hakney, ...	Ashfield, ...

WEXFORD.

Extent of Holding. Statute	Poor Law Valuation.	Former Rent.	Judicial Rent.	Observations.	Value of Tenancy.
A. R. P.	£ s. d.	£ s. d.	£ s. d.		£ s. d.
43 0 0	16 10 0	30 15 2	16 10 0	The rent in this case was fixed by consent of the parties at the sitting of the Court in Dublin.	
108 3 26	67 15 0	66 0 0	50 0 0	do.	
73 3 31	33 0 0	45 0 0	27 0 0	do.	
97 2 28	41 15 0	58 6 0	39 0 0	do.	
319 3 4	151 0 0	195 1 2	132 10 0		

WICKLOW.

181 2 10	175 0 0	250 0 0	173 10 0	The rent in this case was fixed by consent of the parties at the sitting of the Court in Dublin.	
79 0 19	61 15 0	61 0 0	50 0 0	do.	
35 1 32	10 15 0	13 10 0	9 0 0		
128 1 11	60 0 0	90 4 0	66 0 0		
413 1 30	297 10 0	394 14 0	299 10 0		

CONNAUGHT.

GALWAY.

30 3 36	4 12 0	10 0 0	6 15 0		
3 0 38	0 3 0	4 0 0	1 5 0		
3 3 34	0 8 0	3 13 6	1 2 6		
57 2 29	47 0 0	85 0 0	42 0 0		
16 2 23	19 10 0	37 19 10	31 0 0		
100 3 20	31 8 0	78 15 5	45 10 0		
44 0 34	31 10 0	33 4 6	29 0 0		
50 0 11	34 0 0	41 0 0	38 0 0		
43 3 19	30 18 0	40 0 0	29 0 0		
54 1 33	36 15 6	50 0 0	35 0 0		
13 0 9	18 10 0	16 10 6	11 0 0		
16 3 19	6 15 0	11 7 3	7 0 0		
13 2 30	4 15 0	9 17 9	6 0 0		
445 1 16	270 17 0	384 9 6	280 12 5		

COUNTY OF

Names of Assistant Commissioners by whom Cases were decided.	No.	Name of Tenant.	Name of Landlord.	Townland.
Assistant Commissioners—				
E. G. MacDevitt (Legal). T. Hall. J. Martin.	37	Augustin Martin, Ltd. Admor. of Pat Martin.	Catherine Hackett and anor., by Cath. Hackett, Guardian.	Cloninane,
	38	Patrick Cahill,	do.	do.
	39	Michael Sarks,	do.	do.
	40	Redmond Bourke,	do.	do.
	41	Darby Kyne,	do.	do.
	42	Bridget Carroll,	do.	do.
	43	Michael Carroll,	do.	do.
	44	Thady Gavin,	do.	do.
	45	William Purdo,	John Mallett and anor., Exors. of Thomas Kyne.	Toberaniday,
	46	John Martin,	do.	do.
	47	Pat Fahy and others,	do.	do.
	48	Pat Reilly (John) and another.	do.	do.
	49	Pat Reilly (William),	do.	do.
	50	Peter Purdo,	do	do.
	51	Pat Cummings and others,	Mary A. Rogers,	Derrinagun,
	52	Michael O'Neill,	William E. Ravenhill,	Carraville,
	53	Patt O'Neill,	do.	do.
E. G. MacDevitt (Legal). A. B. Montgomery. W. G. De La Poer.	54	Thomas Kelly,	Ross G. Browne,	Sheanaliva,
	55	Do.,	do.	Ashgrovelis,
	56	Patrick Houghan,	Miss Mary Lynch and anor.,	Kotskin,
	57	James Brennan,	do.	Knockbuy,
	58	Margaret Gerry, Ltd. Admx. of Richard Gerry.	do.	do.
	59	Patrick Kirby,	do.	do.
	60	Owen Collins,	do.	do.
	61	Michael Durkin, Ltd. Admor. of M. Durkin.	do.	do.
	62	Mary Collins, Rep. of Pat Collins.	do.	do.
	63	Thomas Hearne,	Mrs. Elizabeth McGlory,	Cloonagloon,
	64	Patt Duffy,	do.	Cloonagharagh,
	65	John Sweeney,	Robert Hunter,	Cloonaloire,
	66	James Roach,	do.	do.
	67	Henry Flynn,	do.	do.
	68	Thomas Moran,	Charles L. Fitzgerald,	Garvanduffe,
				Total,

TABLE OF JUDICIAL RENTS.

Former Rent.			Judicial Rent.			Observations.
£	s.	d.	£	s.	d.	
13	7	4	8	15	0	
[illegible]	0	8	16	17	0	
25	5	6	14	0	0	
[illegible]	5	6	12	0	0	

Names of Assistant Commissioners by whom Cases were decided.	No.	Name of Tenant.	Name of Landlord.	
Assistant Commissioners—				
M. T. Crean (Legal). H. G. Gremmey. W. F. Magill.	32	Michael Mullany, ...	Countess of Kingston,	
	33	James Molloy, ...	do.	...
	34	Bernard Morahan, ...	do.	...
	35	Lawrence O'Hara, ...	do.	...
	36	Cornelius Conlon, Junior,	do.	...
	37	Thomas Casey, ...	do.	...
	38	Patrick O'Hara, ...	do.	...
	39	Charles Devaney, ...	do.	...
	40	Edward Regan, ...	do.	...
	41	Edward McGowan, ...	do.	...
	42	John Brader, ...	do.	...
	43	Margaret Tonghrin, ...	do.	...
	44	Margaret McGreevy, ...	do.	...
	45	Edward McGreevy, ...	do.	...
	46	Peter Campbell, ...	do.	...
	47	Edward Little, ...	do.	...
	48	Thomas Reilly, ...	do.	...
	49	Pat Malone, ...	do.	...
	50	Bernard McHugh, ...	do.	...
	51	John McGlore, ...	do.	...
	52	Patrick Gaffney, ...	do.	...
	53	Michael Regan, ...	do.	...
	54	Pat Dunne, ...	do.	...
	55	Thomas Morahan, ...	do.	...
	56	Patrick Furey, ...	do.	...
	57	Do., ...	do.	...
	58	Thomas Carty, ...	do.	...
	59	John Carty, ...	do.	...
	60	Tervan Harden, Limited	do.	...

TABLE OF JUDICIAL RENTS.

ROSCOMMON.

Extent of Holdings, Statute.	Poor Law Valuation.	Former Rent.	Judicial Rent.	Observations.
A. R. P.	£ s. d.	£ s. d.	£ s. d.	
16 3 19	8 18 0	9 5 6	7 6 0	
22 3 30	10 10 0	11 5 8	9 0 0	
21 0 23	8 18 0	9 0 8	9 0 9	
44 3 27	22 0 0	26 11 1	22 0 0	
9 3 5	3 18 0	6 6 0	4 0 0	
17 1 2	4 10 0	7 12 6	6 10 0	
16 3 14	18 0 0	14 1 2	10 0 0	
148 3 20	119 10 0	187 6 0	150 0 0	
22 1 23	13 17 0	12 14 6	10 0 0	
69 0 32	65 18 0	28 14 0	22 10 0	
13 3 0	9 0 0	8 1 0	7 0 0	
13 3 24	5 16 0	6 3 0	4 8 0	
8 1 29	6 15 0	4 18 0	4 19 8	
10 2 4	4 5 0	7 9 10	5 6 0	
15 1 25	7 15 6	8 8 0	6 10 6	
72 0 0	84 5 0	41 14 6	30 0 0	
17 3 17	5 0 0	9 0 0	7 10 0	
27 3 32	9 8 0	10 9 10	8 0 0	
20 1 23	7 8 0	6 11 2	5 16 0	
23 3 8	4 3 0	8 8 0	8 15 0	
25 1 19	8 8 0	10 10 0	7 10 0	
16 2 16	10 0 0	9 0 0	6 17 6	
27 3 6	14 5 0	18 18 8	18 0 0	
17 0 0	13 0 0	10 6 0	9 0 0	
13 0 25	5 6 0	11 0 0	6 0 0	
16 0 25	20 10 0	10 18 6	8 14 0	
11 3 8	4 0 0	5 0 0	3 10 0	
11 3 6	4 0 0	5 0 0	3 10 0	
17 3 8	7 0 0	9 1 4	6 2 4	
17 3 0	6 10 0	7 5 9	6 10 0	
21 1 1	9 0 0	10 15 0	8 0 0	
15 1 0	5 0 0	10 0 0	6 10 0	
165 1 35	126 18 0	131 0 0	110 0 0	

COUNTY OF

Names of Assistant Commissioners by whom Cases were decided.	No.	Name of Tenant.	Name of Landlord.	Townland.
Assistant Commissioners—				
M. T. Cullen (Legal). H. C. Garrett. W. H. Maxwell.	66	Owen Murphy, ...	Fanny Bugh, ...	Armagh, ...
	67	John Dowd, ...	Andrew N. Comyn, ...	Ryefield, ...
	68	James Murphy, ...	Thomas Russell, ...	Tully, ...
	69	Do., ...	do.	do. ...
	70	Do., ...	do.	do. ...
	71	James Mayne, ...	Company of Kingston, ...	Drinkybonaville,
	72	Joseph E. Beckham, ...	Michael Keogh and another.	Derrycork & anor.,
	73	Thomas Moran, ...	Barbara H. Hamilton, ...	Knockmagowna,
	74	Edward Shanley, ...	Frederick Jones, ...	Ballymannin, ...
	75	Luke Padian, ...	Jane Hague, ...	Ballymacshivrus,
	76	Stephen Barnett, ...	Robert Cahill, ...	Moylick, ...
				Total, ...

COUNTY OF

Names of Assistant Commissioners by whom Cases were decided.	No.	Name of Tenant.	Name of Landlord.	Townland.
Assistant Commissioners— E. G. MacDevitt (Legal). M. Kelly.	79	Michael Coyne, ...	Mrs. Jane W. Irwin, ...	Moyrush, ...

PROVINCE OF

COUNTY OF

ROSCOMMON—*continued.*

Extent of Holding. Statute.	Poor Law Valuation.	Former Rent.	Judicial Rent.	Observations.	Value of Tenancy.
A. R. P.	£ s. d.	£ s. d.	£ s. d.		£ s. d.
79 2 30	42 0 0	83 13 8	46 0 0		
78 0 16	56 0 0	67 18 4	60 0 0		
34 1 8	20 0 0	37 13 3	15 0 0		
19 3 20	11 15 0	14 5 6½	11 20 0		
9 1 29	5 0 0	12 6 0	7 0 0		
17 3 3	6 10 0	9 1 0	6 10 0		
113 3 17	100 0 0	116 10 5	95 0 0		
29 0 21	16 5 0	25 6 8	18 0 0		
91 3 31	63 6 0	103 15 4	65 0 0		
44 3 39	36 0 0	44 17 6	33 0 0		
77 3 23	48 0 0	40 16 0	36 0 0		
1,556 2 27	994 14 0	1,168 13 6½	891 19 6		

SLIGO.

21 3 3	9 0 0	13 0 0	7 10 0		

MUNSTER.

CLARE.

177 0 0	80 0 0	98 0 0	72 10 0	The rent in this case was fixed by consent of the parties at the sitting of the Court in Dublin.	
89 0 0	37 15 0	51 0 0	37 10 0	do.	
60 0 0	26 15 0	34 3 8	23 10 0		
36 2 34	12 10 0	16 0 0	10 0 0		
48 0 0	24 5 0	30 0 0	23 10 0		

COUNTY OF

Names of Assistant Commissioners by whom Cases were decided.	No.	Name of Tenant.	Name of Landlord.	Townland.
Assistant Commissioners—				
J. S. Green (Legal). J. Ambrose. J. Gale.	302	Michael Gavin and others,	Dr. P. M. Callinan, ...	Lavally, ...
	303	Patrick Geary, ...	Francis S. Whitestone, ...	Gragg Kirwan,
	304	Peter Kerin, ...	do.	do. ...
	305	Francis S. Whitestone and another.	Colonel Edward A. Gore, ...	Knockalahan, ...
	306	Martin Ryan, ...	William Crowley, ...	Furnace, ...
	307	John Meehan, ...	Colonel Richard B. Lloyd, ...	Lissurnock, ...
	308	Michael Nealon, ...	do.	do. ...
	309	Martin Moloney, ...	do.	do. ...
	310	Charles Myers, ...	John C. Smith, ...	Shanakenna, ...
	311	Michael Lorigan, ...	do.	do. ...
	312	Patrick Garry, ...	do.	do. ...
	313	Michael Griffin, ...	Kate O'Shaughnessy and anor.,	Coolagappaun and another.
	314	John Greene, ...	John McC. O'Leary, ...	Lackanimbaugh,
	315	Patrick O'Connor, ...	Jeremiah Vaughan, M.D., ...	Cranberry, ...
	316	John Garry, ...	Rowland S. Davenport, ...	Burren, ...
	317	Michael Harvey, ...	Mrs. Susan Sullivan, ...	Furrow, ...
	318	Patrick Garry, ...	Jane G. O'Grady, ...	Sheepark, ...
	319	Bridget Scanlan, ...	Miss M. Bavagh, ...	Ranfa, ...
	320	John Scanlan (East), ...	do.	do. ...
	321	Martin Doolan, ...	do.	do. ...
	322	Thomas Ryan, ...	do.	do. ...
	323	Anne Scanlan, ...	do.	do. ...
	324	Thomas Scanlan (Mahir),	do.	do. ...
	325	Michael Egan, ...	do.	Cloondrinan, ...
	326	John Considine, ...	do.	do. ...
	327	Michael Murphy, ...	do.	do. ...
	328	John Donlan, ...	do.	do. ...
	329	Thomas Scanlan (Michael),	do.	Ranfa, ...
	330	James Chambers, Rep. of Pat Chambers.	Lieut.-Col. Charles W. White,	Collina, ...
	331	John Kelly, ...	do.	Cahernaun, ...
	332	Michael Deegan, ...	do.	do. ...
	333	Michael Chambers, ...	do.	do. ...
	334	James Malone, Rep. of	do.	Millbank, ...

CLARE—*continued.*

Extent of Holding Statute			Poor Law Valuation.			Former Rent.			Judicial Rent.			Observations
A.	R.	P.	£	s.	d.	£	s.	d.	£	s.	d.	
18	2	20	20	0	0	17	18	8	11	5	0	
18	0	25	17	0	0	30	16	6	18	15	0	
85	1	0	18	0	0	22	18	5	18	10	0	
141	0	0	102	5	0	159	3	4	92	0	0	
50	3	28	6	0	0	13	0	0	8	16	0	
81	2	35	13	16	0	20	7	0	13	0	0	
77	1	32	31	18	0	34	4	0	31	0	0	
13	0	36	14	10	0	21	10	0	14	0	0	
48	0	0	23	15	0	36	18	0	18	0	0	
66	1	31	25	5	0	36	18	0	25	10	0	
63	0	25	29	0	0	56	18	0	23	0	0	
104	0	25	55	15	0	65	0	0	45	0	0	
37	1	17	32	15	0	38	16	6	33	0	0	
21	0	0	10	10	0	9	12	6	8	18	0	
18	0	0	8	15	0	10	0	0	7	0	0	
4	2	30	Unascertained,			9	15	0	1	16	0	
45	3	0	67	0	0	73	0	0	46	18	0	
63	3	13	10	5	0	10	0	0	11	10	0	
87	0	13	8	15	0	14	0	0	7	10	0	
44	3	8	5	15	0	20	0	0	10	0	0	
85	1	6	7	0	0	18	0	0	8	8	0	
23	2	8	7	15	0	15	0	0	9	0	0	
65	2	3	5	5	0	15	10	0	7	10	0	
47	0	20	17	5	0	87	0	0	37	15	0	
17	3	0	4	15	0	9	0	0	5	5	0	
68	2	0	15	0	0	25	0	0	16	10	0	
76	3	31	13	16	0	30	0	0	16	0	0	
25	3	0	4	10	0	16	0	0	7	15	0	
35	2	33	20	10	0	32	10	9	20	10	0	
33	1	0	20	6	0	21	2	8	15	10	0	
15	0	0	16	0	0	16	7	8	10	16	0	
45	3	8	35	0	0	60	0	0	28	0	0	
10	3	13	7	5	0	7	0	3	4	5	0	
52	3	20	24	15	0	21	2	4	17	0	0	
4	1	8	unascertained,			3	8	0	1	15	0	

COUNTY OF

Names of Assistant Commissioners by whom Cases were decided.	No.	Name of Tenant.	Name of Landlord.	Townland.
Assistant Commissioners—				
J. R. Greer (Legal). J. Armstrong. J. Carr.	337	John Crowley, ...	Thomas E. Hoare, ...	Glanbeg, ...
	338	Do., ...	do.	Reenadiff, ...
	339	Timothy Kelly, ...	do.	Farran, ...
	340	Patrick Crowley, ...	do.	do. ...
	341	Catherine Maloney, Rep. of Patrick Maloney,	do.	do. ...
	342	John Doolan, ...	do.	Ballyvodane, ...
				Total, ...

COUNTY OF

Head Commission.	1801	Patrick Drury, ...	Henry J. Hungerford, ...	Glanaghasla, ...
	1802	Michael Driscoll, ...	Alexander G. Anderson, ...	Ballyvannane, ...
	1803	Michael Leonard, ...	Mrs. Jane Gibbings and others,	Dromanig, ...
	1804	James Rourke, ...	Mrs. Eliza Harding, ...	Annagcully, ...
	1805	John Cronin and another,	John Hurman, ...	Kilnacaha, ...
	1806	Do., ...	do.	do. ...
	1807	Jeremiah J. Howard, ...	Mrs. Ellen Hoare and others,	Clonmeen, ...
Assistant Commissioners—	1808	Owen Casey, ...	Countess of Kingston, ...	Gurrane, ...
L. Doyle (Legal). E. O'Neill. J. Gernaine.	1809	George Beleher, ...	Colonel and Mrs. Grant, ...	Kilgobnet, ...
	1810	Do., ...	do.	Curraghlower, ...
	1811	John Sullivan, ...	Robert H. E. White, ...	Curryglass, ...
	1812	Patrick Hurley, ...	do.	Maulavanig, ...
	1813	John Sullivan, ...	do.	Curryland, ...
L. Doyle (Legal). W. J. Goodman. W. Walpole.	1814	Michael Sheehy, ...	Kate Atkins, ...	Ardagh, ...
	1815	Michael Trinder, ...	John R. H. Becher, ...	Knockearagh, ...

CLARE—continued.

Extent of Holding. Statute.	Poor Law Valuation.	Former Rent.	Judicial Rent.	Observations.
A. R. P.	£ s. d.	£ s. d.	£ s. d.	
14 3 30	unascertained,	5 10 0	6 0 0	
67 0 0	do.	10 0 0	7 0 0	
[illegible] 0 34	5 16 0	15 0 0	8 5 0	
75 3 6	9 5 0	12 15 0	9 10 0	
64 1 28	5 0 0	9 0 0	5 0 0	
101 0 24	14 0 0	30 0 0	16 0 0	
1,149 1 [illegible]	297 16 0	1,295 13 10	520 15 0	

CORK.

64 0 0	13 15 0	33 0 0	15 0 0	The rent in this case w… consent of the par… sitting of the Court f…
12 2 4	9 10 0	7 10 8	5 18 8	do.
183 5 0	57 5 0	48 11 0	80 0 0	do.
60 0 0	7 18 0	18 0 0	10 0 0	do.
8 3 1	6 10 0	13 0 2	4 15 6	do.
[illegible] 0 15	57 10 0	59 16 10	35 14 6	do.
181 0 0	33 10 0	75 1 2	45 0 0	do.
77 0 16	24 0 0	62 0 0	21 0 0	By consent.
111 2 23	46 10 0	87 0 0	60 0 0	do.
216 3 0	56 16 0	105 0 0	78 0 0	do.
63 0 0	unascertained,	7 10 0	8 0 0	
10 1 6	do.	5 0 0	4 10 0	
22 0 0	5 7 10	7 16 0	6 0 0	

Names of Assistant Commissioners by whom Cases were decided.	No.	Name of Tenant.	Name of Landlord.
Assistant Commissioners—			
L. Doyle (Legal). W. J. Corcoran. W. Walpole.	1218	Michael White, ...	W. H. F. Barry and ano., by W. F. Barry, thei
	1219	Patrick Donovan, ...	Helena Donovan, Rep. Daniel Donovan.
	1220	Richard Driscoll, ...	Becher L. Fleming an Reps. of S. R. Town
	1221	Andrew Donovan, ...	Kate Deasy and other
	1222	Jeremiah Donovan, ...	Hester G. Nagle and
	1223	Catherine Driscoll, Ltd. Admix. of Jer. Driscoll.	do. ...
	1224	Mary Hungerford, ...	Mary B. McCarthy, an Louisa G. McCarthy,
	1225	William Hart, ...	do. ...
	1226	George Wycherley, ...	do. ...
	1227	Patrick Keohane, ...	do. ...
	1228	John Shea, ...	Pierpoint H. Mundy a
	1229	Timothy Carey and anor.,	S. D. Wright, Reps.
	1230	George Sweetman, ...	Becher L. Fleming an Trustees of S. R. To
	1231	Andrew McCarthy, ...	Joseph Sheppard an
	1232	Daniel McCarthy, ...	do. ...

CORK—*continued.*

Amount of Holding. Statute.			Poor Law Valuation.			Former Rent.			Judicial Rent.			Observations.
A.	R.	P.	£	s.	d.	£	s.	d.	£	s.	d.	
44	3	1	18	10	0	[illegible]	0	0	22	5	0	
97	1	19	13	0	0	50	0	0	50	0	0	
37	0	3	11	10	0	[illegible]	0	0	[illegible]	17	6	
44	2	0	13	0	0	25	0	0	17	10	0	
73	0	0	26	5	0	60	0	0	40	0	0	
[illegible]	0	0	8	15	0	21	0	0	13	10	0	
11	0	0	8	8	0	14	18	5	9	10	0	
19	0	0	6	10	0	20	0	0	15	0	0	
61	0	0	21	0	0	30	0	0	22	0	0	
14	2	0	15	0	0	24	0	0	19	17	6	
17	[illegible]	13	11	0	0	16	0	0	13	0	0	
69	2	21	79	16	0	34	0	0	23	3	5	
60	0	34	35	10	0	50	0	0	41	0	0	
96	2	18	31	0	0	58	0	0	40	0	0	
104	1	9	31	0	0	60	0	0	43	0	0	

Names of Assistant Commissioners by whom Cases were decided.	No.	Name of Tenant.	Name of Landlord.	Townland.
Assistant Commissioners—				
J. H. Edge (Legal). A. N. Garvey. C. O'Keeffe.	453	Patrick Brennan, ...	Johanna Brown, Rep. of Daniel Brown,	[illegible], ...
	454	Bridget Kealy, ...	Robert S. Palmer, ...	[illegible],
	455	Terence McAuliffe, ...	do.	Farrihy, ...
	456	James Larkin, ...	George Allen, ...	[illegible], ...
	457	Maurice Kelly, ...	Sir Stephen E. De Vere, Bart.,	[illegible], ...
	458	James Larkin, ...	Richard Jenkins and another,	[illegible], ...
	459	James Callaghan, ...	Robert B. Sealy, ...	[illegible], ...
	460	Stephen Geary, ...	Auster F. Walker, ...	[illegible], ...
	461	John O'Connor, ...	Richard R. Chute, ...	[illegible], ...
	462	James Harris, ...	Nicholas U. Darcy, ...	Ballinahown, ...
	463	Ellen Moran, ...	Colonel W. White, ...	Gortown, ...
	464	Cornelius Harnett, ...	Rowland Bateman, a minor, by Elizabeth Bateman, his Mother,	Park, ...
	465	Maurice Harnett, Rep. of Eliza Harnett,	do.	do. ...
	466	Denis H. O'Brien, ...	do.	do. ...
	467	Denis Collins, ...	do.	do. ...
	468	James Harris, ...	Thomas Newman, ...	Ballynahown, ...
	469	Nicholas O'Keeffe, ...	Major Richard Plummer, ...	[illegible],
	470	Cornelius O'Keeffe, ...	do.	do. ...
	471	Edmond O'Keeffe, ...	do.	do. ...
	472	John Leahy, ...	do.	do. ...
	473	Michael Roche, ...	Gilbert O'Grady, ...	[illegible], ...
	474	John Baggot, ...	Thomas R. D. Atkinson, ...	Clonagh, ...
	475	Michael O'Connor, ...	Richard R. Chute, ...	[illegible], ...
	476	Mary Flanagan and mother,	James A. Russell, ...	[illegible], ...
	477	Daniel Fraughery, ...	do.	do. ...
	478	Patrick Sullivan, ...	Godfrey C. Massy, ...	[illegible], ...
	479	Mathew O'Brien, ...	Robert S. Palmer, ...	Farrihy, ...
	480	David Condon, ...	Le Marchant Della Rosalie,	[illegible], ...
	481	Michael King, ...	Michael Scanlan, ...	[illegible], ...
	482	Charles McCarthy, ...	do.	do. ...

TABLE OF JUDICIAL RENTS.

LIMERICK—*continued.*

Extent of Holding. Statute.	Poor Law Valuation.	Former Rent.	Judicial Rent.	Observations.
A. R. P.	£ s. d.	£ s. d.	£ s. d.	
30 1 37	12 0 0	15 0 0	13 10 0	
[illegible] 1 [illegible]	27 10 0	[illegible] [illegible] 3	30 0 0	
[illegible] 3 13	[illegible] 0 0	51 13 6	37 0 0	
[illegible] 1 0	unascertained,	13 0 0	8 10 0	
34 3 9	16 15 0	20 0 0	18 0 0	
[illegible] 1 0	unascertained,	10 9 2	6 10 0	
45 3 30	16 10 0	36 10 0	16 0 0	
[illegible] 1 0	23 0 0	41 13 0	34 0 0	
42 0 34	14 0 0	26 10 0	18 0 0	
10 2 34	8 10 0	12 18 10	9 0 0	
81 1 34	[illegible] 10 0	80 0 0	40 0 0	
[illegible] 2 0	16 15 0	[illegible] 0 0	16 0 0	
36 3 0	18 15 0	23 0 0	16 0 0	
30 0 11	7 5 0	13 8 0	10 0 0	
41 3 34	19 10 0	34 0 0	18 10 0	
[illegible] 3 [illegible]	13 10 0	[illegible] 13 0	[illegible] 11 9	
44 3 0	unascertained,	11 18 8	6 5 0	
61 2 13	15 0 0	37 13 6	19 0 0	
73 0 37	3 0 0	[illegible] 0 0	13 0 0	
19 1 30	1 10 0	4 9 8	3 0 0	
[illegible] 0 [illegible]	17 5 0	31 10 0	19 10 0	
67 1 0	[illegible] 5 0	[illegible] 16 0	[illegible] 15 0	
105 0 [illegible]	[illegible] 15 0	76 10 0	[illegible] 0 0	
[illegible] 0 11	27 5 0	[illegible] 0 0	30 0 0	
30 0 0	18 5 0	[illegible] 0 0	22 10 0	
91 3 0	[illegible] 0 0	51 19 4	45 0 0	
111 3 14	[illegible] 5 0	46 1 8	[illegible] 0 0	
[illegible] 1 37	[illegible] 15 0	95 17 4	73 0 0	
13 2 33	9 10 0	30 10 0	15 0 0	
[illegible] 0 16	[illegible] 0 0	59 7 11	41 0 0	
147 0 33	91 0 0	139 1 8	[illegible] 0 0	
40 3 0	19 0 0	[illegible] 8 11	18 10 0	
46 2 0	[illegible] 8 0	[illegible] 9 2	18 10 0	
[illegible] 0 0	40 5 0	61 10 0	46 0 0	
47 2 36	36 15 0	41 8 0	[illegible] 10 0	

COUNTY OF

Names of Assistant Commissioners by whom Cases were decided.	No.	Name of Tenant.	Name of Landlord.	Townland.
Assistant Commissioners.— J. H. Edge (Legal). A. N. Curtis. G. O'Keeffe.	488	Daniel Healy,	Lord Muskerry,	Ballinlongane,
	489	Catherine Ryan,	do.	do.
	490	Roger Green,	Earl of Dunraven,	Cratloe,
	491	Thomas Flahiy,	do.	Cloonlatrick,
	492	John P. Flahiy,	do.	do.
	493	Daniel McEniry,	do.	Cratloe and anor.,
	494	John Cunningham,	do.	do.
	495	Michael Enright,	do.	Cratloe,
	496	John Sheahan,	John B. Hamerton,	Mahoonagh,
	497	Catherine Mahoney,	do.	do.
	498	Patrick Bridgeman,	do.	Fanes,
	499	James O. Nolan,	Mary E. Cussen,	Ballyane,
	500	Patrick Costello,	Marchese della Rosella,	Glin,
	501	James Conway and anor.,	Knight of Glin,	Killeentyvane,
	502	Mary Meade,	do.	do.
	503	Michael Scanlan,	do.	Kinard,
	504	Michael Shea,	do.	Ballyengland and another,
	505	Timothy Higgins,	do.	Kinard,
	506	John Hogan,	do.	do.
	507	Thomas Costello,	do.	Killeenagh,
	508	Mary Costello,	do.	Killacolla,
	509	Honora Sullivan,	do.	Fermoyle,
	510	James Enright,	do.	Killeenagh,
	511	Michael Dillane & anor.,	do.	Killeany,
	512	Mary Costello, Admix. and Devisee of Daniel Costello, deceased.	do.	Cloghanagh,
	513	Margaret Fitzgerald,	do.	do.
	514	Patrick Enright, junior,	W. B. Goggin,	Drumreask,
	515	John Scanlan,	do.	do.
	516	James Foran,	do.	do.
	517	Patrick Normoyle,	do.	do.
	518	Nicholas Greaville,	do.	do.
	519	Bridget Culhane, Limited Admix. of Michael Culhane, deceased.	Sir James H. Pelle,	Ballyguiltenane,
	520	Denis Cregan,	do.	Tullabeg,
	521	John McGuinane & anor.,	Francis Ryan and another,	Knockaderry,

LIMERICK—*continued.*

[illegible]			Poor Law Valuation.			Present Rent.		
A.	R.	P.	£	s.	d.	£	s.	d.
64	3	5	45	0	0	70	0	0
186	1	14	85	0	0	126	0	0
37	3	34	21	8	0	35	17	0
21	2	28	10	10	0	14	15	0
26	2	[illegible]	18	10	0	28	14	0
[illegible]	1	30	61	10	0	76	0	0
48	1	19	41	10	0	65	16	0
17	2	20	14	0	0	13	0	0
108	1	0	80	0	0	80	0	0
66	1	26	82	15	0	89	5	0
9	1	7	6	0	0	8	0	0
91	1	0	61	15	0	93	4	10
70	1	34	14	15	0	25	18	0
[illegible]	2	20	10	5	0	16	0	0
22	0	[illegible]	7	15	0	13	0	0
34	2	14	11	5	0	22	10	0
71	3	0	85	15	0	60	0	0
23	3	18	9	10	0	14	12	6
40	3	18	6	10	0	13	0	0
19	0	16	11	0	0	12	0	0
27	3	0	11	10	0	18	10	0
43	2	37	34	5	0	50	0	0
36	1	7	9	0	0	20	0	0
20	0	18	13	10	0	20	0	0
31	1	6	14	0	0	26	5	0

COUNTY OF

Names of Assistant Commissioners by whom Cases were decided.	No.	Name of Tenant.	Name of Landlord.	Townland.
Assistant Commissioners— J. H. [illegible] (Legal). A. N. [illegible]. G. O'Keeffe.	622	John Courtney, ...	Francis Royse and another,	Knockaneboyle, East.
	623	[illegible] Taylor, ...	do.	Knockaneboyle, West.
	624	James McMahon, ...	do.	Ballynash [illegible],
	625	Patrick McMahon, ...	do.	do. ...
	626	Johanna [illegible] and another.	do.	do. ...
	627	James C. Nolan, ...	do.	do. ...
	629	Denis Cregan, ...	James F. Winder, ...	[illegible], ...
				Total, ...

COUNTY OF

Head Commission.	665	Michael Conway, ...	Edward U. Quin, ...	[illegible], ...

COUNTY OF

Head Commission.	110	John R. Tobin, ...	George A. Wood, ...	[illegible], ...

CIVIL BILL

PROVINCE OF

COUNTY OF

No.	Name of Tenant.	Name of Landlord.	Townland.
5	William Archdale, ...	Anne M. Brownrigg and another, ...	Kilgortnaleague,
6	Robert G. Glenn, ...	William Darcy Irvine, ...	Ballindullagh, Inward, & another,
			Total, ...

COUNTY OF

No.	Name of Tenant.	Name of Landlord.	Townland.
1	John Wiley, ...	Richard Olpherts, ...	Cashelkenny, ...
2	Robert Stitt, ...	do.	do. ...
3	Charles Durnan, ...	Richard Olpherts and another,	do. ...
4	Robert Wm. Patterson,	do.	do. ...
5	Alexander McCloskey,	The Drapers' Company, ...	Drumnaspraddy,
6	Patrick Bradley, junior,	do.	Carntogher, ...
			Total, ...

PROVINCE OF

COUNTY OF

No.	Name of Tenant.	Name of Landlord.	Townland.
14	Thomas Flynn, ...	George S. Rowland, ...	Knocktopher, ...
15	Thomas Barnewall, ...	Duke of Bedford, ...	Chamberstown, ...
16	Michael Brady, ...	John R. Battersby, ...	Loughanstown, ...
17	Hugh Farmer, ...	do.	do. ...
18	Margaret Smith, ...	John Coddington, ...	Grange, ...
19	Anne M. Bailey, ...	Colonel Richard Donaldson,	Harristown, ...
20	Nicholas Duff, ...	Hon. Mrs. Isabella H. O. Egerton,	Primatestown, ...
21	James Kilroy, ...	James L. Napier, ...	Derrypatrick, ...
22	Peter Gaffney, ...	Edmund O'Connor, a minor, and another,	Ross, ...
23	Michael Maguire, ...	H. O. Ramadge, ...	Faganstown, ...
24	Michael Keegan, ...	M. Sweetman, ...	Clarkernagh, ...
25	Ellen M. Cradwell, ...	Ralph Smith, ...	Loganstown, ...
26	William Lacy, ...	F. W. Waring, ...	Bremore, ...
27	William Ryan, ...	George Wilson, ...	Rahinstown, ...
			Total, ...

COURTS.

ULSTER.

FERMANAGH.

Extent of Holding. Statute.	Poor Law Valuation.	Former Rent.	Judicial Rent.	Observations.	Value of Tenancy.
a. r. p.	£ s. d.	£ s. d.	£ s. d.		£ s. d.
20 1 38	17 0 0	25 15 9	20 8 0		
84 0 25	80 0 0	78 4 0	60 0 0		
104 2 23	97 0 0	103 4 2	60 8 0		

LONDONDERRY.

15 2 0	9 10 0	12 10 0	6 12 0		
13 1 26	8 18 0	9 14 8	6 14 8		
10 3 37	7 15 0	8 2 10	5 10 0		
5 1 33	3 15 0	4 2 0	3 3 4		
11 3 36	7 6 0	6 5 6	6 10 0		
11 2 8	7 0 0	5 6 0	6 10 8		
73 1 13	41 0 0	45 16 10	35 19 0		

LEINSTER.

MEATH.

65 0 23	34 0 0	47 0 0	34 15 0		
178 4 30	134 0 0	186 4 4	188 0 0		
48 0 30	30 18 0	42 15 8	20 0 0		
81 3 21	18 10 0	26 18 8	15 0 0		
55 2 12	30 0 0	40 0 0	30 0 0		
44 2 28	39 0 0	71 8 8	55 0 0		
147 0 0	127 0 0	232 0 0	165 0 0		
108 3 0	68 0 0	87 4 0	87 0 0	By consent.	
19 0 13	9 10 0	16 1 8	9 0 0		
84 0 19	23 0 0	36 0 0	25 0 0		
70 0 8	63 10 0	42 16 4	45 10 0		
21 0 37	19 0 0	28 5 5	16 10 0		

PROVINCE OF

COUNTY OF

County Court Judge.	No.	Name of Tenant.	Name of Landlord.	Townland.
T. Rice Henn.	9	George Johnstone, ...	Burton W. Persse, ...	Cloonkee, ...

COUNTY OF

County Court Judge.	No.	Name of Tenant.	Name of Landlord.	Townland.
J. H. Richards.	45	John McLoughlin and another.	Letitia A. McDonnell and another.	Brackloon, ...
	46	T. Wilson Walpole, ...	Lieut.-Colonel R. Rutledge,	Ballygarris, ...
				Total, ...

PROVINCE OF

COUNTY OF

County Court Judge.	No.	Name of Tenant.	Name of Landlord.	Townland.
R. Ferguson, Q.C.	127	John O'Brien, ...	William Wolfe, ...	Cashel, ...

COUNTY OF

County Court Judge.	No.	Name of Tenant.	Name of Landlord.	Townland.
John A. Curran, Q.C.	29	Charles Heffernan, ...	Arthur [illegible], ...	Dungeel, ...
	30	Daniel Healy, ...	Timothy Cronihan, ...	Carrigcannaquilla,
	31	Garrett Prendiville, ...	Charles Drummond, ...	Killowarig, ...
	32	Denis Neligan, ...	Markham L. Marshall, ...	Mounidrinn, ...
	33	Robert Glasser, ...	John Mullings, ...	Tullig, ...
	34	George McElligott, ...	do.	do. ...
	35	James Leary, ...	Francis McCarthy and anor., Exors. of Alex. McCarthy.	Sleghin, Lower,
	36	Martin Connor and anor.,	The O'Donoghue, ...	Tooreenmough, ...
	37	Catherine Moriarty, ...	do.	Caslin, ...
	38	Ellen Curtin, ...	William L. Ross, ...	Ardmoneel, ...
	39	Nicholas Donoghue, ...	George Raymond, ...	—
	40	Cornelius Callaghan, ...	Benjamin Smith and others,	Bonnemore, ...
	41	Michael Purtill, ...	do.	do. ...
				Total, ...

CONNAUGHT

GALWAY.

Extent of Holding. Statute.	Poor Law Valuation.	Former Rent.	Judicial Rent.	Observations.	Value of Tenancy.
A. R. P.	£ s. d.	£ s. d.	£ s. d.		£ s. d.
87 0 27	43 16 0	65 10 4	64 10 6		

MAYO.

25 0 17	7 15 0	8 5 0	6 13 0		
119 3 23	72 13 0	95 0 0	72 18 0		
145 0 4	80 8 0	103 5 0	79 12 0		

MUNSTER.

CORK.

89 3 5	61 10 0	70 0 0	57 0 0		

KERRY.

51 0 16	24 0 0	27 11 0	25 16 0		
67 0 31	—	8 0 0	8 10 0		
63 0 0	59 10 0	64 10 0	41 0 0		
80 1 11	4 15 0	15 0 0	10 0 0		
69 2 10	23 10 0	35 0 0	25 0 0		
67 5 0	11 5 0	23 0 0	19 0 0		
115 3 9	77 0 0	45 0 0	33 16 0		
129 1 10	17 15 0	40 0 0	21 10 0	With right to graze eight cows on adjoining mountain during summer.	
45 2 0	7 15 0	10 10 0	8 0 0	With right to graze ½ of adjoining mountain.	
53 3 7	34 10 0	70 0 0	61 0 0		
41 0 12	11 0 0	31 0 0	17 0 0		
1 0 24	5 0 0	1 5 0	0 15 0		

www.ingramcontent.com/pod-product-compliance
Lightning Source LLC
Chambersburg PA
CBHW032212230426
43672CB00011B/2531
9783742805829